INTRODUCTION

Freedom's Cry by Pamela Griffin
In 1777, Sarah Thurston looks forward to Philadelphia's first celebration of Independence Day. To her, the day heralds the end of her five-year term as an indentured servant. When her greedy master threatens to draw out her servitude, cabinet-maker Thomas Gray comes to Sarah's defense. Will he and Sarah ever be free to express their love?

Free Indeed by Kristy Dykes
Winkie Williams, a freewoman, makes her living as a milliner on a back alley of Charleston, South Carolina, in 1859. She meets Joseph Moore, a slave, at the Independence Day celebration, but her heart holds so much bitterness from the past that she rejects him and his words of peace through God. When will Winkie really be free?

American Pie by Debby Mayne
At the annual July Fourth pie auction in 1897 Mississippi, Sophia Manfield finds her creation in the center of a bidding war between two men. She has known William all her life, but she wants to be kind to Hank, the new guy in town. Will a simple pie auction spawn a lasting relationship?

Lilly's Pirate by Paige Winship Dooly
Lillian Appleby longs for adventure. She slips away from her Florida town's July 4, 1900, celebration planning to comb the beach and meets a Bible-reading "pirate." No one believes her story, and plans proceed for her to marry the postmaster, a man she doesn't love. But her heart says "wait."

SWEET LIBERTY

Freedom and Love Reign at
Four Historical Fourth of July Celebrations

Paige Winship Dooly
Kristy Dykes
Pamela Griffin
Debby Mayne

BARBOUR BOOKS
An Imprint of Barbour Publishing, Inc.

Freedom's Cry ©2002 by Pamela Griffin
Free Indeed ©2002 by Kristy Dykes
American Pie ©2002 by Debby Mayne
Lily's Pirate ©2002 by Paige Winship Dooly

Cover photo: ©PhotoDisc, Inc.

ISBN 1-58660-506-2

All Scripture quotations, unless otherwise noted, are taken from the King James Version of the Bible.

Published by Barbour Books, an imprint of Barbour Publishing, Inc., P.O. Box 719, Uhrichsville, Ohio 44683, www.barbourbooks.com

ecpa Member of the
Evangelical Christian
Publishers Association

Printed in the United States of America.
5 4 3 2 1

SWEET LIBERTY

FREEDOM'S CRY

by Pamela Griffin

Dedication

First, I want to say a special thank you to all the courageous men and women in the military who've fought for our country. You are very much appreciated, and my prayers are with you. May God bless America!

And to my wonderful critique partners on this project, Tracey Bateman, Paige Winship Dooly, Tamela Hancock Murray, Jill Stengl, and my mother, Arlene Trampel—I never could have done any of this without your help and encouragement. Also to my historical researcher and brother, John Louis, and my dad, John Trampel, who designs my bookmarks and web site—thank you, all of you.

As always, I dedicate this story to my Lord and deliverer, Jesus Christ, who freed me from the bondage of sin that once ensnared me and gave me victory over all the powers of the enemy.

Chapter 1

1777 Philadelphia

Sarah Thurston hurried from the humid kitchen, her grip tight on the platter of steaming dishes. Swiftly she moved down the dim corridor toward the dining room where the master entertained his guests.

"Best look lively," Belle, a housemaid, warned as she bustled by Sarah. "He looks to be in a foul mood despite the occasion. Likely because his wife lies abed."

Grimacing, Sarah turned the corner. The master's five-year-old son stood near the entrance to the dining room and peeked around the doorframe.

"Rupert," Sarah scolded softly, "away with you. If your father catches sight of you spying on him and his guests, there will be trouble—and well you know it." Soon Rupert would be six and ready for breeching, the step initiating him into manhood. Sarah would miss seeing his blond curls, which would be shaved off so the boy could be fitted with a wig, as the gentlemen of the township wore.

The child spared her the briefest of glances, then looked back into the well-lit room. "They are toasting the thirteen colonies now," he whispered. "Mr. Rafferty belched horribly after Father toasted Maryland. Father doesn't look happy."

"Nor will he be if he catches sight of you. Run along."

Rupert reluctantly moved away. "Will you play quoits with me later, Sarah? It is so dull here, and Father will not allow me to go into town to watch the celebration."

"If my duties allow it. Now go, Child," Sarah whispered before entering the room.

Wealthy gentlemen in powdered wigs, colored coats, knee breeches, and white stockings sat around the long table. Frills of lace or scarves in white donned their throats above their buttoned waistcoats. Sarah's master, Bartholomew Wilkerson, stood at the head, his wine glass raised high. Catching sight of Sarah, his heavy-lidded eyes remained on her seconds longer than usual, and Sarah shuddered. How thankful she would be when her indenture was completed and she could be away from this place.

"And finally, I propose a toast to the Commonwealth of Pennsylvania," Mr. Wilkerson said. "And to our most esteemed town of Philadelphia, the City of Brotherly Love, which William Penn founded almost a century ago, establishing this great township for religious and civil liberty—that all therein should not suffer persecution of the same."

Sarah clenched her teeth as she served the twelfth cake for dessert, unable to bear the man's hypocrisy. It was common knowledge that shipping magnate Bartholomew Wilkerson had friends who were loyal to King George. Though he spoke of liberty, Sarah suspected Mr. Wilkerson of secretly being a Tory sympathizer. With recent local arrests of pro-British citizens, two of whom were Mr. Wilkerson's friends and prominent men such as he, it stood to reason he would now hide any sympathy he might feel toward the British.

"On this fourth day of July, in the seventeen hundredth and seventy-seventh year of our Lord," Mr. Wilkerson said, "we declare to Great Britain our right of independence. No, we demand it! And as the most esteemed John Adams decreed a year previously, upon the signing of our Declaration of Independence, we shall celebrate the day with great rejoicing, with parade and cannon fire—this, our Independence Day. May God hasten this war to a glorious end, so that we may not only declare our freedom but live it in the fullest sense."

"Hear, hear," a portly gentleman cried.

"And may the Tories return with all Godspeed to their native England—and keep their accursed tea with them," another man exclaimed. His remark brought a round of laughter from all except the master.

Sarah saw Mr. Wilkerson frown, then quickly give a feeble smile to his comrade who turned to speak with him. The tea incident in Boston led to the start of the war two years ago and was still talked about in drawing rooms. She had heard how the Sons of Liberty disguised themselves as Indians and dumped a ship's cargo of highly taxed tea into the harbor.

Though she herself was a native of England and had sojourned in Pennsylvania only five years, Sarah felt the people's cry for freedom deep within her heart. Soon she would be free from her indenture, free to pursue personal interests and no longer bound to serve a wealthy family's every whim. That the master's interests had not been of a more personal nature these five years past was a blessing to Sarah; he exerted those particular interests in another direction. Sarah felt sorry for the young and beautiful indenture named Grace, who at twenty-one was four years younger than Sarah. However, lately Mr. Wilkerson had been eyeing Sarah the same way he eyed Grace.

Determined not to dwell on ill thoughts, Sarah hurried to the kitchen to resume her duties to Mrs. Leppermier. The elderly cook was bossy at times but had a fondness for Sarah, and Sarah knew it was because she reminded the woman of her daughter, now deceased.

Once dinner ended, they worked in the kitchen, scrubbing dishes while quietly conversing. Suddenly Belle swept into the room. "Where is that young scamp Morton? I have searched and searched for him!"

"Whatever is the matter?" Mrs. Leppermier asked.

"The matter?" Belle screeched. "The mistress has run out of her tonic, and whenever she lies in such ill humor with her complaints, without fail she asks for it the following morning. If I tell her she has no more, she'll cause a ruckus we'll all regret. I have need of Morton to hasten to the apothecary's shop at once."

"I'll go," Sarah said, removing her water- and gravy-spotted apron. "I know where the apothecary resides."

"You?" Belle said in shock.

"Aye, 'tis a good thing for Sarah to go," Mrs. Leppermier quickly intervened. "If Mrs. Wilkerson doesn't have her tonic, the entire household will suffer her ill temper come morning."

"Very well," Belle said to Sarah, her thin lips compressed in disdain. "I suppose there is no other recourse, but do not dawdle." Because Belle had willfully signed a contract of indenture, unlike Sarah, she considered herself superior and let Sarah know it at every opportunity.

"Take your time," Mrs. Leppermier corrected after Belle exited the kitchen. "Mrs. Wilkerson will have no need of the tonic until the morrow, and Katie and I can finish here. Linger and watch the celebration if you so desire."

"You are too kind," Sarah murmured with a grateful smile, looking forward to the reprieve. Before setting off, she adjusted her ruffled mobcap, which had gone askew during her work. Hurriedly she tucked a few errant tendrils beneath the white puffy circle of cloth that was fitted to her head by use of a drawstring. Smoothing her ankle-length gray skirt, she hurried outside into the sunny afternoon.

The Wilkersons' home, a stately two-and-a-half-story Georgian manor of buff stucco and red brick with gabled roof and dormers, was in Fairmount Park, as were other mansions. Tall poplar trees lined the walk, shielding the sun's brilliance. Beneath the fresh smell of grass and flowers, the acrid odor of gunpowder filtered through the air. In the distance, Sarah could see white fogs of smoke drift toward the delft blue sky, marking where guns had been discharged. Throughout the day she'd heard muffled explosions of cannon and musket fire, and the revelry had not yet ceased. Nor would it until the day was spent.

The glaring sun had dropped a couple of notches by the time Sarah drew near the heart of the city. Loud huzzahs and more reports of musket fire rang through the air. Buildings of red brick trimmed with white painted wood, soapstone, and marble lined the straight, paved streets. Charming gardens and shade trees were in abundance. White towers could be seen on the roofs of a few important public buildings, and inside the belfry of the State House on Chestnut Street, the great Liberty Bell hung.

To Sarah's left, three boys laughed and raced along the cobbles, propelling their hoops with their sticks. A dirty terrier scampered at their heels. To her right, a group of men stood in a circle, cheering the day with loud acclaim. One decreed certain victory for the Patriots and discharged his pistol in the air to the excited cheers of others. A few men threw their tricorn hats upward in jubilation.

Sarah strode the crowded footpath, paying little attention to any horses and carriages that traveled the road alongside her. Only men of means and men of trade used coaches or wagons. Most, like Sarah, walked everywhere they needed to go. In honor of the holiday all businesses were closed, and she wondered too late if she would have trouble finding the apothecary.

Through the thin soles of her shoes, Sarah could feel the heat radiating off the cobbles in the stifling summer day. Five years she had worn these shoes and was in dire need of another pair. When she left the Wilkersons, she would have to acquire a job. Widow Brown ran a coffeehouse near the wharf. Perhaps Sarah could find work there. Once she gained enough money to provide for her immediate needs, she could save up her guineas to do the one thing she desired, the one thing she longed for each night as she stared at the moon suspended above tree-dotted hills. . . .

"Well, gentlemen, what have we here?"

Sarah came to a halt, startled by the mocking voice. Three guests from the Wilkersons' dinner party moved to block her path.

"I'm on an errand," she stated with an air of false bravado, her heart skipping a beat. "Please, stand aside and let me pass."

"Bartholomew's estate must be in a sorry state of affairs that he would send his kitchen maid on an errand," Samuel Fenston, the biggest of the three said. His dark eyes narrowed beneath his tricorn hat. "Why does Morton not attend to such a task?"

"Me thinks I detect treachery afoot," William Reilly inserted, the odor of liquor heavy on his breath. A smirk distorted his pockmarked face. "Mayhap the girl lies and has slipped away to meet a lover. Perhaps we should interrogate the wench. We owe it to our friend to right a wrong if we discern trouble in his household."

"Aye," Clay Riggs, the youngest, agreed. "A private interrogation might be just the thing to loosen her tongue."

Alarmed by the sudden gleam in the eyes of all three men, Sarah backed up a step. "I tell the truth. The mistress needs a potion for her ails, and I've been sent to the apothecary to fetch it."

"A likely story," William sneered.

Clay reached out to fondle the curl hanging by her face. Sarah tried not to flinch, but the brand of fear was leaving a deep impression on her soul. People flocked everywhere. Yet if she cried out, the merrymakers would likely think her cries ones of revelry in the day and not pleas spurred from alarm. Indeed, jubilant screams, along with repeated gunfire, filled the city streets.

"My friends, let us not judge the lass too quickly or too harshly," Clay said, his gaze never leaving her face. "The matter is easily settled. We shall retrieve Samuel's coach and return with the wench to the estate to inquire there." A slow smile spread across his face, and he grabbed her arm above the elbow. "A most expedient solution for all involved, I daresay."

William laughed. "An excellent suggestion, Clay. I do admire your rapier intellect."

Sarah panicked when William took his place on the other side of her and also grasped her arm. "Please," she said, the word lost in the surrounding din as she was forced to move with them to a narrow alley between brick buildings. She struggled to be heard. "Unhand me! I have done no wrong."

"We shall soon see," Clay said. "Do not be anxious, Sarah. We will deliver you safely to your master. In due course."

At this the other men laughed.

"You heard the girl," a calm masculine voice spoke from

behind. "Unhand her."

Along with the others, Sarah turned. . .to observe the most handsome man she'd ever seen. One hand behind his back, he stood with a casual, masculine grace she had not perceived in many of his gender. Though his shirt, breeches, and leather jerkin were those of a commoner, he filled the clothes out well. His pleasing face was strong, unafraid. His head was bare, and Sarah would wager that the thick, dark hair gathered back to hang in a queue and tied with a black ribbon was his own and not a wig. His deep blue gaze briefly lit on her, then made a scan of each of the two men holding her against her will.

William tensed. "You dare to address us in such a manner? Do you know with whom you speak? Be gone with you, Cur!"

The man did not move a muscle, only stared at them in a way that showed he wasn't easily intimidated. Sarah felt her heart flutter with both interest in him and fear concerning her predicament.

"Though it's true I'm not aware of the identity of those I address," the man said, his rich voice sending flutters through Sarah again, "I am well acquainted with the manner of men to whom I speak. I repeat, unhand the girl."

Samuel stepped forward, his face a mottled red. "You, Sir, are overstepping your bounds! By your manner of dress it's plain to see you're nothing more than a common laborer. What entices you to presume that you can address us in such a manner?"

Clearly unruffled, the handsome stranger calmly brought his arm from behind him. He held a pistol, which he raised to aim at Samuel.

"This."

Chapter 2

His grip on the weapon strong, Thomas eyed the last man to speak. The woman fidgeted, but Thomas did not risk glancing her way again. Her loveliness was engraved upon his mind, and he feared that if he looked into her pale green eyes once more—eyes so clear and riveting they could disarm a man—he would forget why he was there.

"You dare draw a weapon on us?" the tallest of the three asked. "I'll have you dancing on the end of a rope for this!"

"When a woman's honor is at stake, Sir, there are a great many things I dare," Thomas replied smoothly, though he felt anything but calm. The woman gasped in what sounded like surprised awe.

"She is an indenture. Hardly worth this bother," the light-haired one who held one of her elbows explained almost cordially. "We were in the process of returning her to her master when you came upon us."

Thomas spared her a glance then. The girl trembled, her breathing labored, as revealed by the rise and fall of her chest underneath the laced bodice. Golden brown hair, the color and shine of honey, escaped in damp ringlets from her mobcap. Although she was not classically beautiful, there was an appeal to her oval-shaped face, which rivaled the color and purity of cream just skimmed off milk. A few light freckles dotted her nose and the apples of her cheeks. Her eyes, thickly rimmed with long, sable brown lashes, beseeched him.

"The lady doesn't appear to desire your company, gentlemen," Thomas said quietly, watching her.

"Lady? Perhaps you misunderstood. She is an indenture—a common servant."

"Ah, but it is you who misunderstood. As my mother once said, a true lady isn't characterized by class but rather by her actions and modesty," Thomas countered softly. The girl's eyes widened.

"What drivel is this you speak?" the man holding her other elbow intoned.

"And yet what more can one expect from a man of such questionable character?" the light-haired man put in with an air of condescension. "Far be it from me to verbally spar with one lacking intellect in the merits of social standing."

"Well said, Clay," one of the men spoke.

Thomas gave a slight mocking bow. "Be that as it may, it's not my character that is in question. I must insist that you release this woman and take your leave, Sirs. Otherwise, you leave me no recourse but to locate the constable. When last I saw him, only moments ago, he was strolling down this very block."

"Call the constable?" one of the men sputtered. "You would dare—what impudence! He would not believe your word over a gentleman's!"

"You may be correct in that assumption. However, I'm willing to find out." Thomas motioned with the gun for them to precede him. "Oh, did I mention that the constable and I are long-standing acquaintances?"

Suddenly the men did not look so cocksure. Thomas was disgusted with their arrogance.

"The wench isn't worth the trouble," the tallest man grumbled. "Let us depart."

The other two seemed about to protest but were silenced by the look in their leader's eyes, and they released the woman. She crossed her arms, rubbing the long sleeves where they had grabbed her.

The leader turned his cold gaze once more to the pistol aimed at them, then upward to Thomas. "Have a care. This is not the end of the matter."

Thomas watched as the three grimly moved away, back to the crowded street, before lowering his weapon.

"Thank you, Sir," the woman said, her voice shaky. "I am in your debt."

Thomas gave her a faint smile. "It is my pleasure. Yet I find it a good thing that your attackers were ignorant of the fact that the pistol is not loaded."

Her eyes widened. "Not loaded?"

He shook his head, rueful. "I doubt this relic would have discharged a lead ball had I tried. The frizzen spring has been defunct for some time."

"Defunct?"

He nodded. "This flintlock was my father's long ago. I also own a matchlock, but alas, I have no match."

"Oh, my."

She looked as if she might swoon, and Thomas put his hand out to steady her. "Are you well?" He scanned the area, looking for a stoop or crate—something for her to sit on—but nothing of that nature was in evidence.

Pink flushed her face, and she moved her arm from his

fingers. "I must be about my business, Sir. Again, I thank you." Though her words were steady, her eyes held a trace of lingering disquiet.

"Might I presume to ask permission to accompany you?" Thomas inquired softly. "Merely to offer protection, of course."

"Oh, but. . .really I don't wish to be a bother—"

His smile grew wide. "It's no bother. All the shops are closed in honor of the celebration—mine as well. I have a wagon I keep at the livery to help me with my deliveries and would gladly take you wherever it is you need to go."

Shyly, she averted her gaze. "I do not know you, Sir."

"How remiss of me! My apologies. I am Thomas Gray, a cabinetmaker. My shop is on the next street." He motioned in that direction with the hand that held the pistol, looked at the weapon wryly, then glanced at her. "Perhaps you would feel more assured if we seek out the constable to give you a character reference on my behalf? I normally don't carry a weapon— much less one that is disabled—but I brought it with me at my young nephew's request."

She regarded him with surprise. "Did you say your name is Thomas Grey? I overheard my mistress tell her company that she acquired a Thomas Gray's services to fashion a bookcase with the faces of the statesmen carved along the top."

"Am I to understand your mistress is the wife of Bartholomew Wilkerson?"

She nodded. "The same."

"Then you are correct. It's the latest fashion among the wealthy to have busts of popular statesmen predominant in their furniture."

The girl's brow lifted. "You must be quite skilled in your trade. Only the finest joiners are capable of such a task, from what I have heard."

"I was an apprentice to Hermann Unger, one of the most talented cabinetmakers there was. Everything I learned was under his tutelage." He shifted. "But let us not stand in the street and converse. Will you not accept the offer of my aid?"

"I do not wish to detain you."

"Detain me?"

"You mentioned a nephew."

He smiled. "I've been invited to my sister's home to partake of a meal with them this evening. First, I thought to enjoy the festivities and should welcome the company."

She hesitated before giving a shy smile. "Then I shall be pleasured to accept your offer, Sir."

Once they secured his wagon and horse, a placid-looking beast with a rough coat of dappled gray, Sarah took a better look at her self-appointed escort.

The sun shimmered off his ink-dark hair and highlighted the clean lines of his profile. His features were most pleasant, though a minor bump at the bridge of his nose prevented his countenance from being too perfect. His mouth was thin, well formed, with a slight tendency to lift at the corners, even when he wasn't smiling. Sarah guessed he must smile often, judging from the laugh lines creased alongside his lips. Realizing she was shamelessly staring, she turned her attention to the road, thankful he'd not caught her frank appraisal.

The traffic on the street was congested. Hearing the *rat-a-tat* of drums, the piping of wind instruments, and the tromp of many boots, Sarah sat up straighter and craned her neck, trying to see the road intersecting the one on which they traveled.

"I believe there is a parade," Thomas said. "Would you care to take a closer look? With this crowd, we would need to walk and dispense with the wagon."

Sarah hesitated. Mrs. Leppermier had made it clear that she should take the opportunity to enjoy the festivities. The mistress's potion would not be needed until the morrow, and Sarah had never seen a parade.

She turned to him and smiled. "I should like that."

This time he hesitated. "Might I ask your name? I know not how to address you."

She flushed. "Oh, of course. 'Tis Sarah. Sarah Thurston."

"A pleasure, Miss Thurston," he said, smiling. With agile grace, he alighted from the wagon and came around to her side, offering his hand.

Sarah felt her cheeks go hot as her fingers touched his warm, rough palm when she stepped down. He treated her like a lady, instead of the commoner she was, and it made her wonder. Very few gentlemen would treat a servant with civility. Though Thomas claimed to be a tradesman and not a gentleman, his deportment stated otherwise.

Curious, Sarah sent sidelong glances his way as they strolled toward the spectacle. Once they reached the flagstone street crowded with commoners and the wealthy alike, Sarah looked over the man's shoulder in front of her. She had to stand on tiptoe to see, but it was worth it.

At the front of the procession, a boy on horseback carried a flag that Betsy Ross was reputed to have created for the budding nation. A circle of stars on a square of blue sat in the uppermost corner, and red and white stripes horizontally filled the cloth. The sight of it made Sarah's throat clench with emotion.

A group of young men followed, playing their instruments,

and Sarah saw four drummers and other men with clarinets, fifes, and oboes. Rigid lines of soldiers, each holding muskets and bayonets over their shoulders, marched in rows of four behind them, looking stately in their brown uniforms with blue facings.

The gentleman in front of Sarah, obviously wealthy, as denoted by his fine coat and the metal buckles on his shoes, turned to his companion, who wore an expensive gown of blue cotton. "The Hessian band that played at the dinner for Congress was much more accomplished than these musicians, do you not think so, my dear?" he asked.

"Yes, my husband. Quite." She gave a disparaging glance at the pressing crowd around her. "Let us be away from this dreadful heat. I've seen enough."

"As you will."

The two left, and Sarah stepped up with Thomas to take their place at the front. It was nice not to have to crane her neck to see. First came the infantrymen, followed by soldiers who rode horses. The animals' coats gleamed in the sun from the currying they'd received. A corps of artillery, hauling cannon and other weapons, trailed behind.

"God bless 'em," Sarah heard the man at her side say to his comrade. "I hear tell they're on their way to join the grand army."

"God go wi' ye," an elderly woman from the crowd cried out. "An' give ye victory over them Redcoats!"

Sarah looked in the woman's direction and suddenly caught sight of her three attackers in the crowd on the other side of the parade. She froze, unable to look away. Clay caught her eye and gave a slow smile fraught with the promise of retribution.

Thomas turned his head toward Sarah, and she flicked a glance in his direction. His brows drawing down in concern, he gently grasped her elbow. "You've gone as white as parchment. Is this heat overly much for you?"

Sarah shook her head, somewhat amused by the prospect. As a kitchen maid, she was accustomed to worse heat than this. "Nay, Sir. I am well. Truly," she added when he looked unconvinced.

His gaze went to the crowd on the other side of the marching soldiers. Sarah knew when he caught sight of Clay and his acquaintances, for his hand marginally tightened around her elbow. Thomas turned to her, understanding in his eyes.

"Perhaps you would care to seek out the apothecary at this time?"

"Aye," she said, relieved. "That I would."

He nodded, keeping his hand on her arm while he accompanied her back to the street where he had tethered the wagon's horse to a lantern post. Sarah appreciated the warmth of his hand for more than the protection offered. Once he dropped his hold from her sleeve, upon helping her into the conveyance, she missed his touch.

Her cheeks grew hot. What folly! This man was a stranger, a kind stranger, to be sure, but still a stranger. Had her aunt known what wayward imaginings traveled through Sarah's mind, she would think her little worse than a doxy.

Thoughts of family made her sober, and tears clouded her eyes. Impatiently, she brushed them away with the heel of her hand, but Thomas had already seen.

"Here, what ails you?" he asked, his words laced with worry.

Knowing it would be inconsiderate to give no reply, as benevolent as he'd been, she spoke. "I was thinking of home. I miss my brother and sister."

"Do they reside in Philadelphia?"

"No. In England." She shook her head. " 'Tis a long, sad tale. I do not wish to burden you with it."

"It would be no burden, I assure you. However, if you do not care to speak of it, then let this be the end of the matter. I have no wish to upset you further."

His words were kind, and Sarah studied his profile. Would he understand? Or would he judge her based on titles alone?

"We shall have to backtrack and take another street." Thomas flicked the reins and turned the horse around. He looked her way again. "Have you family in town?"

"Not a soul." Her gaze dropped to her lap. "My father was a scholar and was killed in a carriage accident when I was but three and ten. My mother died a year later. Afterward, my two siblings and I were taken in by poor relations—an elderly aunt and uncle in Dorchester. Besides them, I'm alone and have been alone for five years, since first I came to America."

"You do not sound pleased with the arrangement," he said, perplexed. "Why then did you leave England?"

Sarah balled her hands in her lap and for a moment chose not to reply. She looked at him then, noticing his brow creased in puzzlement. His midnight blue eyes regarded her sympathetically, and she wondered if they would remain so once he knew the truth.

"I had no choice in the matter," she said slowly. "I did not come of my own free will. I was transported on a convict ship."

"A convict ship?" he repeated, taken aback.

"Aye. I was sent to the colonies to serve out my sentence."

Chapter 3

Thomas's mind brimmed with questions. He struggled to contain them and waited for Sarah to continue.

"My sister has been sickly all her life," she said and looked away, as if the memory were painful to recall. "One day we were at the market. I was procuring vegetables for my aunt, who's an invalid. Dorrie, my sister, who was then ten and six, had left my side. I heard a ruckus and looked up to see an elegantly dressed, old gentleman holding Dorrie by one ear and yelling. Dorrie was crying."

Moisture filmed Sarah's eyes when she looked at Thomas again. "He accused her of stealing his wallet. Dorrie insisted it fell from his waistcoat and that she was returning it to him at the same time he discovered it missing. Yet he didn't believe her and called a constable. Though I didn't know it at the time, Dorrie's accuser was visiting our city and was a prominent man from the House of Lords. He demanded a high sentence."

Sarah let out a mirthless chuckle, her eyes despondent. "You see, the fault was mine for Dorrie being there in the first place. I thought the outing might do her good. They were going to take her away and put her on a convict ship, and I begged them to let me go in her stead."

"And they allowed it?" Thomas asked in surprise.

Sarah nodded. "I was in full health, and anyone with eyes could see my sister was not. She was still weak from a recent illness and continuously coughed. Her skin had a gray pallor. It was apparent Dorrie would not last the voyage on such a ship and they would receive no payment for her labor."

He stared, silent. Again she looked away, obviously uneasy. "After a harrowing voyage, with sickness and death abounding everywhere, the convict ship arrived in Philadelphia. Mr. Wilkerson paid the asking price for me and acquired me to be one of his kitchen maids."

"A remarkable story," Thomas said pensively.

Her chin sailed up. "You don't believe me, but I shouldn't be surprised. Few people who know my story do."

"I didn't say I doubted you," he quickly inserted. "Only that your story is remarkable. There are few people—blood related or not—who would willingly take another's sentence."

Sarah gave a slight shrug. "Dorrie is my sister, and I've always taken care of her. I could not let her be sent away to die."

He eyed her with respect. "A commendable action on your part, Miss Thurston. And how much longer is your indenture?"

"Three weeks." Her eyes sparkled with anticipation. "And then I shall be rid of the Wilkersons, though I must admit I'll miss young Rupert's company. He has taken to me since his father and stepmother show him no interest. I spend time with him when my chores are done."

"What will you do once you leave?"

"I shall find work here in town and save my money so that I may send for my sister and brother one day."

"You will not return to England?"

"No." Her expression sobered. "I am a Patriot at heart. I

admire this nation's fight for liberty, as I have long wished to be free, and want to call such a land my home. England never held anything for me except my siblings, of course."

Thomas nodded, thinking of his older sister, Anne, whose husband was off fighting in the war. She was looking for a cook, and Thomas wondered if she would consider Sarah for the position. He planned to bring up the topic that night.

When they reached the apothecary's shop, Thomas pulled on the reins. The building's two narrow windows were shuttered, and he frowned. "It appears empty. I'll look into it." He stepped down to investigate, finding the shop was indeed vacant. Noticing a group of children nearby, Thomas approached them.

"Have you seen the apothecary?" he asked a freckle-faced little girl nibbling on a chunk of rock candy. Blue ribbons adorned her light hair.

She nodded but did not speak. The boy next to her, sharing the same facial characteristics and coloring as she, pointed down the road. "Last I saw, Sir, he was heading in that direction, he was. He closed up shop, due to the holiday."

"Did he mention where he was going?"

"Why should he speak to the likes of us?" an older boy responded. "We ain't his keepers."

Thomas nodded stiffly. "Thank you," he said to the first boy, then headed back to the wagon and told Sarah the news.

She sighed. "Well then, that is that. I thank you for assisting me in my quest." She made as if to get down.

"You are giving up so soon?"

"No, I shall look for him—I must. Yet I cannot take up more of your time and ask you to search with me. You've done so much already."

"I have nothing else to occupy my time at present. I don't

mind." Thomas slapped the reins against the horse's neck before she could exit the wagon. He did not approve of her wandering about town alone.

"Oh!" A surprised gasp escaped her lips as the conveyance lurched forward, and she moved her hands to the seat to hold on. She looked at him curiously. "Well, Sir, if you are sure you don't mind. . ."

"Quite sure," he said, sending a grin her way.

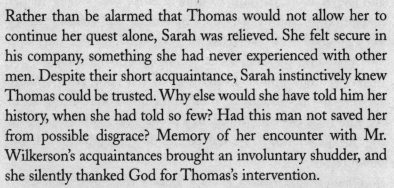

Rather than be alarmed that Thomas would not allow her to continue her quest alone, Sarah was relieved. She felt secure in his company, something she had never experienced with other men. Despite their short acquaintance, Sarah instinctively knew Thomas could be trusted. Why else would she have told him her history, when she had told so few? Had this man not saved her from possible disgrace? Memory of her encounter with Mr. Wilkerson's acquaintances brought an involuntary shudder, and she silently thanked God for Thomas's intervention.

They slowly drove along the road, searching the people walking along the sidewalks. Thomas came to a stop before a tavern. "I'll look inside. You stay here."

Relieved, Sarah nodded. She preferred to avoid such places. Alehouses in the colonies were the same as in England, with men well into their cups, foul language afoot, and frequent brawls. Her uncle frequented just such a place, and it was due in part to his ill reputation that the convict sentence Sarah had taken for Dorrie was so stiff, she was sure.

Within minutes, Thomas was back. "The apothecary was here but left a short time ago. We shall find him."

The glowing ball of the sun had dropped lower toward the

horizon by the time they found the portly, ruddy-cheeked man walking with a taller gentleman along Cherry Street. The apothecary's wig hung askew, and his clothes appeared rumpled, but Sarah was relieved to see he was not inebriated. She explained her reason for seeking him out.

He clucked his tongue in disgust but said a farewell to his companion and moved to take a place beside Sarah. Quickly she slid over to make room for his wide girth on the short bench. Pressed up against Thomas's solid build as she now was, Sarah found it hard to draw breath; the pulsing of her heart reverberated in her ears. His clothes had a fresh, musky smell coupled with the aromatic odor of wood shavings, and she inhaled his pleasing scent, feeling a trifle lightheaded.

When they pulled up in front of the apothecary's shop, Sarah found it difficult to stand. Her limbs were shaky from being in such close proximity to Thomas. He said nothing, yet his eyes questioned as he helped her down. Embarrassed, she looked away.

Inside the dim shop, the apothecary went to a back room behind the counter. Avoiding Thomas's gaze, Sarah studied the shelves filled with labeled jars and bottles containing colored liquids and powders. Several stone mortars and pestles were strewn atop the wooden counter, one mortar still bearing grains of white powder. A huge jar of live leeches sat at the other end, and Sarah hurriedly turned her gaze away from the sight of the blood-sucking creatures crawling inside the glass.

"Here it is," the apothecary said when he rejoined them, a bottle of dark liquid in his hand. "I realized Mrs. Wilkerson's supply would be running low and had the foresight to prepare this a few days past. I'll put it on her account."

"Thank you, Sir," Sarah said, slipping the bottle through a

slit in her skirt to one of two bags suspended from a rope tied around her shift. The pockets, as they were called, helped her carry all manner of things and leave her hands free.

She strode to the door, Thomas behind her. At the wagon, she turned his way. "You've been of great help to me, Mr. Gray. Again, I thank you."

His expression was incredulous. "You don't think I'll allow you to walk to the Wilkersons' estate when I have a wagon to drive you?"

"But you've spent so much time helping me already," Sarah protested. "Look, it's approaching nightfall. You'll miss dinner with your family."

"Anne will understand. I cannot let you traverse these streets alone, especially with night falling as you have pointed out."

The sound of many bells pealed throughout the streets, interrupting their conversation, and Sarah started in surprise. The great gongs of the Liberty Bell, hanging in the State House a few streets over, mingled with the more delicate sound of hand bells the excited townspeople rang. The mellow tones of nearby church bells added to the delightful clamor.

"The sweet sound of liberty," Thomas said, his gaze meeting hers.

Before Sarah could reply, a small urchin with the biggest and brightest dark eyes scampered between them, laughing. Her short black curls bounced under her ruffled cap and over the collar of her gown as she shook her brass hand bell. Her older sister trotted after, catching up with the plump child and scooping her up and onto one hip. The toddler giggled and rang her bell some more.

"Shall we join in the fun?" Thomas asked, smiling.

Though to spend more time in this man's company was

exactly what Sarah did want, she knew she shouldn't. "I've been gone a long time. I best return before they think I've run away."

"As you will." He stepped toward the wagon and held out his hand to assist her. She hesitated but accepted his aid, reasoning he could get her to Fairmount Park much faster than she could walk.

Thomas drove slowly along the roads to avoid hitting the people—children mostly—who sometimes darted across the street. Everywhere citizens rang their bells and gave loud huzzahs. Sarah smiled, wishing she too had a bell to ring. On such a day as this, it was easy to get caught up in the merriment.

The dusky purple twilight had deepened to inky darkness by the time the bells stopped ringing, though throughout the town a few could still be heard, the merrymakers not wanting to cease in their revelry. All of a sudden, myriad explosions of color shattered the air to Sarah's left, painting spectacular starbursts of light against the dark sky.

"Oh, look," Sarah gasped in awe, taking hold of Thomas's shirtsleeve, barely cognizant of the fact she'd done so. "Let us stop and watch."

Thomas pulled the wagon to the side of the road, and they lifted their faces toward the heavens. For the next several minutes, they watched the vibrant rockets explode above the commons, one by one.

"How exquisite," Sarah whispered. A spark lit inside her, quickly fanning into flame. "America must win this war and gain her freedom. She must!"

Thomas turned her way, his eyes understanding. "She will. God is for us. He forever stands on the side of justice."

"Aye," she whispered. "That He does."

During her absorption with the display, Sarah hadn't realized that she had moved closer to Thomas. Against the backdrop of the illuminated sky, she could easily see the dark lashes that framed his eyes, feel his warmth, smell the sweet scent of herbs on his breath. A colorful finale of numerous fireworks filled the heavens beyond, highlighting his features all the more. His eyes were gentle, soft, like liquid velvet might appear if there were such a thing. . . .

Feeling faint, Sarah moved back, putting distance between them, and averted her gaze. "We should go."

He lifted the reins from his lap where he clutched them. "Aye. The day is long spent." His words seemed terse and rocked Sarah a great deal more than the deafening bangs from the fireworks had done.

As the wagon bounced along, Sarah shot several discreet glances his way. The flame-lit globes of lantern posts that lined the wide streets shed a pale glow over Thomas's sober profile, until the wagon moved into the shadows between posts once more. Would she see him again? Or was the scope of their acquaintance destined to be limited to this one extraordinary day?

At the manor, the wheels crunched over pebbles while Thomas drove to the side of the house, as Sarah directed. Once the vehicle came to a stop, she looked at him. "It has been wondrous, and I appreciated the company."

He inclined his head. "My pleasure."

Before she could say more, he leaped down and came around to her side to assist her. This time, his hands briefly spanned her waist as he lifted her from the wagon and set her on the ground in front of him. The action took no more than a few seconds, yet his touch flustered Sarah, sending her heart racing.

She opened her mouth to frame a cordial farewell, but the faint sound of crying coming from the vegetable garden stopped her.

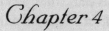

Chapter 4

S arah stared at Thomas, wondering if her mind was playing tricks on her. "Do you hear?"

"Yes," he said, already ahead of her. Sarah followed him to the garden, the moon lighting their way. Upon leaving the cloak of trees, they came to the grassy clearing. With bowed head, Grace sat on the ground near the rows of vegetables.

"Grace! What ails ye?" Sarah asked in alarm, rushing over to the young woman. She knelt before the housemaid, feeling the reassuring presence of Thomas behind her.

The girl lifted a face wet with tears, her dark eyes forlorn. "Sarah," she murmured. "Whatever shall I do?" Suddenly she threw her arms around Sarah and buried her face in her shoulder, starting to cry again.

"I should be going," Thomas inserted quietly, obviously recognizing Grace's need for privacy.

Sarah nodded with a grateful smile.

"We will meet again, Sarah Thurston." His eyes glowed with promise in the moonlight. "Farewell."

"Farewell," she breathed, watching his tall form move away. Even concern for her friend could not dispel the flutter of her heart at his words.

When Grace's tears were spent, Sarah pulled back. "Tell me," she chided gently, "what causes you to weep as though the world were coming to an end? Have you ill word of your family?"

"I am with child," Grace blurted out numbly. "Which means another year will be added to my indenture, as the law states." Like Sarah, Grace's servitude was almost at an end.

Indignation rose up in Sarah. "You must take this to the constable, Grace. You mustn't let Mr. Wilkerson get away with such a deed."

"I'm only a servant, and he's an important man. Who would give heed to what I say?"

Such deeds were common among masters, Sarah knew, to prolong an indenture's servitude. Yet there had been cases of a penalty being slapped on the offender and the servant being removed from his custody. "You must try, Grace. You don't want to work for him another year, do you?"

Grace helplessly shook her head. "I've not your courage, Sarah. I'm afraid to let my plight be known. Likely, I will be publicly whipped and ostracized." She clutched Sarah's arms, and her tone grew cautious. "Your indenture ends soon. Now that the deed is done, the master will look to others for his entertainment. You must be on your guard, Sarah, lest he do the same to you."

Sarah clenched her teeth. "He dare not try!" Remembering her earlier encounter with Mr. Wilkerson's three friends and her timidity in the face of danger, she sobered. "I will be cautious. And I'll consider a solution for your dilemma, as well, though I know not what. You shouldn't be forced to serve that ogre another year! But come, let us talk of this no more. The night air grows cold."

Helping Grace, who leaned heavily on her shoulder, Sarah

rose with her friend, keeping an arm around her waist. Together, they moved toward the house.

Tuesday was baking day. Up at four, Sarah and the other servants served the family scrapple, eggs, and other foods to break the fast, then made quick work of building a fire inside the oven, using finely split wood. After the fire burned awhile, Katie scraped the oven out, swept the ash away, and stuck her arm into the heated box to test the temperature. Both her arms were smooth, the hair singed off them long ago from this practice. First in went foods that needed more baking time—the meat pasties, the duckling, and the mutton. Sarah turned the hourglass upside down to let the sand trickle to the bottom. When that was accomplished, the breads would go in.

Swiping her forearm over her moist brow, Sarah released a weary breath. Next came making the fruit pastries and sweet breads of which Mrs. Wilkerson was so fond.

As Sarah stirred the ingredients for another piecrust and lifted the bowl to dump its contents to be rolled out, Mrs. Leppermier spoke. "Tell me, Sarah. Did you have a good time at the festivities? Did you meet anyone special?"

Sarah almost dropped the bowl. The celebration was a week ago, though she had not ceased thinking of Thomas since. Feeling her face flame even more than the heat in the room had already caused it to, she stared. "Pardon?"

"Grace mentioned a man brought you home that night," Mrs. Leppermier said as she sliced the apples thin. "Would ye care to talk of it?"

Sarah immediately focused on her job, rolling out the dough. "Aye, there was such a man. He saved me from a dangerous situation and helped me to find the apothecary."

"What's this?" Mrs. Leppermier stopped chopping, her knife still. "A dangerous situation?"

Sarah nodded and told the woman all that had transpired. The cook looked thoughtful. "Perhaps it was a mistake to let you go into town alone on such a day of revelry. . .then again, perhaps not." Her smile was mysterious. "Whatever the case, the good Lord protected you, Sarah, and He will go on doing so."

"Aye." Sarah smiled. In her prayers, she'd pleaded with God for protection in light of what had happened to Grace and had felt His reassurance. Had He not sent her Thomas when she needed him? Sarah wished she could share the gospel with Grace, but when she'd tried in the past, the woman had shaken her head.

"We are the masters of our own lives, Sarah. As such, we are responsible for our destinies," Grace had said, a sad smile on her face, as though she felt sorry for Sarah's gullibility. "Besides, how can a God who is real allow horrible things to happen to people?"

Sarah hadn't been able to respond, since that same question sometimes filtered through her mind. It made her ashamed that she also harbored doubts. Growing sober, she focused on her work.

The hours passed with dogged slowness, like a stubborn mule with a burden upon its back, plodding along a trail. Once the food was baked for the week, Sarah used a wooden peel to scoop the items from the oven. Afterward, she and Mrs. Leppermier cleaned the mess they had made, washed pots and pans, and swept flour and other food droppings from the flagstones. Katie, her skirt pulled up and tucked in to give her some relief from the oppressive heat, put bread pudding into a fabric bag to steam over a kettle. Pepper pot, the spicy beef and vegetable stew everyone in the family loved, boiled in the container.

"Fetch the butter, Sarah," Mrs. Leppermier ordered. " 'Tis soon time to put the meal on."

Sarah exited the house, carrying a basket laden with perishable food they would not eat that day. Rupert came skipping out of the trees to join her.

"Play with me, Sarah?"

She shook her head, never diverting from her trek. "This is baking day, and there's still much to do." At his downcast face, she relented. "Tonight, I will tell you a story."

His face beamed. "Will you tell me more about the celebration? I heard a friend of father's say thirteen galleys and armed ships were gathered in the harbor, all with red, white, and blue streamers, and each of them fired thirteen cannon! Did you see it? That must have been what made all the noise and scared the hens from laying eggs."

"I don't doubt it," she said with a laugh. "No, Child, I didn't see the ships. That must have taken place afore I arrived. Now off with ye! There is much to be done."

Once she entered the springhouse, Sarah set the basket down. The soothing sound of the stream rushing over small rocks filled the building. She turned to retrieve the container of freshly churned butter from the cool water. A shadow filled the door, and she looked up in surprise.

Mr. Wilkerson stood in the entrance. "Sarah. We have need to talk."

Sarah's body went as cold as the brook. "Something I've done displeases you, Sir?"

"Nay, your conduct has been exemplary. Rather, I have looked through my papers of late, and I see that your term of indenture is almost at an end."

"Aye," she said through numb lips.

He regarded her where she knelt by the gurgling spring. Slowly, he walked closer and came to a stop beside her. Reaching out, he laid his hand upon her shoulder. Petrified, she looked up at him.

"Would you consider signing another contract, this one of your own will?" he asked, his voice silky. "The boy has taken a liking to you. Therefore, I would give you a different position, as a companion to Rupert. You would find such an arrangement comes with numerous benefits, especially the closer our acquaintanceship grows. Know ye what I am saying, Sarah?"

"Aye," she said stiffly, clenching her teeth. She averted her gaze to the clear water, wishing he would go. Fear struggled with resentment for first position in her mind.

A long, unnerving pause followed. Sarah swallowed over the lump that had formed in her throat.

"Think on it," he said finally, his voice harsh as he wrenched his hand away.

After he exited the small building, Sarah took time to gather her composure before returning to the house. She uttered a brief prayer for safety during her remaining days in Mr. Wilkerson's employ but couldn't help feeling apprehensive about her future.

"I did it!" Rupert cried with glee, clapping his hands and jumping up and down.

"That you did," Sarah said with a congratulatory smile. "And now we shall see if I can fare as well."

She lifted her wooden ring, brought it back, and slowly

lifted it again, her eye on the stake. Quickly she drew back her arm and flung the ring at the target. The edge of the wooden disc bounced on top of the stake and went awry.

"Oh too bad, Sarah!" Rupert sympathized.

"Your stance is incorrect," a masculine voice said from behind, startling Sarah into dropping the rings in her other hand. Spinning around, she spied Thomas standing near the flowering dogwood trees.

"Forgive me," he said. "I delivered the bookcase and heard the sound of laughter so decided to investigate." The noonday sun painted silvery-blue highlights in his dark tresses. Again he wore no tricorn, and his trim form was clad in a billowy white shirt with leather vest and breeches. He looked magnificent.

Sarah dropped her gaze to the rings on the ground. Hurriedly she bent to retrieve them, not overly surprised when Thomas joined her in the task. He picked up two and placed them in her hand. Their gazes met, and Sarah felt a jolt go through her.

"Would you care for me to give you some pointers? I was quite accomplished at quoits in my day." He grinned, his laugh lines becoming more pronounced.

Sarah's heart flipped. If his referral to "in my day" suggested he were advanced in years, he was obviously jesting. He could be no older than his late twenties, she was sure.

"Sarah?" Rupert asked. "Are you going to swoon? You look ill."

She sent a rapier-sharp glance to the young scamp. "I am fine." Turning to Thomas, she said, "If you care to coach me, I'll not refuse you." Sarah looked away from the amusement dancing in his eyes as he moved beside her.

"Put one foot in front of you and bend slightly at the knees," Thomas instructed. "Now, raise your arm to shoulder level—slightly bend it—keeping your back straight. No, you're too stiff. Permit me."

Before Sarah knew what he was about, she felt his warm touch on her wrist. He came alongside her while lifting her arm and pushing against the inside of her sleeve to bend her elbow, as though she were pliable clay and he were the potter. Indeed, she felt as stable as mushy earth. He stood so close she was aware of his form lightly pressed against her side. She tried to draw a firm breath, but it, too, felt shaky.

"Steady," Thomas said close to her ear. "Steady. . ." He pulled her arm back until the disk brushed her skirt. "Now bring the ring up swiftly and release it!" He let go of her wrist but otherwise did not move.

Sarah brought her arm up with a snap and let go of the ring. Her hand was trembling so that she was surprised the ring made it as far as it did, though it came nowhere near the stake.

"You are too tense," Thomas said. "You need to relax."

Ha! As if she could do such a thing with him standing so near, reminding her she was a woman and he was a man. "I think I have the gist of it," she said, not daring to look his way. In the position they were in, his lips would be at a level with hers if she faced him. She continued to stare at the stake until it swam before her eyes. When at last he moved from her side, she was relieved. Almost.

"Will you play with us, Sir?" Rupert asked hopefully.

Sarah stole a peek at Thomas and felt another bout of lightheadedness when she noted him staring at her.

"No, Lad. I'm in the process of making deliveries. I thought only to bid you good day." He nodded at Sarah. "Again, it was a pleasure."

Sarah's heart raced as she watched his erect form stride

toward the front of the house. *Aye. A true pleasure.*

"Sarah?" Rupert asked, his voice holding a superior air. "Should you not offer him cider? He looks thirsty, and the day is hot."

Already he was beginning to sound like a master giving orders. Sarah had noted the perspiration beading Thomas's fine brow when he stood close. And the boy was right. The day was hot.

"Mr. Gray!" she called, taking a few running steps after him. He turned in surprise.

"Would ye care for refreshment before you go? We have cider." She motioned to a nearby decanter sitting on the step.

Something lit the deep blue of his eyes, as though a candle's glow shone beyond them. "Yes, thank you."

Feeling suddenly flustered, Sarah quickly turned to the task at hand.

Thomas watched her flurry about. Her upswept hair was in disarray underneath the mobcap, several damp curls sticking to the slender column of her neck. Her cheeks glowed from exercise. Or was it from embarrassment?

Thomas realized he had inadvertently made her ill at ease, standing close to her as he had while showing her how to throw the wooden rings. At first his action had been one of courtesy. Yet when he stood near her, inhaling the sweet apple scent that undoubtedly came from the cider she'd prepared, and felt the brush of her silken curls against his cheek, he had not wanted to leave. Propriety demanded he step away, and he had, albeit reluctantly.

Sarah handed him a brimming glass. Thomas was surprised to see shaved ice floating in the liquid. Yet it shouldn't astonish him that the wealthy Bartholomew Wilkerson owned an icehouse, where huge blocks of ice from winter's frozen river were stored in hay and buried deep within the ground to provide refreshment in summer.

Thomas gratefully swallowed the tangy, cold mixture, draining the glass without removing it from his lips. Afterward, he handed it to Sarah. She smiled, a twinkle in her eyes.

"More?"

"No, thank you. I need to complete my deliveries." Normally, he might have let such a task fall to Jeremy, his apprentice. Yet the hope of seeing Sarah again had Thomas going in Jeremy's stead.

"Thank you for coaching me in quoits." Sarah's face reddened, and Thomas grinned and gave a small bow.

"My pleasure. Good day, Miss Thurston."

"Good day."

Thomas resumed the trek to his wagon. Before entering it, he again looked toward the mansion. Mr. Wilkerson stood at the front, his gaze raking over Thomas. Thomas wasn't sure why, but he felt the man boded no good. Hesitating, Thomas returned the stare, then climbed into his wagon.

Chapter 5

Several days later, Sarah had just finished preparing a currant pudding when Mrs. Leppermier came sailing into the kitchen. "Sarah, put away your apron. You have need to accompany Morton into town."

Sarah looked up in surprise. "Morton?"

"Aye. Mrs. Wilkerson was so pleased with Mr. Gray's work that she wants him to design another piece of furniture." She handed Sarah a slip of paper. "This tells what the mistress wants. You're to give it to Mr. Gray along with a small advance." She placed a guinea in Sarah's hand.

"I don't understand," Sarah said, looking first at the guinea and paper, then at the cook's wrinkled face. "You want me to go with Morton to talk to Mr. Gray? Mrs. Wilkerson asked this of you?"

"No, Belle spoke of it," Mrs. Leppermier corrected. "And since you answer to me, I'm ordering you to go." She winked, smiling. "That young scamp Morton is not to be trusted; yet, since he's the master's illegitimate son, he gets away with more than most. With you along, I know Mr. Gray will receive his guinea—and that it won't go toward a round of drink for Morton and his disreputable friends."

Moved, Sarah nodded, putting her hand through the slit in her skirt and sticking the note and money in the pocket. Mrs. Leppermier's faith in Sarah spoke volumes to her.

Hurriedly she untied her apron and fixed her mobcap. The thought of seeing Thomas again brought excitement, something she tried to hide. Yet the knowing smile on Cook's face when Sarah bid her farewell proved her efforts were useless.

Morton, who was all of eight and ten years, regarded Sarah with effrontery when she joined him on the lawn. "So, Cook won't let me go on my own, won't she?" He snorted, fixing his flop hat over his head. "Well, you best keep up then. I won't be trailin' behind for the likes o' you!"

Sarah rolled her gaze heavenward, then quickly followed Morton as he turned on his heel and kept a few paces ahead of her the entire way. Morton was an enigma. Though he held the station of a servant, he was treated better than all of them combined and given finer clothes. It would seem that to be so blessed, his attitude might be kinder. Yet he was often surly—aided, no doubt, by his desire for rum. Or perhaps his dour behavior stemmed from the fact that the master barely acknowledged him, though Morton was his offspring.

As they approached Thomas's street, a sense of alarm made Sarah halt in her tracks. Columns of thick gray smoke rose in the humid air over the rooftops of the buildings, and she could smell the fumes from where she stood. Picking up her skirts, she ran ahead of Morton.

In the distance, flames licked a roof not far from Thomas's shop. A volunteer fire brigade worked to put out the flames. Axmen opened and stripped the roof, hookmen pulled down burning timbers, and others manned the two-handled pump on the engine and held the hose. The townspeople helped.

One long row of men passed full water buckets in the direction of the blaze, while an opposite row of women passed the empties to children, who filled them at nearby pumps.

Sarah searched, shading her eyes from the sun with one hand. Relief seized her when she spied Thomas's strong form in the long line of men, though she was alarmed at how close to the burning structure he stood. Wanting to help, she filled buckets, then ran with them and transferred them to the last man in line.

Finally, the crackling flames dwindled. A loud hiss filled the air, as though the dying fire were protesting, while gallons of water continued to be tossed upon it.

When all that remained was smoke, several men closest to the fire moved away, their faces blackened. The crowd began to disperse, the people finding and taking their leather-covered buckets, which each household was required by law to possess.

Thomas moved from the crowd, and Sarah hurried to join him. Now that the danger of the fire had passed, she suddenly realized she'd lost Morton. Exasperated, she made a quick scan of the crowd before continuing her trek toward Thomas.

Soot covered his face and streaked his white shirt, the sleeves of which were rolled up, exposing sinewy forearms. His queue hung askew, long strands of dark hair hanging near his lean face, but he looked no less striking.

"Miss Thurston," he said, surprised. "What brings you here?"

"Business—with you," she said, averting her eyes from his steady gaze. She felt somewhat embarrassed by the admiration she felt toward him upon surveying his form and wondered if he could sense her thoughts. "Mrs. Wilkerson wants you to fashion another piece of furniture. I have the description with me."

"Really? Well, come along. I need to find my bucket, and

we will talk. Thank the good Lord the fire is out. Old Mr. Fogherty is a kindhearted man, and I would have been dismayed had he lost his livelihood, though surely there will be damage to his merchandise."

Sarah walked behind Thomas to the fire-blackened, smoking building. Several bystanders eyed the ruined structure. One man gazed at the fire plaque on the outside wall, the symbol of an eagle showing from which company the fire brigade would receive their reward for putting out the fire. Along with other townspeople, Thomas searched through the pile of discarded buckets on the ground until he found the container with his initials. Straightening, he headed Sarah's way, his expression sober. "Did you come alone?"

Sarah thought she detected a note of disapproval in his voice. "I came with another servant. Yet he seems to have disappeared."

"He knows my shop was your destination?"

"Aye." She hesitated. "Perhaps I should wait on him."

"He will show. Come, and I'll have a look at what Mrs. Wilkerson desires."

Sarah accompanied him to his shop. Several people greeted them along the way. Most mentioned the recent fire and the relief that it had not spread. Many looked at Sarah with raised brows and curiosity plainly written on their faces.

Their frank appraisal made her wonder. Did Thomas have an understanding with a woman? Was that why they looked at Sarah so? Or was the opposite the case? That he was rarely seen in the company of the fairer sex, and so the prospect provided interest to his neighbors?

Sarah hoped the latter were true, though as attractive and kind as Thomas was, she doubted it.

Thomas led Sarah into his shop, his gaze darting around the room to make sure everything was in its proper place. He winced when he noted his dark coat draped over the bench instead of hanging from the wooden peg in his living quarters above his shop. When the fire had started, he had been in the process of donning his coat. An empty tankard and pewter plate sat nearby, an old, dog-eared copy of Franklin's *Poor Richard's Almanac* beside it, and both table and floor were littered with wood shavings.

Thankfully, she made no comment, and Thomas began to roll down his shirtsleeves, at least hoping to make himself presentable. He stopped upon catching sight of his blackened hands and forearms. Realizing for the first time that his appearance must be shocking, he hurriedly excused himself and rushed upstairs. After using the washbasin to cleanse his face and hands to the best of his ability, changing into his one spare shirt, and redoing his queue, he clomped down the wooden stairs, worried he had taken too long and Sarah would not be there. Her form was bent over a maple candle sconce he had recently carved, and relieved, he shrugged into his coat.

"Now, then," he said, out of breath. "What is it your mistress fancies?"

Sarah withdrew a note and coin from within her skirt, handing them to him. His brows lifted at the advance of the guinea, and his eyes skimmed the missive: *A chest press carved to portray "The Fox and the Grapes" from Aesop's Fables.* And she wanted it in two weeks.

Thomas frowned. "I can deliver the item she requested, but I'll need more time than she's allotted me." He looked up from the paper. "I have orders from other customers to fill."

"I'll deliver the message," Sarah said, her gaze on an unfinished secretary in one corner of the room. She strode toward it and moved her hand over its many pigeonholes. "What beautiful work! And such fine detail!" She turned her shining face his way. "How long have you been a cabinetmaker?"

"I became an apprentice at the age of thirteen. When I was twenty-four, I opened my own shop, using all that Mr. Unger taught me. He died three years ago." Realizing she was still standing, he motioned to the bench beside the table. "Please, have a seat."

She stared, her expression curious, but did as he asked.

He inclined his head. "You wish to say something?"

"Aye. But I don't want you to think me impertinent."

Thomas chuckled. "I could never think that of you, Sarah." Realizing his slip of the tongue, he sobered. "Pardon me, Miss Thurston."

"I don't mind you using the name given me at birth," she assured. "All at the estate call me Sarah. You're the only one who addresses me otherwise." A curious expression lit her face. "It does make me wonder—and that is the question I wish to ask—how can a tradesman have the manners of a gentleman?"

"Ah," he said with a smile. "I'm a mystery in need of solving?"

At this, she blushed. "Aye."

" 'Tis a simple matter. My father was the youngest son of an English earl. As such, he did not stand to inherit the property or the title. He was given an allowance and came to the colonies to pursue his living as a practitioner at law. Soon patriotism fired his blood, and he joined the cause, though he was a nobleman's son—unheard of, you understand. For his "impudence and betrayal" as my grandfather posed it, my father was ostracized from the family. Being raised a gentleman, he taught his sons that same trait."

"Sons?"

"I have two brothers. I am the youngest of all my father's children."

"And your mother?"

"She died in childbirth, as did the babe. My father never remarried."

Sarah nodded, her eyes sad as she studied the room filled with the tools of his trade. "And so this is the life you lead, though you were born to one of wealth?"

"Do not pity me, Sarah. I am satisfied with my 'plight,' as some have called it. Since I was a small lad, I was fascinated with the exquisite carvings on the mahogany furniture in my father's house and even took a kitchen knife to a block of wood one day to fashion one of my own. I was but seven at the time, and this is what I received for my troubles." His words were light as he held out one hand to show her the long white scar racing along his palm.

"Oh," she murmured in sympathy.

What Thomas did not expect was for her to lift her fingers and brush the old wound with lingering feather softness, sending his nerve endings tingling into awareness. Stunned, he yanked his hand back before he could think twice. She looked up, her eyes full of embarrassed dismay.

"Forgive me," she blurted, hurriedly rising to her feet and moving across the room.

Feeling like a fool, Thomas shook his head. "There's no need. You've done nothing wrong." Though she was by proxy a customer, they were alone, nevertheless. Because of this, he considered it wise to keep his distance, as attracted to her as he felt.

She moved toward the sash window and gazed through the square-shaped panes of glass. "Morton is taking a long time. I should look for him."

"Sarah, please stay," Thomas encouraged, his voice steady. "I don't think it wise for you to wander the town alone."

"I've done so before. What happened with those men during the celebration was the first time such an incident had occurred," she said, addressing the window.

"It is my hope you'll not invite a second incident. I may not be there to protect you."

Her gaze swung his way, her face flushed. "Tell me, why is it that one in such fine form as yourself and forever spouting of protection is not off fighting in the war?" As soon as the rash words left her mouth, she looked distressed, as though she wished she could take them back.

Her soft question struck him hard, ramming at the door of his defenses. "I make a better craftsman than I do a killer."

"A killer?" A trace of censure filled her tone. "Then you secretly despise the men who are fighting for freedom, yours included?"

"Not at all. I have great admiration for them. Would I could do as they have done."

"I fail to understand your reasoning, Sir." Her eyes brimmed with confusion and, Thomas was saddened to see, disappointment. Before he could reply, the door swung open and a young man half stumbled inside.

"There you are," he said, his words full of reproach. "I been lookin' for you."

Sarah eyed him without flinching. "Then you have searched the wrong place, Morton. You would not have found me in the alehouse." She wrinkled her nose at the strong stench of liquor that cloaked his breath, her expression one of disdain. "Imbibing in rum again, I see. Never mind. I have taken care of all the necessary arrangements. We are free to take our leave."

She looked at Thomas, her manner detached. "I wish you good day, Sir. I will deliver your message to my mistress." She swept out the door, Morton in her wake.

Thomas stared into space, his mind replaying her cutting words. He thought of another day, another time. . .two mischievous lads, nowhere near old enough to shave, behind the springhouse—one the master's son, one a servant's. The master's pistol in the son's hand. . .the curiosity and excitement involving the danger of being caught with the forbidden weapon. . .the haughty order from the master's son for the servant's son to shoot first. . .the blood when the gun misfired.

Thomas had been to blame for the death of his young friend, a heavy load he still bore. Turning his gaze to the mantel, he looked at his father's old pistol. He kept the relic as a reminder that human life was precious. And because of those feelings mingled with those of his faith, he had never killed a man. As a child standing beside his friend's grave with tears running down his cheeks, Thomas had vowed never again to be responsible for another's death. Yet neither had he reckoned that, one day, the land he dearly loved would be at war in a fight for its freedom.

Chapter 6

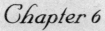

Before retiring, Sarah lit a candle and went upstairs to bid Rupert good night, as she always did. The boy was so often lonely, and Sarah felt sorry for the young scamp. His eyes stared up at her with love as she walked toward his cot.

"Have ye said your prayers?" She smoothed his golden locks from his forehead.

He nodded. "Will you tell me a story?"

"Aye." Sarah smiled. "That I will."

She related the Bible account of the Israelites gaining freedom from the wicked pharaoh and thought of her master. Though Mr. Wilkerson had toasted religious freedom, he forbade his servants from attending church on the Sabbath, claiming it a lot of nonsense designed to prevent them from doing their chores. Yet once a week, a handful of indentures and slaves took a few minutes to gather by the springhouse and hold their own service, while Mrs. Leppermier recited Scripture from her Bible.

"The Is-il-rites wanted freedom, like the colonies do from England," Rupert murmured sleepily when Sarah paused after relating how Moses had taken God's people across the Red Sea.

She smiled and kissed his cheek. "Aye. Something like

53

that." When she straightened, he regarded her sadly.

"I miss my mother. She used to kiss my cheek every night."

Tears stung Sarah's eyes at the admission. "I'm certain she looks down from her home in heaven every evening to blow you a kiss on that same cheek."

Her words erased his frown, and he closed his eyes. "Good night, Sarah. I'm glad you'll never leave us."

Alarm shot through her, but before she could question him, Rupert turned on his side and burrowed into a ball. She picked up the candle and left. Did he know her indenture was almost at an end? She had not told him. Yet what did he mean by those last words?

Telling herself she was looking for problems that did not exist, Sarah sank to her mat above the kitchen where the kitchen servants slept. She had been given permission by Cook to go into town the next morning and search for employment. Less than a week remained until her term was complete.

Smiling, she floated into sleep but was troubled by disturbing dreams that woke her well before four, when she usually began her day. Sarah decided to get an early start. She donned her clothes over her shift and laced up her bodice in the dark, not bothering to light a candle.

Quietly, she slipped downstairs and tore off a hunk of bread from the shelf. A rustle and series of footsteps from beyond the wall caused her heart to lurch. Gathering courage, she peered into the main room. No one spoke to her from the still darkness. Uneasy, she let herself outside.

The air was cool against Sarah's skin. Up ahead in the distance she could see ships' masts, their mammoth bows almost touching

the row of buildings facing the harbor. The vessels were out-
lined in the lanterns' glow against the sky now lightening from
inky black to murky gray.

"Sarah! Is that you?"

Without realizing it, she had walked down the street with
Thomas's shop and was not overly surprised to hear his voice
quietly call out.

In the stillness, his footsteps echoed on the cobbles as he approached. Early morning mist from the Delaware River clouded
the air but not so much as to make it impossible to see. Thomas's
expression was one of surprise as he came upon her. "Whatever
brings you to town so soon? It is not yet daybreak."

"I've been granted permission to seek future employment
and have only the morning to do so. I thought I would get an
early start and ask at the coffeehouse the Widow Brown runs."

"It is early," Thomas agreed. "Many have not yet tumbled
from their beds, though I notice several are up and about now."
With a wry grin, he motioned to the tobacconist, who swept
his stoop across the street and cast interested glances their way.

"Your neighbors watch you often?" she asked. "Are they so
inquisitive?"

"Only when their curiosity is aroused. I am not often in the
company of an attractive woman."

The soft compliment made her eyes widen. He took her
elbow. "Come. Let us walk and not provide Mr. Coppel with
further information to tell his wife. I have something I need to
discuss with you."

"Oh?" Sarah asked, her heart tripping a beat at his light
touch. He turned her away from the direction of the river, and
they began walking.

"I spoke with my sister. She is married to an army officer

and has a fine house in town. At present, she has much to do with six children to look after. Her cook has departed, and Anne is helpless at the craft." He grinned. "In short, she's open to the idea of hiring you."

Tears pricked Sarah's eyes. Was there no end to this man's benevolence? Memory of how shoddily she'd treated him when they last parted made her face go hot, despite the cool mist bathing her skin. Thomas did not lack courage. Whatever his reason for separating himself from the fighting, it must be a worthy one.

"I owe you an apology," she said softly.

"An apology?"

"Aye. I never should have spoken to you as I did when last we were together. I was mistaken."

"Never mind, Sarah," he said, his voice gruff. "Let us put the matter behind us."

She nodded, relieved.

"Would you care to meet my sister? She, too, is an early riser. Her house is on the other side of town, though, so you might prefer for me to fetch my wagon."

"No." Sarah sent him a shy smile. "I think I'd rather walk with you."

"As you will." His voice was as soft and warm as the look that suddenly lit his eyes.

When they finally reached the large, two-story plain brick building, the sun, visible through the leafy boughs of sycamore trees, was just peeking over the horizon. Thomas sensed Sarah was nervous and gave her a reassuring smile. "Never fear. Anne is quite companionable," he said before knocking at the door.

A sour-faced woman answered and glared at them. Sarah started, obviously taken aback. Thomas quickly spoke. "Good morning, Matilda. Is my sister available?"

The maid opened the door to let them in, but her stiff countenance did not change. "She's in the garden."

When Matilda continued to stare, Thomas blew out a quiet, exasperated breath. "Then if you will not announce us, we shall go and make our presence known."

"As ye will." The maid turned her back to them.

Thomas caught Sarah's shocked gaze at Matilda's disrespect. "She, too, is an indenture," he explained. "And as lazy as an old hound."

At the back of the house, they found Anne kneeling on the soil in a losing battle against a carrot that refused to be tugged out of the earth. Her belly was great with child, and Thomas caught Sarah's surprised gaze toward him before she hurried to his sister.

"Milady, allow me." Sarah knelt beside her and gave one hard tug to the carrot Anne had let go of in surprise, freeing it from the earth. His sister smiled.

"Thomas, please tell me this is of whom you spoke."

He grinned. "Anne, may I present to you Miss Sarah Thurston. Sarah, my sister, Mrs. Anne Rollins."

Sarah nodded and averted her gaze, obviously still uneasy. Anne touched her arm. "Let us go inside for coffee, though perhaps I've had too much of that already." She shook her head. " 'Tis a craving I've had since first I was with child. The weakness that has come upon me in months past is also due to the babe within my belly, I suppose—"

Thomas cleared his throat and looked away, uncomfortable with the womanly conversation. Anne laughed. "But, lo! I've offended my brother's sensibilities. Without a man around the house of late, my talk has become quite frank." She gave

Thomas a grin sparked with mischief, then faced Sarah. "Come, let us get acquainted."

Thomas hurried to help Anne to her feet, a trifle amused at how awkward his normally graceful sister had become. The three went into the hall, and Sarah admired the small glazed pictures, framed in black molding with gold-leafed corners, on the whitewashed walls. "How lovely," she murmured.

"Aren't they? I procured them from the Kennedy's Print Shop on Second and Chestnut. I do so love the one showing Jesus with the little children."

Almost as if on cue, Nancy and Frank, the two youngest of Anne's brood, ran into the hall still in their bed gowns. Seeing Sarah, they stopped in surprise. Anne smiled and held out her arms to the pair, who shared the same dark hair and hazel eyes as their mother. "Come along, children. 'Tis all right."

Frank ran across the hall and hurtled himself into his mother's arms to receive his usual morning kiss, but Nancy moved more slowly, her wide gaze fastened to Sarah.

"Hello," Sarah said with a smile.

Nancy giggled shyly and, after receiving her mother's affection, scurried from the room, Frank close to her heels. Immediately Martha came to the door, the eldest of Anne's children. Where Anne was dark, Martha was fair like her father.

"Oh, hello," Martha said, first looking at Sarah, then to Thomas and her mother. Her pale blue eyes were curious. "I've started the porridge, and Fran has set the table. Willis is chopping more firewood, and Clive is gathering the eggs."

"You are a blessing, Child." Anne glanced at Sarah. "I had no need to learn to prepare food until our cook left, shortly after Phillip went to war," she explained. Her eyes clouded, but only momentarily. "Tell me about yourself, Sarah, and why you wish employment here."

"Will she be the new cook?" Martha asked hopefully. Thomas hid a smile. Neither his sister nor his nieces knew how to prepare food. Thomas had endured charred meat and stew with vegetables boiled to mush more times than he cared to remember.

"She might," Anne said with a conspiratorial grin at Thomas. Yet his sister's look said more. Realizing she wanted to interview Sarah alone, Thomas rose. "When last I visited, you mentioned the window shutter in the girls' room sticks," he said. "I will see to it."

Before leaving, he glanced Sarah's way. She smiled, her shoulders relaxed, all anxiety vanished. Anne had that way about her, putting people at ease. He was certain this arrangement was an answer from heaven. Returning Sarah's smile, Thomas strode from the room.

Humming a little ditty, Sarah let herself in through the servants' entrance. The interview had gone well, and both women admitted they eagerly awaited the day when Sarah would join Anne's family. Though Sarah's title would be cook, Anne had also asked for help with the children after hearing of Sarah's experience with her siblings and with Rupert. As such, her wages would reflect both positions. God was good!

The cook turned from stirring the stew in the kettle over the fireplace trivet, her actions edgy.

"I received a position!" Sarah exclaimed, her words brimming with happiness.

The woman did not reply. The uneasiness in her countenance and the warning look in her eyes alerted Sarah that something was amiss. "Mrs. Leppermier?"

The door banged open, admitting the master of the house. His features were grave. "Sarah," he clipped. "I would have a word with you."

Before she could speak, he exited the room. Aghast, Sarah looked at the cook, hoping for an explanation.

"I'll be praying, Child." The woman's look was sympathetic. "No matter what is said, I hold ye in high regard."

Sarah gave a faint nod, moving to the door on stiff legs. The fangs of dread bit deeply into her soul.

Chapter 7

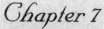

Mr. Wilkerson looked at Sarah grimly from where he stood behind his desk. "You are a thief, and I have the proof," he said quietly.

Certain she'd not heard correctly, Sarah stood frozen in disbelief. His accusation sank to the bottom of her being like a heavy rock disturbing peaceful waters.

"Sir?" she said, her voice raspy.

Mr. Wilkerson arrogantly surveyed her, his hands clasped behind his back. "You were seen skulking about the house this morning and entering the room where the ivory frame was kept. I have no alternative but to believe you are the thief."

Sarah shook her head. "I took no ivory picture frame. You have my word on that."

"You were seen, Sarah. Why else would you move about in the dark without lighting a candle if you were innocent of the crime?"

Sarah desperately tried to think of a reply. Only Mrs. Leppermier knew of Sarah's quest for another job. Sarah had purposely kept the fact from her master for obvious reasons. Yet for all her caution, she stood here, accused.

He narrowed his eyes in speculation. "You do know the

punishment for such crimes, Sarah. The least you can expect is a day in the stockades."

Dread dug its talons deeply into Sarah's heart. "Please, Sir, you must believe me! Search my sleeping area, if you so desire."

"For what purpose?" He slowly shook his head, as though addressing a child. "You could have transferred the frame to your partner—perhaps the man I saw here recently? The cabinetmaker. Are you conspiring with him, Sarah? Do you sell stolen merchandise for money?"

"No! I would do no such thing—nor would Thomas."

His brows bunched at her familiar use of Thomas's name, then his forehead smoothed and he offered a tight smile. "Very well. I am a reasonable man. I'll not turn you over to the constable to be publicly punished. Instead, I will lengthen your term of indenture by one year and issue a contract for you to sign."

Sarah's eyes widened. Was such an action lawful? Yet it made no sense. If he considered her a thief, why would he want her to continue working for him?

The answer was obvious, so obvious it kindled her anger. He knew she had not taken the frame. This was only a scheme devised to keep her here.

"No," she said bravely, lifting her chin. "I will sign nothing."

His fleshy lips narrowed. "You'll do as I tell you!" He walked over to her and grabbed her elbow. "Or I'll see to it that you are publicly whipped—forty-nine lashes to be carried out at one time. My three friends, whom you met during the celebration, would be most eager to testify to the constable on my behalf and swear how you've also stolen from them. Especially after the unforgivable treatment you and your friend meted out to them."

Sarah's blood turned cold. Few people survived so many

lashes given at one time. No one would believe the word of an indentured convict against that of four prominent gentlemen.

Mr. Wilkerson began to walk with her to the door. She dragged her feet, now very afraid.

"A night in the springhouse might help you think differently," he said, forcing her to move as he tugged her arm. "When you're given time to dwell on the choices, another year of indenture might not seem so horrible in comparison."

Tightness clenched Sarah's throat, but she couldn't speak. He pulled her, struggling, to the springhouse. Roughly he pushed her inside, and Sarah went tumbling to the ground. Her palms stung as they scraped hard earth. The door slammed shut, and the suffocating cloak of darkness fell. A heavy thump and scrape of a wooden bar being dropped across the outside of the door sounded ominous in the chilled room.

Disbelieving, her mind too numb to grapple with the enormity of the plight that had befallen her, she struggled to sit up and stared into the darkness.

Sarah was unaware of the passage of time, though she knew it must be hours. Crossing her arms, shivering, she determined to escape. The cry of freedom demanded to be heard, its peal reverberating throughout her soul. If she would not be granted liberty, then she would seize it! She had waited too long for the day.

Despite her doubts and questions of how God could allow such a thing to happen, she breathed a prayer. "Heavenly Father, help me! If I am forced to stay, You know what he will do. Please protect me from the evil intentions of that man. . . ."

Sarah staggered in the direction of the door, careful to avoid the narrow brook that bubbled to her right. Her hands made contact with stone, and using it as a guide, she slowly walked along the wall until she found the door. She pushed against it, though such efforts proved futile since it had been barred from the outside. From earlier visits to this structure, she knew the walls were strong. The place was as secure as a fort.

In frustration, Sarah repeatedly banged her fists against the door, until her hands throbbed with heated pain. Angry tears filled her eyes. "Why, God? Why did You let this happen to me? Why?" At last, spent, she allowed her fists to slide down the wooden door while her forehead dropped to its rough surface.

"Sarah?"

The voice was weak, muffled, coming from the other side. Instantly alert, she lifted her head, her eyes going wide with hope. "I'm here! Rupert, is that you?"

"Yes," the boy replied. "I waited for you to come bid me good night, then said my prayers without you. I heard a voice in my head telling me to go to the springhouse."

The hairs on the back of Sarah's neck prickled, but she didn't dwell on his words. "Rupert, you must let me out. Can you lift the bar?" Sarah's brows drew together. The boy was so small, and the beam was heavy.

She heard a grunt and the slight scraping of wood, followed by a thump. "I can't," he said, his words remorseful.

Sarah closed her eyes and tried to think. "Find Mrs. Leppermier or Grace and bring one or both of them here. But tell no one else."

There was a pause. "Sarah? How did you get in there?"

She clenched her hands on the wood. Despite the truth—that Bartholomew Wilkerson was a horrid man with wicked motives—she could not hurt his son by telling him so. "Never mind. 'Tis not important you should know. Go find help, there's a good lad."

Silence met her plea. Sarah prayed that the boy would not be offended but would do as she asked. Intolerable minutes passed before she heard the wooden bar slide up. In sudden caution, she backed away from the entrance as the door creaked open. What if the master had returned with an even more despicable act in mind?

A cloaked form stood silhouetted against the starlit sky, the smaller form of Rupert behind it. Sarah stood still, her heart hammering in her ears, her fist pressed to her mouth to still the scream that wanted to escape.

"Sarah?" Grace whispered.

Relief melted through Sarah, dissolving the ice that had frozen her blood. She stepped forward and hugged her friend.

"What will you do?" Grace whispered solemnly.

"I don't know." She clutched Grace's forearms. "Yet I cannot stay."

"But you have only a few more days left of your contract!"

In the hours she had sat in the dark, pondering her dilemma, Sarah had reached a decision. "I would rather risk being publicly whipped or put in the stockades than to stay here and wait to see what he will do to me."

"Sarah, the penalty for an escaped convict may be death—"

"So be it," Sarah stated firmly. "This country's brave men are fighting to the death to procure our land's freedom. I'll do no less when it comes to mine. Though my oppressor is of a different nature than the foe that the colonies wage war against, it is through meditating on this country's courage that I have found a measure of my own. Do ye understand, Grace?"

Grace shook her head, her brow wrinkled in confusion.

Sarah attempted a smile. "Never mind. I must go."

"Sarah?" Rupert asked, his voice fearful. "Will they kill you?"

She knelt to better see his face in the moon's glow. A pang struck her heart at his woeful expression. "I pray not. You mustn't tell a soul about tonight, especially the part you played."

He nodded, and Sarah kissed him on the forehead. She clutched Grace's arm once more, then hurried away.

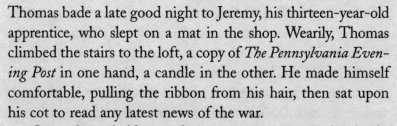

Thomas bade a late good night to Jeremy, his thirteen-year-old apprentice, who slept on a mat in the shop. Wearily, Thomas climbed the stairs to the loft, a copy of *The Pennsylvania Evening Post* in one hand, a candle in the other. He made himself comfortable, pulling the ribbon from his hair, then sat upon his cot to read any latest news of the war.

One column held an update concerning a recent battle. As Thomas read the numbers killed and wounded, a strong sense of self-reproach came over him. He lifted his gaze from the print and stared at the opposite wall, watching the shadow from the flickering flame dance on the whitewashed surface.

How long he sat, staring, he did not know, but when the frenzied pounding came at the shop door, it was shocking enough to make his hands jerk and tear the half sheet of crown paper.

Irritated, he laid aside the ruined newspaper and hurried downstairs in his stocking feet, the pounding at the door never ceasing. Jeremy stood near his mat and stared at Thomas, his eyes wide.

"Think you, Sir, that the Redcoats have come?"

Before opening the door, Thomas offered a reassuring smile. "Nay, Lad. Nothing so tragic." He lifted the beam and stared at the dark figure on the doorstep—a woman. She stepped forward into the light. "Sarah!" he exclaimed in shock.

A mass of tangled ringlets covered her shoulders, and the mobcap was missing. Her dress was dirty as though she had lain on the ground. Smudges of dirt covered her pale cheeks. Her eyes were wide with fear, but something else as well. Determination.

"What happened?" he asked. "Are you hurt?"

She shook her head, as if she didn't want to discuss it. "I need sanctuary. Will ye help me?"

"Is there trouble at Wilkerson's estate?" Thomas asked, confused.

"Nothing of that nature," Sarah stated impatiently. "Please, Thomas. I've nowhere else to turn!"

Knowing he must calm her before he could get her to make sense, Thomas put an arm around Sarah's shoulders and shepherded her to the low fire. Jeremy had not moved, but curiosity had replaced the fear in his eyes as he stared at Sarah.

"Stop your gawking and make yourself useful, Lad," Thomas said quietly as he helped Sarah sit at the table's bench by the fire. "Bring her a cup of that coffee you made earlier."

Jeremy nodded and scurried toward a high shelf. He pulled down one of two pewter mugs and set about his task.

"Now," Thomas said, turning his attention to Sarah, who stared blankly at the waning fire. Her eyes focused on him, traveling to his unbound hair that touched his shoulders and reminding Thomas he was unfit for company. Rather than bring attention to that fact by rising to tuck his shirt into his breeches and fasten the shirt's top four buttons, he tried to focus on the problem at hand.

"Tell me, Sarah. What tragedy brings you here in the middle of the night—and in such disheveled condition?"

Jeremy walked over to her, offering the pewter cup. Accepting it, she took a steadying drink before staring into Thomas's eyes. "I will tell you everything, but, in turn, will ye promise to help me, no matter what I say?"

Thomas felt a twinge of unease, but the anxiety in her eyes stilled his qualms. "Aye, Sarah. You have my word."

Chapter 8

T he boy apprentice, seeming to realize his presence was not desired, went upstairs. Once Sarah told Thomas everything, including her fear of Mr. Wilkerson doing to her what he'd done to Grace, she waited for his response.

His eyes had deepened to a stormy blue, and his mouth was drawn tight in anger. Sarah thought his ire might be directed at her, so she opened her mouth to defend her actions, but he shook his head.

"It's not you I'm angered with, Sarah. I understand your reasons for escape." His features softened with concern. "Yet you have put yourself in a precarious position. A runaway is still a runaway and subject to punishment by law."

"Think you they will truly give me forty-nine lashes?" she all but whispered.

Again Thomas's expression grew grim. "Is that what he told you?"

She nodded.

"Sarah, I seriously doubt they would give a woman accused of theft forty-nine lashes on her first offense."

"But they would not see this as a first offense. Few people know I took my sister's place. I'm looked upon as a true convict."

To her shock, he dropped down on the bench beside her and took hold of her hand. "Then, if necessary, I'll testify on your behalf. My word holds some merit because of who my father was." His voice was low, determined. "However, you must return to the Wilkerson estate. Otherwise the sentence could be extreme."

The wave of gratitude that first swept over her was replaced by one of fear, and she snatched her hand away. "How can you say such a thing? You know I cannot go back."

"It's the only way. To escape makes you appear guilty. Such an action will not aid your case."

"And what if he attacks me?" she asked, her voice strained. "What if he does to me what he did to Grace?"

A flicker of anger shot through his eyes, then disappeared. "We will pray to the heavenly Father and ask Him to bestow on you His divine protection."

Giving a faint nod, she looked down at her lap.

He put his hands to her shoulders, startling her into meeting his gaze. "You must put your hope in God, Sarah, as all of this land is doing in its fight for liberty. Trust that He will take care of you and that His righteousness will prevail so that you may win your own freedom."

" 'Tis a hard thing," she whispered, the tightness in her throat cutting off her voice. "And yet, I do so want to trust. . . ."

Sympathy gleamed in his eyes, and he drew her close. Suddenly the swift beating of her heart stemmed not from fear but rather from the powerful feel of his arms encircling her. Her ear lay against his solid chest, beneath which his heart pounded just as erratically. The soft brush of his hair tickled her cheek while the pleasant musk, combined with the sweet aroma of wood shavings—a scent uniquely his—made Sarah woozy, yet strangely alive.

In wonderment, she lifted her head. Her stomach tumbled when he touched his warm lips to her brow. Their gazes briefly met before he slowly dipped his head to brush his lips across hers. Sarah's heart ceased beating. The kiss lasted mere seconds, but she knew she would remember this moment for a lifetime.

When he pulled away, self-consciousness wouldn't allow her to meet his gaze. "I'll see you home," he said after a long moment, his voice strange.

At this, she swiftly looked up. "Please, Thomas. I promise to return, as you have advised. But I need time—just this night—to reconcile my feelings in the matter."

"Sarah," he said, his voice hoarse. "You cannot stay here."

Her cheeks flamed at what he must think of her after she so readily accepted his kiss. Embarrassed, she pushed him away and rose from the bench. "Never fear, Sir. I am no doxy to seek a man's bed! I thought only to sleep by the fire. If you won't help me, I'll find another place to rest my head. I've slept beneath the stars before and in worse places than that, I assure you."

He also stood to his feet. Still feeling the sting of humiliation, she stepped back—and came against the wall.

"Sarah, I never gave nor suggested any ill construction to your words," he said patiently. "I know you're a woman of pure heart." He stepped forward and gently pulled one of her stiff hands from her crossed arms. "Regardless of how innocent it may seem to let you take my cot for the night while I sleep down here with Jeremy, the townspeople are likely to misconstrue the situation and regard you as a woman of ill repute."

The truth of his words made her bow her head in shame. "Forgive me, Thomas. I didn't think."

He placed a finger beneath her chin, lifted it, and offered a tolerant smile. "It's understandable. You are overwrought. I'll take you to my sister's house for the night. There you'll be safe."

Grateful, she nodded.

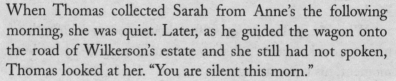

When Thomas collected Sarah from Anne's the following morning, she was quiet. Later, as he guided the wagon onto the road of Wilkerson's estate and she still had not spoken, Thomas looked at her. "You are silent this morn."

Brow furrowed, she turned to him. "I've been mulling over the conversation I had with Anne." She paused, ashamed. "I hesitate to speak so, but I was having a difficult time understanding how God could let this happen to me."

When she didn't expound further, Thomas nodded. "Permit me. Anne told you that God wasn't responsible for bringing misfortune but rather it was the result of evil men who make evil choices. Since man has been given the gift of free will, God will not interfere with those choices. Yet to His children who obey His commands and confidently rely and trust in Him, He will deliver them from the hands of the enemy and to a place of safety."

She lifted her brows, surprised. "She spoke of our discussion?"

"No. Anne would never divulge a confidence. In years past, she has also told me as much. My sister is an intelligent woman of strong spirit. Tell me, has she eased your fears?"

"She answered the question that has long plagued me, 'tis true. Yet I am still apprehensive of the future."

"Shall we pray?"

To Sarah's amazement, Thomas pulled the wagon over and held out his hand. Shyly, she gave hers to him, and he bowed his head. His words were confident as he asked God to give them peace, wisdom, and protection, also asking for His divine intervention.

"Thank you," she said, touched.

His eyes reassured, and he squeezed her fingers before returning his hand to the reins. "Remember, Sarah. God is bigger than the difficulty you face."

Once they arrived at the estate, Sarah clung to Thomas's words as she watched Mr. Wilkerson storm outside. She had barely stepped off the wagon before the man grasped her arm and pulled her toward the house.

"You'll be greatly sorry for attempting to escape," he snarled.

"I returned of my own free will," Sarah argued, trying to wrest her arm from his iron hold.

"Tell that to the constable when he arrives. I have sent Morton to fetch him." He shoved her inside, but before he could shut the door behind them, Thomas moved to the entrance.

"Be gone," Mr. Wilkerson said. "This is none of your concern."

"I beg to differ, Sir. Anything relating to Sarah is of the utmost concern to me."

Despite the grave situation, Sarah's heart leaped. Had Thomas stated his intentions, or was she reading more into his words than was there?

"Sarah is my indenture. She is under a convict's contract, and as such, she has sorely abused the law."

"As have you, Sir, in your treatment of her, as well as other indentures in your household—namely a woman named Grace," Thomas rejoined quietly.

Mr. Wilkerson regarded him in incredulous anger. "You dare speak to me in this manner and in my own home? I have broken no law!"

"I speak not of the written law man has devised, but rather of God's Law, as revealed in His holy Word."

"What insolence! Leave my house at once!"

Thomas did not budge. "I shall not go until I am assured of Sarah's safety."

"Now you accuse me?" the older man sputtered. "What lies has the wench told you?"

"I merely state the facts as I perceive them."

"Though he may not accuse you," a sober voice abruptly announced from the doorway, "I, and others, most certainly do."

Sarah turned in shock to see the constable standing near the open door, a solemn expression on his lined face.

Her master pointed an accusatory finger Sarah's way. "This indenture has stolen an item of worth from my household. I demand you arrest her. And this man," he continued, pointing his finger at Thomas, "I suspect to be her accomplice."

"I have stolen nothing," Sarah countered firmly. "Nor has Thomas. You have no proof."

"My proof is my word. I am a gentleman of means, and that should be testimony enough against the word of a convict and her, her. . ." He sought for a fitting word to describe Thomas.

"Father?" a small voice broke into the discord.

Everyone looked toward the entrance near the stairwell. Rupert stood in his bed gown, sleepily rubbing his eye with one fist. With the other hand he held an ivory picture frame clutched to his chest.

"What have you there, Lad?" Thomas asked, moving his way. "May I see?"

Rupert eyed Thomas, uncertain, then nodded and held his treasure out. " 'Tis my mother, Sir." He looked toward his father. "I know I wasn't supposed to take it, but. . ."

His words trailed off in fear, and Sarah stepped forward and knelt before him. Remembering their conversation the previous evening, she finished the boy's sentence. "But you were lonely for your mother and slept with her likeness since you couldn't have her with you. Is that not true, Rupert?"

Hanging his head, a great tear rolling from his eye, he nodded. Thomas faced Mr. Wilkerson. "Is this the item which you accused Sarah of taking?" The older man frowned, gave a stiff nod, and Thomas turned to the constable. "Then it would appear there is no longer a need for an arrest. Correct, Edward?"

"Unfortunately, Thomas, that is not the case."

Shocked, Sarah watched the newcomer step in front of her master. "Bartholomew Wilkerson," the constable said, "through the authority invested in me by the township of Philadelphia, I place you under arrest for a suspected liaison with the enemy, as well as for harboring pro-British sympathies."

"Outrageous!" the accused man sputtered. "I'm as much a Patriot as you are."

"On the contrary, several highly venerated men have come forward stating otherwise," the constable rejoined. "Will you leave peaceably, or need I exert force? I have men at my disposal to aid me, should such a task prove necessary."

The estate owner opened his mouth to speak, cast a look at his son staring up at him in confusion, then shook his head and marched out the door. The constable followed.

Sarah blinked, startled by the speed with which events had progressed. Only seconds ago she'd stood accused, and now her master was going in her place?

Sensing the child tremble, she gave him a hug. "Go ask Mrs. Leppermier to give you a dish of plum pudding. Tell her I said it was all right."

The boy's eyes widened. "Before breakfast?"

She grinned. "This time only."

The thought of a sweet in the morning brought a smile to his face. After he left, Thomas spoke. "You truly love him."

"Aye," she said, as Rupert skipped to the kitchen with thoughts of his father temporarily forgotten. "Think you that Anne would agree to Rupert coming to visit? His stepmother cares naught for him, so she would likely condone the arrangement."

"I believe Anne would agree."

She hesitated, then looked at him. "I have a second favor to ask. Would your sister consider hiring another indenture? I believe Grace would be an asset. Her term here as a housemaid is almost at an end as well."

"Anyone would be an improvement over Matilda," he said with feeling. "I'll discuss the matter with Anne."

"Thank you." Suddenly the enormity of what had transpired struck Sarah fully. "God answered our prayer," she whispered. "He delivered me from the hands of my enemy, as Anne said He would."

Thomas nodded. "Yes, He did. . .as He will do for all who serve Him."

Something about his manner made her peer at him more closely. "Is anything the matter?"

He was quiet a moment. "I had not thought to tell you at this time, but in light of the circumstances. . ." He released a breath. "Let us go to the garden and talk."

Perplexed, she rose to go with him.

They walked side by side in the shade of the chestnut trees. Thomas gravely stared ahead, clasping one of his wrists behind him. "For long weeks I have agonized over a decision. A childhood tragedy shaped my beliefs, and I made a vow never to take a life. Yet I can no longer idly stand by and watch while my friends and neighbors fight for this country's freedom." He halted on the path and faced her. "I'm going to join the war."

"Oh, Thomas," she breathed, feeling faint. She clutched her skirt. "When?"

"After my last work order is filled. A month, perchance." He took her hand. "Do not fear for my life, sweet Sarah. God will protect me."

Before she could formulate a response, he volleyed another cannonball through the unsteady foundation of her whirling emotions.

"Forgive me if I speak too rashly, but I must say more. I care deeply for you, Sarah—nay, I love you and want to protect you always. Bartholomew Wilkerson is detained, but for how long? Then, too, there is the matter of those who harassed you during the celebration. . . ."

She only stared, the chambers of her mind still echoing with his words, "I love you and want to protect you always."

Thomas paused, seeming to realize he'd lost her. "Sarah, I'm asking you to consider becoming my wife and marrying me before I go to war. In bearing my name, you'll be protected from those who mean you harm. Until my return, you shall live with Anne as a member of the family, not as a servant."

His *wife?* Sarah struggled to retain his words, but she could not think. Everything was happening so fast.

"I respect your desire to bring your siblings to America," he continued, "but until this conflict is over, it is impossible to do so. Yet I give you my word that I will acquire passage for them as soon as is feasible." His hands tightened on her fingers when she did not respond. "What say you, Sarah? Will you have me?"

She looked away from his penetrating blue eyes and down

at the grass while she endeavored to express herself. "I know not what to say, Thomas. My heart is full, and my thoughts are in a muddle." She shook her head, overwhelmed. "So much has happened this morn—"

Dismay clouded his face, and briefly he closed his eyes. "Forgive me. I spoke too soon. Attribute my blunder to my eagerness at the prospect of sharing my life with you as well as to my concern for your protection. I'll not speak of the matter again." Swiftly he brought the backs of her hands to his lips, released them, and turned away.

Bewildered, Sarah watched him go, the sun's rays highlighting his striking form. Nowhere had she met such a benevolent man, a man who lived his faith without apology, who was not afraid to face danger for righteousness' sake. . .and soon he would be entering the very heart of danger. He was going to war.

The thought frightened her. Would she see him again?

With each step Thomas took away from Sarah, her heart beat harder within her breast, as though punishing her for her foolishness. *Dear Father in heaven, what should I do? I need Your guidance. I do care deeply for him. . . .*

With astonishing clarity, her rampant thoughts melded into one, and she was assured of the course to take.

"Wait!" she cried.

Picking up her skirts, she ran down the path and came to a stop in front of Thomas, where he, too, had halted. "Aye, Thomas," she murmured, suddenly bashful. "I will have you."

His eyes were tender, his smile sad. "No, Sarah."

No? She blinked, certain she had misunderstood. Did he not just ask her to marry him?

"I was wrong to seek your response so soon," he explained. "I see that now. I don't wish you to speak in haste, only to regret doing so later. 'Tis my earnest hope that should you ever seek me out it will be love that compels you. I know many enter a match for convenience's sake, but I want mutual love to be the bond that holds us together."

Awed, Sarah stared at his handsome countenance, convinced of one thing. It didn't matter how much time passed, whether it be a day or a year. Thomas's unselfish words only further persuaded her that this was the man God had chosen for her. She wanted no other.

Placing her hands on either side of his face, Sarah looked deeply into his eyes. "I never have been more certain of anything. And I do love you, Thomas Gray."

Hope lit his features. "You are certain?"

She grinned, her heart buoyant. "Aye."

To her delight, he pulled her into his strong embrace and kissed her, sealing the pledge of their future together.

Sarah didn't know what lay ahead in their land's fight for freedom, but she vowed to be grateful for the moments God gave her with Thomas. Every day was a gift, and she would treasure each one.

Epilogue

In the darkening twilight, Sarah stood on the grassy hill and scanned the crowd of merry-goers. Grace's daughter, Hannah, played with Phillip and Anne's seven children, while Anne strolled nearby, carrying her newest daughter, Beulah.

Laughing, the children stood in a circle and threw a ball to one another. Hannah's hands were too small to catch it well, and she could only throw it a few feet; but everyone loved the cheerful six year old and couldn't refuse her in the game. Grace stood nearby, looking at her child with a mother's loving pride. In the years she'd worked for Anne, she'd responded to the love and kindness showered upon her and grown to know the Lord.

Sarah sighed. So much had happened in the past few years. Two weeks after Thomas left for war, her old master, Mr. Wilkerson, had been banished, though his wife and son were allowed to stay behind. The next day, Sarah had heard the guns of battle at nearby Chadd's Ford. On September 26, the British marched into Philadelphia and occupied the town for nine months. During the following five years, as all other soldiers' wives did, Sarah waited, wept, and prayed for word from her husband. Then last year, two months after the war's end, her beloved had come home. A short time later, Thomas kept his promise to Sarah and answered another strong desire of her heart. That of bringing her family to America.

"Sarah?" Her sister, Dorrie, hurried her way. "Have you seen Charles?"

"I imagine our young brother is with Thomas," Sarah said with a smile. "The two are inseparable since Charles has shown an interest in woodworking."

"Would they have gone to the shop this night?" Dorrie asked in surprise.

Though still frail, she was beautiful, with her cobalt eyes and ginger brown hair. Happiness made her face glow. That and the attentions of a certain young blacksmith who lived nearby.

"All the shops are closed," Sarah said. "Though I know Thomas is eager to finish the cradle before the time arrives."

Several loud, popping explosions interrupted their conversation, and both women looked toward the heavens, where brilliant starbursts of color painted the evening sky.

"Oh," Dorrie murmured in awe. " 'Tis beautiful."

"That it is," Thomas said, coming up behind them. Charles and a smartly dressed, thirteen-year-old Rupert flanked his sides.

"A wondrous spectacle," Rupert agreed, his voice cracking with manhood.

In the shielding cloak of night, Thomas looped his arm around Sarah's waist, gently drawing her back so that her shoulder blades rested against his chest. " 'Tis the triumphant cry of freedom," he said softly. "One this nation has longed to hear."

Suddenly the babe within Sarah's belly kicked hard against Thomas's arm, and he chuckled. "It would seem our son agrees."

"Aye," Sarah said with a smile, leaning back against him. "How thankful I am that our child will be born in a land that is truly free." Her hand covered Thomas's where it rested against her swollen stomach. "And how thankful I am for you, and men like you, whose bravery made it possible."

She felt his lips brush the top of her head.

"I pray all generations, henceforth, will remember this day and hold it in high regard," Sarah said, watching the rockets light the sky. "That the meaning is not lost and the sacrifices made are not forgotten. . . . Thomas, do you think our country will ever again have to fight a war?"

"Sarah. . ." He turned her to face him. "Why question what we cannot possibly know? I cannot predict the future, yet I can tell you this: God stands for righteousness and looks after His own. Let us thank Him for our liberty this Independence Day and put all worries behind us."

"Aye," she murmured, grateful for this man. Thomas was a strong tower when she needed reassurance, and he was right. God would take care of them, come what may, as He had always done. Through past years, Sarah had finally learned that lesson, and her faith had grown.

"I love you, my husband."

"And with all that I am, I love you."

The glow from the fireworks lit his tender expression as he lowered his head. His lips met hers, and myriad explosions—both in the sky above and in her heart—filled Sarah with joy.

At last, freedom was theirs.

"Proclaim Liberty throughout all the land
unto all the inhabitants thereof."
INSCRIPTION ON THE LIBERTY BELL
FROM LEVITICUS 25:10

PAMELA GRIFFIN

Pamela lives in Texas and divides her time between family, church activities, and writing. She fully gave her life to the Lord Jesus Christ in 1988, after a rebellious young adulthood, and owes the fact that she's still alive today to a mother who steadfastly prayed and had faith that God could bring her wayward daughter "home." Pamela's main goal in writing Christian romance is to help and encourage those who do know the Lord and to plant a seed of hope in those who don't, through entertaining stories. She has four titles with **Heartsong Presents** and several novellas published by Barbour. Pamela invites you to check out her website (please note the changed address for those who've visited before): http://members.cowtown.net/PamelaGriffin/

FREE
INDEED

by Kristy Dykes

Dedication

To my hero husband, Milton,
who is my collaborator in the deepest sense of the word—
he's believed in me, supported me,
and cheered me on in my calling to inspirational writing.

Author's Note:

In 1859, there were many black dialects in the South,
including Geechee, Gullah, combinations of various kinds,
even Elizabethan-sounding ones. I considered using Gullah,
which is the authentic Black dialect in Charleston,
South Carolina, but the dialogue would be hard to read.
In an effort to maintain the flavor of the setting and time,
I've sprinkled in off-grammar vernacular,
the most easily-read form of dialect.

*"If the Son therefore shall make you free,
ye shall be free indeed."*
JOHN 8:36

Prologue

1856, Laurel Ridge Plantation
The outskirts of Charleston, South Carolina

T wo important days have shaped my future, and they both had to do with freedom. I'll never forget the first day as long as I live.

That afternoon, I was helping Mrs. Williams, my master's wife, get dressed. She was to entertain her friends, and I took particular pains with her light brown hair, coiling the back into the new figure-eight style chignon, fluffing the front and sides into frothy curls. I wanted her to look her very best and had even suggested she wear her rose-colored silk, which she did. Then I refashioned her maroon velvet hat, adding ribbons and peacock feathers, something I'd seen in her ladies' magazine.

When she dismissed me, I came down the staircase of Laurel Ridge, intent on going to my quarters and checking on my little daughter, Cassie. She was asleep when I left her, and I wanted to be there when she woke up. After that, I planned to bring her to the kitchen house so I could watch her while I ironed Mrs. Williams's fine lawn underpinnings.

As I reached the last step, I lingered for a moment, thoughts of my Sweet Love Roscoe making my head swim and my heart race. My Sweet Love Roscoe lived on a neighboring plantation, and we had been allowed to jump the broom—that's slave talk for getting married—the summer of my seventeenth year, though I was still required to keep my master's surname.

Our blooming union, as Sweet Love Roscoe joshingly called it, had a bright spot. It had given us little Cassie. But dark clouds of despair overshadowed us when his bedeviled master issued a cruel edict after Cassie was born. He refused to let Sweet Love Roscoe see me, something that caused both of us great grief. The rare moments we spent in each other's arms were brief and on the sly.

I wept many a night over this. Other times, I got downright angry. The only things my people would ever know were ownership by other human beings and long dreary lives of servitude— if they were lucky enough not to be lashed into early graves, something that was a real possibility for my Sweet Love Roscoe.

The thought turned my stomach, as if I'd swallowed rancid meat, and I gripped the banister more tightly to steady my footing.

Oh, Roscoe, I cried out in my heart. *Oh, my Sweet Love Roscoe. . .*

I felt so woebegone, I couldn't even hang words on my thoughts. Then I shook myself. Work waited, always waited. As I proceeded across the wide hall of Laurel Ridge, I heard a door open behind me.

"Winkie?" called my master, Mr. Williams.

I turned around, my long skirts swishing in my quick movement. "Sir?"

"I've something to discuss with you. Come into my study?"

"Yes, Sir." In moments, I was seated in front of Mr.

Williams's large mahogany desk, wondering what he had to say. Though he was far different from Sweet Love Roscoe's stony-hearted master, still he was. . .my master, and inside, I chafed at this thought.

Mr. Williams sat down in his high-backed leather chair, reached into a drawer, and pulled out some papers.

Again, I wondered why he'd called me in here.

"You are a free woman," he said, eagerness in his voice, kindness in his eyes. "Here are your official papers. Winkie Williams, I'm proclaiming you free as of this moment."

I looked at him as if thunderstruck. "Free?" I finally said, trying to fathom the meaning of the word that held no meaning for the likes of me.

"I'm selling the plantation, and Mrs. Williams and I are moving back to the North. I'm freeing my slaves. You're the first one I've told because you've always been special to our family." He pushed a paper across the desk. "Here. Take it."

I reached for the document, dazed. Where would I go? What would I do? How would I support myself? And most importantly, what would this mean for my Sweet Love Roscoe and me? Living at Laurel Ridge, we enjoyed a few stolen moments here or there. When I left, I would never see him again.

Not ever.

Anger boiled in me. Of course I wanted my freedom. All of my people wanted their freedom. Now I had it in my hands. I squeezed the document, and it rustled in my grip. But freedom for me meant parting with my Sweet Love Roscoe.

A venomous chuckle roared up my throat as the irony of the whole thing struck me. Slavery had been forced on me, and now freedom was too.

"Winkie?" Mr. Williams said, concern in his tone.

My presence of mind returned, along with my manners. "I–I don't know wh–what to say, Mr. Williams," I stammered as I stood up. "Except th–thank you, kind sir."

"Godspeed to you, Winkie."

With a nod and a smile and a confident step, I made my way across the room, but inside, I was reeling from this news. I closed the door behind me and leaned against the wall, knocking a brass sconce askew. I righted it and moved a few paces down the hall, sank into a chair, my legs too wobbly to hold me.

Tears welled in my eyes as I bunched and unbunched the fabric of my skirt, fretting over my future, a lifetime without my man. Then a thought came to me that sent thrill chills speeding down my spine.

Strike for freedom, I would urge Sweet Love Roscoe. *Go to Canada. We'll start a new life together, one founded in the sweet light of liberty.*

Now was our chance. We could live in Canada, where we'd been told blacksmiths easily obtained work. I knew Roscoe would do as I bid. He'd been thinking about it for months, years even.

"I'll escape to Canada on the Underground Railroad," he would say, "and you and Cassie can follow me when I get settled."

Every time he mentioned it, I would put my fingers across his lips. "No," I always said, fear gripping me with an ironclad hand. "If the slave hunters were to catch us. . ." I would shiver, and then I would say, "You know what they do if you're caught."

Now, though, courage welled up in my breast, and I knew it was time for Roscoe to strike for Canada. And with my freedom granted, Cassie and I could follow him legally and unafraid. The thought comforted me like a coat in the cold.

But how would I keep body and soul together during the

time Cassie and I waited on Sweet Love Roscoe to reach Canada?

My mind ran a hundred different ways. I could dress a lady. I could sew. I could take care of children. Would any of these skills help me find work once I left Laurel Ridge? I could cook. I could clean. Why, I would even scoop dung from the streets if that's what it took.

But would I be able to find work? Jobs were scarce for free people, I knew. And where would Cassie and I live? And what would she do while I worked? Who would look out for her?

The ponderations pounded in my brain until my head ached with a ferocity I had never known. If I were a lady woman, I would take to my bed with a vinegar compress on my brow. But I was not a white lady.

I was a former slave, now a free woman, alone in the world except for little Cassie, with no prospects of a job under my belt or a roof over my head. . . .

Chapter 1

Three years later, 1859
Charleston, South Carolina

Winkie Williams stood in front of her millinery shop, sweeping vigorously. Only two hours past cockcrow, the July sun was already high in the sky, and she stopped her work and swiped at her brow with a handkerchief.

Grasping the broom handle, she stood staring at her strong brown hands, hands that had picked cotton as a child, dressed the master's wife as a girl, and were now making hats for Charleston society ladies.

She looked across the pastel-colored buildings and drew in a breath of sharp briny air drifting in from the harbor. In the distance, she could hear horns blowing, flutes trilling, drums beating, and she knew that somewhere in downtown Charleston, band members were practicing for the Independence Day parade that would soon commence.

She could picture the parade scene as if it were before her. She had watched the parade in the past, but not last year, and not today either. Today marked two years since she had gotten the awful news, and she doubted she would ever go to another

Independence Day parade again. How could she celebrate when her Sweet Love Roscoe lay in a cold, dark grave?

She willed herself not to succumb to the grief that often overwhelmed her. "Think about the parade," she mumbled as a drummer banged out a fast beat.

"At the parade," she said to herself, "the streets will be lined with ladies and gents and boys and girls. Most will be dressed in red, white, and blue. Some of the ladies will be wearing hats that I made with my own hands. They're going to shake their noisemakers and toot their tin horns and sing their patriotic songs and wave their flags high in the air. They're going to shout, 'Let freedom ring.' They're going to holler, 'Liberty, sweet liberty.' They're going to say, 'God bless America.'"

She continued sweeping, intent on getting every speck of dirt off her front stoop, something she did at least twice a day. "Yes, God has blessed you, America. You are free from the bondage of your mother country. And I am free from the bondage of slavery."

She leaned down and picked dead petals off the flowers that were clumped in pots by the door. "But what good does that do?" she almost spat out. "My people will never be free men and free women, like me. They never know what it mean to have a kind master release them."

From her pocket she withdrew a cleaning rag and rubbed at a streak on the windowpane. Her musings brought to mind her dear departed mother, a slave brought over from Africa before the turn of the century, a woman whose existence had been one of unspeakable inhumanity, sorrow, and despair.

Burdens—that's all there be to life, Mama said many a time. *We be tasked hard.*

"Mama, look—"

"Goodness, Child," Winkie shrieked, dropping the rag, "I be so deep in the land of emptiness, you plumb scared the pudding out of me." She reached over and patted her six-year-old daughter where she stood in the open door, then lifted Cassie's chin and smiled down at her. "I got a surprise waiting for you, Sugarbun."

"We going to the parade?" Cassie exclaimed, her eyes lit up like the sidewalk firecrackers the white children set off every Independence Day. "Oh, Mama, thank you, thank you. Just what I wanted—"

"Now what you go bringing that up for?" Winkie snapped. "I done told you my answer about the parade. It's no. *N-O,*" she spelled. "Madam is expecting three more bonnets from me in the morning. I got work waiting."

She turned back to the window and rubbed the pane furiously. "Always, the work is there. There's never no letup. I be tasked hard."

Cassie grew as still as a statue, her eyes downcast, and immediately Winkie was ashamed of her outburst. She knelt down and drew Cassie to her, squeezing her in a tight embrace, head to head, heart to heart.

"Mama's sorry, Cassie, my mama-look baby. My surprise is a sweet potato pie. I made it this morning. Your favorite. Mama don't mean to be such a sore head all the livelong day. It's just that I. . .well, I got troubles pressing on my mind—"

"Winkie," a high-pitched female voice called from down the street. "I'm sorely in need of your services."

Winkie stood up, her fingers locked with Cassie's as she looked toward the lady, her girlhood friend, the master's daughter who had taught her how to read. Miss Willie was coming pell-mell down the street, her blond ringlets bouncing with every step, her bell-shaped skirts swishing and swaying with every movement.

"Why, do tell," Winkie said, when Miss Willie drew near, forcing cheerfulness into her voice. "What brings you here on Independence Day? Shouldn't you be heading to town for the festivities?"

"I'm on my way," Miss Willie huffed out. "But I had an item of utmost importance to attend to." She swooped down and tickled Cassie on the side of the neck, and Cassie giggled in delight. "Look what I've brought you, Cassie dear." From her large reticule she pulled out a charming doll dressed in an ex- quisite red, white, and blue silk gown.

Cassie hugged the doll to her. "Thank you, Miss Willie. This be better than any old parade," she said softly as she turned and headed inside.

"She's a quiet child," Miss Willie said.

"Yes, Ma'am. Now, what can I do for you today?" Winkie looked to her left, then to her right. It wouldn't be fitten for a fine lady like Miss Willie to be seen standing in the alleyway conversing with the likes of her. "Come on in. Whatever it is you need, we be seeing to it right away."

Inside the little shop that wasn't really a shop, only a work- room with a curtained-off sleeping area, Winkie offered Miss Willie a chair, then put the broom away.

"Willie and Winkie," Miss Willie said as she settled back in the chair and smoothed her ruffle-flounced, white brocade gown. "We were a lively duo growing up, weren't we?"

"That we was."

"Had ourselves some escapades, didn't we?"

"That we did." Winkie sat down in the other chair, leaned her elbow on the table, and lightly drummed her fingers. Miss

Willie's family, the Williamses, had come from the North and purchased Laurel Ridge when both girls were about thirteen.

From the moment they'd met, they'd become fast friends. Miss Willie—Wilhelmina was her given name, but everyone called her Miss Willie—had married at seventeen. That same day while the white folks' wedding festivities were going on up at the big house, Winkie and her Sweet Love Roscoe had been jumping the broom down at the quarters.

Winkie fiddled with the folds of fabric stacked neatly on the table. Growing up, she and Miss Willie had shared many commonalities. Their flair for fashion. Their interest in reading after Miss Willie taught her how. Even the similarity of their names. Willie and Winkie. Perhaps those were the things that had bonded them together so strongly.

But now one profound difference stood between them. Miss Willie had a husband and no child. Winkie had a child and no husband. She had no husband because her Sweet Love Roscoe had died fleeing the tyranny of a cruel master. Halfway to Canada, the slave hunters had captured him and dragged him back, and in the process, Sweet Love Roscoe had lost his life. And it was all because of her. She had urged him to escape.

Oh, Roscoe. She rubbed her temple where it throbbed.

"I came by this morning to see if you'd make a few of these rosettes you made for my bonnet." Miss Willie touched the red, white, and blue fabric flowers on each side of her hat. "And sew them onto my sash." She fingered the red silk sash at her waist. "I thought a touch of red, white, and blue somewhere on my gown would look even more patriotic."

"Sure thing, Miss Willie." Winkie stood and in one quick movement gathered her sewing basket and some swatches of red, white, and blue silk fabric from a shelf overhead. Then she sat back down. "Won't take me no time."

"I knew that. Otherwise, I wouldn't have troubled you."

"No trouble at all." She could spend a lifetime helping Miss Willie, yet it would never repay her for her kindness. A few years after Miss Willie had married and moved to a plantation in Georgia, her father had decided to sell Laurel Ridge and move back to the North. It was then that Miss Willie convinced him to free his slaves.

It was then that Winkie had become a free woman.

Winkie threaded her needle, stuck it in a pincushion, cut narrow strips of red, white, and blue silk skillfully, just as her milliner patron had taught her. She would be indebted to Miss Willie for life.

It was Miss Willie who had traveled to Charleston and secured Winkie's apprenticeship with the grand milliner, Madam Henderson. It was Miss Willie who had given Winkie the guidance to set up her own shop. It was Miss Willie who was responsible for Winkie's present life—living as a free woman and productive citizen on a busy street in Charleston, even if it was a back alley.

Though the ladies of Charleston had turned up their snooty noses at her back-alley shop—causing Madam Henderson to agree to front for Winkie for a fee and no credit for her hatmaking—still, the small profits kept body and soul together for Winkie and Cassie, and she would be eternally grateful to Miss Willie.

As long as Winkie lived, she could never do enough for the kind and gracious Miss Willie. Never. Why, there was no guile to be found in the blue-eyed, blond-haired belle, only sweetness down to the bone.

"I've come to ask a second favor of you, Winkie." Miss

Willie's sparkling blue eyes were sober now.

"Anything."

"Come to the parade."

"I couldn't do that." Winkie silently reprimanded herself. Hadn't she just been thinking she'd do anything for Miss Willie? Here she was, refusing her request. But she couldn't help it.

"It's time."

"That's something I need more of," Winkie said, trying to hide the anger in her voice, thinking that she'd had far too much time to brood this morning. "I have three bonnets yet to trim."

"It's time, I repeat. I think you know what I mean."

Winkie pushed the needle into a bunching of fabric, then deftly pulled it out. In the fabric, out the fabric, in the fabric, out the fabric.

"It's been two years since. . ." Miss Willie's voice trailed off. "There's someone I'd like to introduce you to after the parade."

The first rosette completed, Winkie bit off the thread, grinding her teeth more than necessary, and rethreaded the needle. A moment ago, she'd been thinking Miss Willie had no guile in her. Now she saw a hint of pretense. *Why, Miss Willie didn't come to the shop to have rosettes made. She came to make a match—*

Winkie couldn't even finish the thought. She pushed the needle into the fabric so hard, it punctured her finger and drew blood. She hadn't done that since her apprenticeship. She wrapped her finger with a piece of cloth, stuck a thimble on it, kept sewing.

"We're going to the parade with our friends, the Fletchers," Miss Willie said. "It's their carpenter I want you to meet. Mr. Fletcher says there's no finer man of all his people. This man I'm talking about—his name is Joseph Moore—is diligent and hard working, just like you, Winkie."

Winkie didn't say a word while she completed the second rosette. She just sat there, pulling the needle in and out, biting off the thread, rethreading the needle as Miss Willie prattled on about the man she wanted her to meet, the carpenter owned by the Fletchers.

"Dolly Fletcher says the talk is," Miss Willie continued, "that Joseph hasn't found the right girl to jump the broom with. You'd be the perfect girl."

"Jump the broom?" Memories seared her mind, and she felt as though she'd been burned by an ember from the cooking fire.

"I know it's hard for you—"

"You don't know no such of a thing." For the third time this morning, Winkie felt remorseful. Silently she reprimanded herself. First, Cassie had gotten the brunt of her malcontent. Then, Miss Willie. Now, Miss Willie again. Still, she couldn't help humming loudly, "Nobody Knows the Trouble I Seen."

"Mama, look," Cassie exclaimed as she skipped from behind the curtain. "Sheena—" She held out her doll as she ran to Winkie. "Her eyes opens and closes. I never held no doll that's eyes opens and closes. Oh, Mama, look."

"Come here, my mama-look baby." Winkie set aside her sewing, swooped Cassie onto her lap, and planted a kiss on each eyelid as Cassie convulsed in giggles.

All the things Winkie had thought about that morning, all the fanciful things Miss Willie was saying now—none of them mattered. Only Cassie mattered. Cassie was her reason for being. And living.

"Show Mama them eyes that opens and closes." Winkie kissed Cassie's eyelids again.

"For her," Miss Willie said, tipping her head in Cassie's

direction, looking intently at Winkie. "If for no other reason, go to the parade for her. She's a child. She needs diversion every now and then. I always said Independence Day is more fun than Christmas."

Winkie fiddled with the doll's eyelids. Perhaps Miss Willie was right. Cassie rarely had the opportunity for pleasure.

"After the parade," Miss Willie said, "the Fletchers are giving a pig roast in our honor—for moving back to South Carolina." She tapped on her hat brim. "I'm so happy you'll be making all my bonnets from now on."

Winkie sat there, contemplating what Miss Willie was saying, glad Miss Willie would be living nearby. That gave her a comfort.

"That's where I wish to introduce you to Joseph Moore—at the Fletchers' pig roast. Dolly Fletcher knows of my desire, and out of courtesy to me, she's extended an invitation to you to eat with their people. There'll be children Cassie's age, and she'll enjoy their games and child play. And the food is going to be simply scrumptious. The Fletcher people have been roasting the pigs all night long. Dolly says their people make the best roast pork in all of South Carolina. She vows and declares it's the wood they cook them over. I believe she said it's—"

"Oak wood," Winkie remarked absently, straightening the doll's hair that didn't need straightening. "Oak wood bring out the flavor of pork like no other."

"And they make a special sauce—"

"Carolina gold, I'd hanker." She untied the ribbon on the doll's bonnet, then retied it, laboriously making the loops as small as possible so they'd be in correct proportion to the doll's chin. "Carolina gold be better than Carolina red by a mile."

"Won't you please come to the parade? If you won't do it

for yourself, and you won't do it for Cassie, do it for me. Please? Help celebrate mine and Mr. Richard's move back to Charleston."

A half hour later, Winkie and Cassie were headed to the parade, dressed in their best gowns, matching feather-trimmed bonnets on their heads, a sweet potato pie in a basket on Winkie's arm. As they walked along, they trailed Miss Willie by a good half a block, as was proper.

"I wonder about. . .Mr. Joseph Moore, isn't that what Miss Willie called him?" Winkie said under her breath, knowing Cassie was paying her no mind.

"There won't be no mama-looks from Cassie right now," Winkie whispered. Cassie was holding Sheena—her first store-bought doll—and as the tyke walked along, she was opening and closing the open-and-close eyes. "I wonder what Mr. Joseph Moore's countenance be like," Winkie said softly.

She shifted the basket to her other arm and caught a whiff of the sweet potato pie. "Miss Willie is sweetness down to the bone. That she is." She breathed in deeply of the pleasant-smelling scent. "I'm going to the Independence Day parade and the picnic afterwards for Cassie's sake," she whispered. "And for Miss Willie's sake."

Deep down, though, she was loathe to admit that she was really going to the parade to meet Mr. Joseph Moore.

"I wonder if Mr. Joseph Moore be dark?" she mused aloud. "Or light? I wonder if he have big eyes or small? I wonder if he be tall, like me? Or short? He be smart, for sure. Double-dose smart. Miss Willie say he be so skilled at carpentering, the carpentry shop in town use his services."

Into her mind came a vision of a tall, handsome man bent over a workbench, his muscles glistening in the sunlight. Would he have understanding eyes and a compassionate soul? Perhaps this Mr. Joseph Moore would take a shine to little Cassie. That would most assuredly cause her to do a joy jig.

Then a second vision appeared, gut-wrenchingly so, of another tall, handsome man, this time bent over a blacksmith's fire, his muscles glistening in the sunlight. This man had understanding eyes and a compassionate soul, and he had loved Cassie with every sinew of his soul.

She drew in a sharp breath at the thought of Sweet Love Roscoe, her husband who'd died fleeing slavery—a word so abhorrent, she had a hard time letting it float through her mind. With brooding ponderations gnawing at her insides, she hurried on down the street.

Chapter 2

Joseph Moore stood amidst a sea of brown faces in the proper section of downtown Charleston, his arms folded across his barrel chest, anticipating with relish the Independence Day parade that was about to commence. He hadn't planned on going with the Fletchers, but at the last minute, the master had sent word that they would need his help transporting the Fletchers' many important guests to their afternoon picnic.

"You're to oversee the carriage caravan after the parade," came the word of direction.

That set well with him. Mighty well. Who wouldn't want to look at fine bands in colorful uniforms sounding out patriotic songs as they marched in rhythmic stride? Who wouldn't want to see ships in Charleston Harbor decorated in the nation's colors? Who wouldn't want to hear cannons along the waterfront discharging, one blast for every state of the Union?

And better than all of those things, he had to admit with a wry grin, who wouldn't want a day off from their labors?

As he stood in the dense throng of people, he rubbed his jaw, which was smooth from his morning's shave. Today, the nation would commemorate the anniversary of the independence of the United States of America.

Here in Charleston, the city fathers, as well as their families, would gloriously celebrate, he knew from years past. The first part of the festivities always began with the parade, followed by cannon fire, then speeches by political figures. All afternoon, picnics would be enjoyed all over the city, from public parks to private homes, including the gala party at the Fletchers' house. The evening would be marked by fireworks lighting the skies.

With the hot sun high overhead, Joseph shielded his face with the crook of his arm, then craned his neck to see above the crowd. When would the parade reach this side of town? In the distance, he could hear the band, but just barely.

Yes, all of Charleston, it seemed, had turned out to honor the brave patriots who had given their lives for freedom.

Freedom? With a sad shake of his head, he knew that word didn't apply to him and probably never would, even though political talk had heated up recently. Despite the hot sunshine beating down on him, he shivered, thinking of the strange words that elicited anger everywhere they were discussed: *Antislavery newspapers, equality, abolitionists, emancipation.*

Into his mind came the image of a large-bosomed black woman cradling a little boy in her arms as she taught him Bible stories and songs.

"Tell me the one about the boy with the coat of many colors, Mama," he'd said with a wide grin, knowing that the boy with the coat of many colors was his namesake.

"Someday, Joseph, I'm going to make you a coat like that," she'd said softly. Time and again she would tell him the story of Joseph-in-the-Bible and how he was sold into slavery and then unjustly imprisoned—

"But that isn't fair," the little boy would say every time at that particular place in the story.

"Life isn't fair," she would say back. "The thing that counts is always doing what's right, no matter what comes our way."

And he would beg her to finish the story because he had heard it a hundred times, and he knew something good awaited the boy Joseph.

"Joseph-in-the-Bible had the right attitude through every trial," she would say, "and in the end, God honored him. Son, hear me well. If you determine in your heart to be like that, God will honor you."

By his tenth summer, his mother had finally saved enough scraps of various-colored material and fashioned a coat of many colors. She presented it to him with great fanfare and pride.

That fall, the master sold him farther south.

He remembered the day as if it were yesterday. He would never forget his piercing cries as he was wrenched from the arms of a loving mother and thrust into the frightful unknown. Even now, he could smell her sweet scent, feel her warm breath on the top of his head.

But echoing through his mind were her words that would stay with him for as long as he lived, an admonition that had stood him well in life, an exhortation that was the reason for the sustaining peace deep in his heart: *Son, be like Joseph-in-the-Bible. Through your trials, keep the right attitude. And God will honor you.*

And that's how he had tried to live, even though he would always be a servant to a master. Instead of letting bitterness eat away at his soul over the inequities of life, he'd decided a long time ago to make happiness wherever he went.

And he tried to help others live that way too. He gave them so many doses of the Holy Book, the people had taken to calling him Bible Thumper—respectfully and with admiration in their voices—a name they called ministers. Even though he couldn't read, he could quote the Scriptures as good as the minister in Charleston, to his way of thinking.

He was so deep in thought, he almost jumped when he heard the loud notes of a lively patriotic song being played close by. To his left, just within his view, he saw a band marching down the street.

When only a few minutes passed, with his toe tapping to the beat of the rousing tune, the crowd closed in tighter, slaves and free people alike, all straining to get a glimpse and enjoy the frivolities of the day. He glanced around to see if he knew anyone, but the crowd kept jostling and shifting.

"Mama, Mama, I can't see," said a child to his right. "Please pick me up one more time."

"You be too heavy, Sugarbun," said a woman's voice, low and melodious. "I plumb give out from holding you."

Joseph glanced down, saw a little girl with a pleading expression on her face as she tugged on a woman's skirts. Then he looked directly at the woman, saw wide somber eyes, smooth-as-buttermilk brown skin, smart hat and gown, and he couldn't help smiling at the pleasant sight before him.

"Mind if I lend my assistance?" He tipped his head in the direction of the child. "I got mighty strong shoulders." In a playful mood, he tapped his shoulders. "I imagine they'd give a commanding view if somebody was to sit on them." He tweaked the little girl on her button nose, and she giggled, but the woman's lips were a straight line.

"Ma'am?" he asked, when the woman didn't answer. "I'd be glad to lift her up. So she can see the pretty uniforms the band be wearing."

"Mama," the little girl said. "Please?"

The woman dipped her chin demurely and lowered her gaze. "Th—thank you, Sir. I—I'm sure Cassie would like that."

He tried not to stare at the woman. Was something wrong? It certainly seemed that way. She was fidgety-acting, like a filly shying at a snake in her path.

But the little girl was of another vein. Her face was one wide grin from ear to ear, and he swooped her up and settled her on his right shoulder. "Cassie—isn't that what your mama called you?—if you smiled any wider, I believe your teeth would fall right out of your mouth." He chuckled, and the woman smiled—finally.

A quarter hour passed, then another as the bands marched by, their horns blowing and their drums beating. The child was as light as a feather on his shoulder, and he knew he could stand there for hours holding her; but with a rueful sigh, he realized he had to leave and see to his duties. The Fletchers, along with the rest of the white folks, were first on the parade route, and their crowd would be dispersing momentarily. He couldn't keep the Fletchers' guests waiting. He had to hurry. If he ran the six blocks back to the wagons, he would just barely make his appointed time.

"Ma'am," he said, "much as I'd like to stay here enjoying the parade with you and your fine little daughter, I have to go." He lifted the child from his shoulders and set her on the ground, and the woman took the little girl's hand. "I have work to attend to. You know."

"Yes, I know. Work." There was a hard edge to her voice. "The likes of us," she mumbled, "is always at the beck and call of—"

"What'd you say?" He pointed toward the band and raised his voice. "The music. I couldn't hear you."

The first cannon boomed, and the crowd let out a united, "Oh." He glanced to his side, and the woman and the girl were gone. He pivoted this way and that, looked in all directions, studied every face within seeing distance. Still, there was no sign of them. The second cannon fired, then the third.

A sharp sense of disappointment—no, sadness—enveloped him, but there was nothing to do but take off on a run as the fourth cannon fired.

Duty called.

Chapter 3

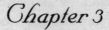

All the way to the Fletcher plantation, Winkie struggled with conflicting emotions. As she and Cassie bumped along in the seat behind Miss Willie and Mr. Richard, she gave her telltale heart a stern talking-to.

You, who didn't care to meet this Mr. Joseph Moore, has gone into public trifling with the first man you meet. Get a grip on yourself.

But I can't help it, Heart said.

Yes, you can, she said.

No, I can't, Heart said back. *He smart-looking and he handsome.*

You been holding with the hare and now you running with the hounds. Shame, shame.

My, but that man be something. He have understanding eyes. And he have a compassionate soul. That be better than any kind of looksome ways, yet he have them too—a right good plenty. Skin—rich nut brown. Teeth—so white they surely shine in the dark. Shoulders—as broad as a tree trunk. Muscles—strong enough to pick up a woman and carry her to—

Stop that, you hear me, Heart? Away with! Away with!

And the best part about him is, he take a shine to little Sugarbun.

Tears trickled down Winkie's cheeks. *Dear heart,* she said, *we'll never see that man again. Oh, what we going to do?*

Heart didn't answer.

With a sadness that settled in her bones, Winkie whispered, "Burdens. That's all there be to life." In a quick movement, she backhanded her tears, willing herself not to let one more fall.

At the Fletcher plantation, streamers dangled from tree limbs and floated in the breeze same as the gray curls of moss, and Winkie took note of the red, white, and blue bunting that draped the porch rails.

"Mama, look," Cassie said in her customary quiet way. "It be a sight to behold."

"You got that right," Winkie whispered, drinking in the prettiness as their carriage continued up the drive that was bordered by towering oaks. The big house was whitewashed until it gleamed in the sunlight, and the windows purely sparkled. Low-growing bushes and flowers of every shade in the rainbow lined the house. A fiddle and other instruments played from somewhere not too far off, and succulent smells of roasted pork scented the air.

Her eyes continued to feast. People dressed in Sunday finery milled about, greeting each other genteel-like; and she saw little girls sitting on the velvety lawn, their pouffy skirts spread about them as they nibbled on cookies.

"Is this heaven?" Cassie asked, her eyes lit up.

Winkie sucked in a long breath of air. "It smell like heaven, that for sure." She hugged Cassie to her. "You in for a treat today, Sugarbun. You can eat till your stomach plumb hurts if that's what you want to do." She touched her midsection. Eating her fill was one of her ideas of heaven.

All afternoon, Winkie and Cassie partook of the people's festivities behind the big house. They ate to their heart's content as they listened to the lively music, and Cassie made friends with several children who were in awe of her store-bought doll.

Winkie was polite when spoken to, but she kept up her usual guard. Why be cordial with people she'd never see again?

Miss Willie had mentioned that Winkie might make some friends today. She snorted as she ate a bite of pie. There was no time for that kind of folderol. There was only time for work, pure and simple. Wasn't that all there was to a body's existence? That's all she knew, anyway.

Toward evening, she helped with the cleanup, taking her turn at the dishpan under the shade of a majestic oak tree.

"Did you get a taste of that sweet potato pie in the basket?" said the woman who was drying the pewter plates as fast as Winkie put them in her hands. "It was gobbled up first thing. I only got a sliver. For sure, for sure, it be better than Bertha's. But don't tell her I said so. She take pride in her cooking, and she would surely be offended if she heard me say that."

Winkie dropped her gaze. She wasn't used to compliments. The woman was saying she was a better cook than the cook on the Fletcher plantation.

"Why, that was your pie, wasn't it? You made it."

"Yes." For the first time, Winkie really looked at the gray-haired, dark-as-ebony woman beside her. She was kindhearted, Winkie could tell, and she reminded her of Auntie, her mother's long-lost sister. For a moment, Winkie let down her stiff reserve. "Yes, it be my pie. I glad you enjoyed it."

"It be the texture that make it so good. It light and fluffy.

Kind of like a cloud." The woman good-naturedly elbowed Winkie as she laughed, her wide smile infectious, and Winkie smiled back.

"Winkie, there you are," Miss Willie said as she approached. "It's time for me to introduce you to the person I told you about."

Winkie hurriedly dried her hands on a dish rag, then rolled down her sleeves. The moment had come. She'd been dreading it and welcoming it at the same time. How could that be?

"He'll be along any moment. He's to meet us under the arbor." Miss Willie drew Winkie's hand into the crook of her elbow and proceeded toward the side lawn.

"What about Cassie?" Winkie looked at the group of children nearby.

"Let her enjoy her play."

Winkie nodded and called out a good-bye to the woman who had befriended her. Then she and Miss Willie made their way to the meeting place.

At the arbor, Winkie stood beside Miss Willie, wringing her hands. It had been so long since she'd been around a man.

Heart, what must I do? Stand a certain way? Strike a pose? Act natural?

Heart didn't answer.

She wrung her hands all the more as she stared toward the east, past the flower garden, into a copse of trees. What would Mr. Joseph Moore be like? Was he a swell? A coxcomb? A man about town? She hoped not. The vision appeared again of a smart, handsome man with understanding eyes and a compassionate soul.

Heart, will he be like that?

Still, Heart didn't answer.

"Miss Willie, I understand I'm to meet you at the arbor," said a man's voice.

The moment was here. Winkie smoothed her skirts, turned around, and got the start of her life. Standing before her was Mr. Joseph Moore. No, the man at the parade. No, the man Miss Willie wanted her to meet. She was confused. How could this be?

"Winkie, this is Joseph Moore," Miss Willie said. "Joseph, this is Winkie Williams."

With a gentle smile on his lips, Mr. Joseph Moore extended his hand.

Almost as if in a daze, Winkie extended hers.

"I've matters to attend to," Miss Willie said as she walked away from the arbor.

It was as if Winkie did not see Miss Willie. All she saw was. . .

A handsome man with understanding eyes and a compassionate soul. . .a man who held her hand in his. . .a man who had taken a shine to Sugarbun.

In response, her feet did a little dance in the dirt.

"Why, Winkie," he said, "I didn't hear the music commencing, but we can dance just the same. So, do-si-do is it, first off?"

She felt her face heat up in embarrassment. "I–I. . .n–no. . . that wasn't my intention," she stammered. "Y–you don't understand." She withdrew her hand, stood ramrod straight, trying to think what to do next, what to say.

He looked directly at her, seeming to search her eyes, but she quickly averted his gaze, glanced at her feet, ground her toe in the dirt.

Gently he lifted her chin so he could look into her eyes. "This isn't going very well, is it? Why don't we start over?" He took a step back, thrust out his hand toward her in play-acting gestures. "Winkie Williams, this is Joseph Moore. Joseph Moore, this is Winkie Williams." He bowed dramatically.

As he drew up to his full height, she saw the smiles in his eyes and felt her face heating up again. This was a man worth getting to know. This was a man who could set her feet to dancing and her face to smiling.

"There it is. A smile. I was certain it was in there somewhere." He picked a camellia off a nearby bush, placed it in her palm, and pressed her fingers around it.

Her heart pounded against her chest, and with her free hand she toyed with the button at her neckline.

Heart, you knew, didn't you? You knew all along.

Heart said, *Yes.*

Under a starlit sky, Joseph drove Winkie and Cassie the two miles back to town in Mr. Fletcher's buggy. As the horse clip-clopped along, he couldn't keep his thoughts off the attractive woman at his side. She had insisted on staying to help with the cleanup, and after knowing her for only one afternoon, he found that Work was her middle name. No matter. Industriousness was a good attribute.

The used key is always bright, his mother used to say.

Winkie's busyness certainly stood him in good stead tonight, he thought with an inward chuckle. Because she'd stayed so long at the dishpan, Miss Willie and Mr. Richard had asked Joseph to deliver Winkie and Cassie back to town.

He reflected about the moment they'd met that afternoon. When Miss Willie introduced them, at first Winkie had seemed. . .confused? Was that the word he was looking for?

Then it was like something dawned on her, and she looked straight at him. Then she did that little dance, right there in front of him, and it warmed the cockles of his heart. As she did her little two-step in the dirt, he was treading on enchanted ground.

Then she acted flustered. What was going on with her? He knew what was going on with him.

This is a woman I want to get to know.

A few blocks from her shop, he stopped the buggy, looped the reins, and leaned forward so he could see Cassie, who was sitting on the other side of Winkie.

"The fireworks ought to be starting soon, Cassie," he said. In the soft glow of the street lamp at the end of the block, he saw her smile in response.

Suddenly, a loud boom sounded, and Cassie jumped. Winkie let out a little shriek.

"The fireworks," he exclaimed. From their close proximity, he felt Winkie tremble, then felt fumbling and saw Winkie put her arm around Cassie protectively.

"Look, Mama," Cassie said. "That one is a wheel in a wheel."

Sitting closely beside Winkie, he was struck by how wiry she was. Why, the woman was so slight-made, he could feel her bones. Probably she ate sparingly so she could feed Cassie well.

The thought tugged at his heart.

Another set of fireworks filled the sky with bursting sprays of color, and Cassie oohed and ahed at the spectacular sight.

Joseph smiled, pleased at the little girl's obvious happiness, as he took the reins and drove on down the street.

"Thank you, Mr. Joseph Moore," Winkie said after a long span of pleasurable silence, "for giving my daughter—and me— a most enjoyable evening."

"It be refreshing for me as well." *Refreshing? No, rapturous.*

"We will never forget this night, will we, Cassie?" She patted Cassie's knee.

I will never forget it either, he couldn't help thinking.

"Look, Mama," Cassie said, pointing upward.

"That be the grand finale." Joseph looked skyward and saw the dazzling display. *Fireworks are not only in the sky. They're in my heart.*

Chapter 4

Two days later, Winkie was on her way home from the fabric shop where she'd ordered some material.

"Sugarbun, don't dawdle," Winkie said. "I got work waiting. Let's take a shortcut."

Cassie didn't respond, just dutifully followed, her doll Sheena clutched in her arms, her fingers working the open-and-close eyes. Winkie took Cassie's hand and led her down an alleyway, passing rows of back doors to shops, every one of them open to let in some air on the hot July day.

The sight she beheld at one door caused her to stop dead in her tracks. In the wide opening, with the morning sun flooding in, a tall handsome man bent over a workbench, his muscles glistening in the sunlight.

The spectacle made her draw in her breath sharply.

Mr. Joseph Moore.

"Why, Winkie, Cassie," he said, looking up from the fluted piecrust table he was working on, "how good it be to see you." He jumped up, made his way to her, rubbed his palms together—sawdust flying—and stuck out his hand for a shake. Winkie shook his hand. Then he tapped the top of Cassie's head, and she smiled up at him.

"We be on our way home. I—I had to order some fabric."
She clutched at her collar. *Be still, my heart,* she ordered.

"I been thinking about you." He was rolling down his
sleeves, covering the glistening muscles. "And what a nice time
we had the other evening."

I been thinking about you too. She was thinking about him now.
He stood towering over her, though she herself was tall. Even
though he was wearing work clothes, he was neat, something very
important to her. He was a real gentleman, she could see.

"I believe those fireworks be the best I ever saw."

She nodded. Why did the cat get her tongue every time she
was around him? What was it about him that made her mute
as a fish, halting of speech even?

Heart whispered the answer.

No, Heart, it be too soon, she whispered back.

With a sweep of his hand, he gestured toward the building
behind him. "This be where I work two, three days a week.
When I'm not here, I'm at Fletchers."

"Fletchers pretty good people?" she forced herself to say for
lack of anything better.

He shrugged. "As good as can be, I suppose."

She studied the toes of her shoes. "We need to be going."

He tipped his head in the direction of the carpentry shop
behind him. "I best be getting back to work." Then he smiled.
His eyes lit up like the fireworks that filled the sky on Independence Day, Winkie noticed.

"I be seeing you," he said softly. "Soon."

The thought thrilled her as she hurried away.

The next morning, as Winkie was fixing breakfast, she heard a gentle tap at the door. She left the spoon in the jam jar and walked to the front of the shop. Who could this be at 7:00 A.M.? She hadn't even opened the door for the day in order to capture the cooling breezes.

"Must be the delivery boy bringing the fabric I ordered," she said.

She swung the door open and faced Mr. Joseph Moore. She brushed at the sides of her hair, smoothed the apron tied about her waist, and fiddled with the knot at the back. "Mr. Moore—"

"Joseph," he corrected.

She glanced back toward the curtained-off living area and a sleeping Cassie. Should she invite him in? Was he expecting that?

"I can't stay but a moment. I didn't want to disturb you this early, but I have something for you."

She saw his hands behind his back. What was he holding? He held out a bundle. "A fresh ham."

She was taken aback. He wanted to give her something this valuable? They hardly knew each other. "I–I couldn't accept it."

"The two to three days I work in town, Mr. Fletcher lets me keep the wages. I can bear the expense."

"But—"

"I be pleasured if you'd receive it."

She bit her bottom lip. What must she do?

"Cook it for Cassie." He put the bundle in her hands. "Cassie would surely like the taste of a slice of ham, wouldn't she?"

She smiled. Then her presence of mind returned. And her manners. "I declare, Mr. Moore—"

"Joseph," he corrected.

"Joseph. You do know how to get the best of my better sense of judgment." But she was smiling. Broadly. "I tell you what. I'll accept your gift, if you'll come back and eat some of it after I get it cooked."

"I never thought of that. . . ." His voice trailed off, but his eyes were fairly dancing. "What time?" he said, eagerness lacing his voice.

"Twelve noon. I believe I can have it ready about that time."

"I see you then."

All morning long, Winkie scurried about, getting her work done, smelling the fresh ham cooking in the iron pot over a low-burning open fire on the side of the building. Not long after the ham went in, she put on a pot of turnip greens.

"Just before serving time," she said to herself as she bent over a bonnet, "I'll make a pan of cornbread."

The way to a man's heart is through his stomach, Heart said, giggling.

Hush up, Heart, Winkie said back. But she was smiling. And singing, "Birdie Went a-Courting."

Only she changed the lyrics.

"Carpenter went a-courting," rang from her lips.

On the half hour before noon, Joseph laid aside his chisel and mallet, rose from his workbench, and went to clean up. He washed in the basin, lathering the lye soap into a rich foam, then changed shirts and brushed off his trousers and shoes with a damp rag.

In no time, it seemed, he was standing in front of Winkie's open door, tapping on the doorjamb. "Hello?" he called. "Anyone home?"

Cassie bounded across the room and into his arms where he stood on the stoop. "Mr. Joseph, we got something good to eat today. Mighty good." She drew out the word mighty.

"That so?" He picked her up and swung her around, then set her down. "I come to eat with you. Your mama invited me—"

"I know. She told me. She been singing all morning."

"That so?" He folded his arms across his chest and rubbed his jaw. "Where is she, by the way?" He tried to temper the excitement he felt.

"Here I am," Winkie said, rounding the corner of the building outside, carrying a heavy pot. "I was taking the ham off the fire."

"Let me help." In three quick strides, he was at her side. He took the pot from her, being careful to keep the hot mitts wrapped around the handles. "Hmm, hmm, this do smell good."

"Taste good too," she said, a twinkle in her eye. "I done partook." She paused and smiled at him. "But only a morsel, to see if it was any good."

"I be relieved," he joked, dramatically wiping his brow. "The hog it come off of was butchered this very morning, but you never know."

"I wouldn't want to serve spoiled meat."

He was enjoying her banter. This was a Winkie he hadn't seen before, and he liked what he was seeing.

"Come on inside." Winkie was already at the door, ahead of him. "Everything else be ready. Will you do the carving?"

"Right happy to."

Inside, his eyes adjusted from the bright sunlight to a cool dimness. He scanned the room, taking in the pleasant sight. Colorful curtains at the window. Another curtain separating the shop, probably to section off the sleeping area. A table set with stoneware plates. A single gardenia in a vase in the center. A rag rug on the floor. Folds of fabric stacked on a shelf on a far wall, millinery items beside them.

Everything was tidy, in apple pie order. And not only that, it was apparent she knew what's what. She was sharp, at home to cleverness. He resisted the urge to shake his head in awe. He was liking what he was seeing more and more.

"Set it here," she said, indicating the table.

He set the pot down, and she handed him a carving knife. After he cut up the ham until there was a heap on a large platter, she filled the drinking cups with fresh water, and the three of them took their places at the table.

"Make your manners, Cassie," she instructed. "Put your napkin in your lap." She shook the folds out of hers and did likewise.

"Would you like me to say the blessing?" he asked.

She looked surprised. After a moment, she nodded.

"Lord, we thank Thee for this, Thy bounty. Bless the one whose hands prepared it, bless her real good. Let us partake of this nourishment so we can be instruments in Thy hand. Amen."

After the bowls and platters went around the table, Winkie hurriedly cut up her food, then picked up the peacock feathers at her side. As she ate with one hand, with the other she fanned the feathers across the table, keeping the flies at bay.

"This be some big eating," Joseph said, relishing every bite. He cut another piece off the slice of ham that nearly covered his plate. "That man I bought this from, he say this hog be fed chestnuts. That—along with your fine cooking—has got to be why the eating be so good. Hmm, hmm. What kind of sauce you put on that ham when you cook it?"

"It be a secret."

"What most cooks say." He chuckled. "Hmm, hmm. This cornbread, why, it melt in your mouth. And these turnip greens, they flavored just right, and they cooked right too. My mama used to claim that greens that wasn't cooked two hours would kill you. She used to say, 'I don't take to the scalding school of cookery.' Yes, Ma'am, you have regaled me with a feast."

She smiled, apparently pleased at his compliments.

When Cassie finished eating, she jumped up and asked for the feathers. "Let me do it, Mama."

"I get the treat then." Winkie handed her the feathers and walked to a shelf along the wall, picked up a rectangular pan, and brought it back to the table. "Blackberry cobbler with heavy cream," she announced as she set it down and began ladling it into serving dishes.

"Have I died and gone to heaven? Where the hams run loose on the streets with forks and knives stuck in them dashing around crying, 'Eat me, eat me'?"

She laughed, and Cassie laughed too. "You certainly know how to set the table in a roar."

"And you certainly know how to cook."

A look of pride filled her eyes. The twinkle he was growing familiar with was back. "Be it as good as Bertha's?" she asked.

"Better by a mile. But don't tell her or anyone at Fletchers I said so."

Winkie took the feathers, seated herself, and fanned as they ate the cobbler.

"Have you ever gone to Sabbath services at the church downtown?" he asked. "I don't believe I seen you there."

"No," she said quickly.

"That so?" He tried to read the expression in her eyes, but he couldn't make it out.

"I never have." This time her tone was soft. "My mama never took to church and such stuff. I guess that be why I never did either."

"What about Cassie? She ever been?"

Winkie shook her head.

"They sing songs and—"

"Oh, Mama," Cassie said, pulling on Winkie's sleeve. "Can I go with Mr. Joseph? Where they sing songs?"

Winkie didn't say anything for a long moment, her brows drawn together as if in contemplation.

"Please?"

"We see about it, Sugarbun. We see."

Cassie jumped up, ran across the room, and within a moment or two was standing at Winkie's side, holding a frayed leather-bound volume. "Show Mr. Joseph your poetry book, Mama."

Winkie lowered her spoon, laden with blackberries, to her bowl, then took the book and ran her fingers across the cover almost reverently as Cassie skipped off to play. "It be a book of poetry. Miss Willie gave it to me when we was girls."

"Read me your favorite."

"My favorite?" Her brows drew together, another frequent mannerism, he noticed. She flipped through the book, stopped at a particular page, withdrew a paper. From the looks of the torn creases, it was apparent it had been handled many times. "This isn't in the book, and it isn't my favorite poem, but it be very important to me." In a strong voice, she read the stanzas:

THE NEGRO'S COMPLAINT
by William Cowper

Forced from home and all its pleasures
Afric's coast I left forlorn,
To increase a stranger's treasures
O'er the raging billows borne.

Men from England bought and sold me,
Paid my price in paltry gold;
But, though slave they have enrolled me,
Minds are never to be sold.

Still in thought as free as ever,
What are England's rights, I ask,
Me from my delights to sever
Me to torture, me to task?
Fleecy locks and black complexion
Cannot forfeit nature's claim;
Skins may differ, but affection
Dwells in white and black the same.

Why did all-creating nature
Make the plant for which we toil?
Sighs must fan it, tears must water,
Sweat of ours must dress the soil.
Think, ye masters iron-hearted,
Lolling at your jovial boards,
Think how many backs have smarted
For the sweets your cane affords.

Is there, as ye sometimes tell us,
Is there One who reigns on high?
Has He bid you buy and sell us,
Speaking from his throne, the sky?
Ask him, if your knotted scourges,
Matches, blood-extorting screws,
Are the means that duty urges
Agents of his will to use?

"Hark! He answers!—Wild tornadoes
Strewing yonder sea with wrecks,
Wasting towns, plantations, meadows,
Are the voice with which he speaks.
He, forseeing what vexations
Afric's sons should undergo,
Fixed their tyrants' habitations
Where his whirlwinds answer—"No."

By our blood in Afric wasted
Ere our necks received the chain;
By the miseries that we tasted,
Crossing in your barks the main;
By our sufferings, since ye brought us
To the man-degrading mart,
All sustained by patience, taught us,
Only by a broken heart;

Deem our nation brutes no longer,
Till some reason ye shall find
Worthier of regard and stronger
Than the colour of our kind.
Slaves of gold, whose sordid dealings
Tarnish all your boasted powers,
Prove that you have human feelings,
Ere you proudly question ours!

When Winkie finished reading, the room filled with silence.
"True," Joseph finally said of the poem. He was too over-come to say more. He lived out its words every day of his life.
A quarter hour later, with proper adieus and plenty of

thanks to Winkie for the delicious meal, he made his way back to the carpentry shop.

There was a bounce in his step as he walked. He would see Winkie again next Sabbath, when he came to pick up Cassie and take her to church.

Chapter 5

F all was in the air, but it was springtime in Winkie's heart. The leaves were turning, changing from their glorious greens to their awesome autumn hues of orange, gold, and brown. The days were shorter and the air cooler, and Winkie put a shawl about her shoulders when she went outside. Yet down in her soul was a warmth so great it was indescribable. It abode with her day in and day out.

She had seen Joseph every Sabbath since Independence Day and a few times more when their paths crossed in town. On Sundays, Joseph picked Cassie up and took her to the downtown church.

Frequently, Winkie had a hot meal waiting when they returned, though sometimes she packed a basket dinner and they went off, the three of them together, spending the afternoon in pleasurable pursuits. Their ventures were always within walking distance. Joseph had no horse or buggy. But the afternoons were highlights in her mind.

And in her heart.

One bright, unusually warm October Sabbath, Winkie watched Joseph rig up a rope swing for Cassie, saw him push her high, heard her peals of delight. Earlier, the three of them had eaten Winkie's fried chicken and biscuits, and now Joseph was approaching her where she sat on a colorful quilt, surrounded by a copse of copper trees.

He plopped down on one end of the quilt, and for long moments, they engaged in light banter, what they did nearly every time they were together. That was Joseph's way, frolicsome-like—coquetry as some people referred to it.

Coquetry? Lightness? She certainly needed some of that in her life. She leaned on one arm. The burdens. . . They were sometimes too hard to bear. But not since Joseph. She knew that the sparking between them was on the surface, but beneath it bubbled a deep bonding.

I'm in love. The thought startled her but exhilarated her too.

"How about a piece of that spice cake you brought?" He reached into the basket and withdrew a bundle in a checkered cloth. "I got a whiff earlier." He held it up to his nose. "Hmm, hmm. This do smell good."

"You like spice cake, do you?" She tried to hide the quakes in her voice. Love was on her mind.

"Grass be green?" He gestured to the expanse of lawn at his side. "Sky be blue?" He pointed upward.

She smiled at his playful antics. Joseph had never voiced his feelings about her. Just the same, she knew it was there between them, love, and she basked in this private knowing. Secretly, she'd taken to calling him her Heart Happy Joseph, not because he made happiness everywhere he went, but because he made her heart happy.

The day after Love Blossoming, Winkie had a keen desire to prepare a Christmas gift for Joseph. One of Miss Willie's friends had frequented her hat shop and placed a sizable deposit on two bonnet orders, and so she had some extra funds for Joseph's gift.

That afternoon, she made a trip to the fabric store and purchased material, two yards of blue broadcloth for a vest, three of white linen for a shirt, five of gray serge for trousers and frockcoat, a yard of elegant patterned silk for a cravat. She would make him a fine suit of clothes and present it to him on Christmas Day.

"This Christmas Day will be the best Christmas I've ever had," she told herself as she hurried home, eager to make her cuts and start the sewing.

Late at night, in the workroom off the Fletcher stables, Joseph labored by lantern glow, what he did every evening until the wee hours, what he would continue doing until Christmas. A carved blanket chest and a child's rocking chair took eons to make, yet he was determined to complete them both by Christmas.

He ran his hand over the smooth sides of the chest, making sure he had sanded them properly. "Winkie gone be plumb lit up when she see this."

Tonight he would start on the hinged top, and maybe he would get the first coat of stain on Cassie's rocking chair.

He thought of little Cassie—Starlight, he'd been calling her because her eyes were as bright as the stars in the heavens. Every Sabbath since Independence Day, he had taken her to church, and nearly every Sunday afternoon, he'd had the privilege of spending time with Winkie. On several occasions during these last few months, he'd asked her if she would go to service with him in the downtown church.

"I can't," she said each time. "I got work waiting."

The woman was a workhorse; that was for sure. But she had to be. The little monies she made went to pay rent and put food on the table, though he tried to be a help, bringing things like sweet potatoes and sacks of grits from time to time.

It was tricky, though, handling her pride. She was known to bristle, scowl even, when the subject of the lack of money surfaced, which inevitably led to the subject of their people's plight.

"The likes of us," she would say, "isn't never going to know real relief—free nor slave."

On one occasion, he confided in her about his sad past. Winkie was sympathetic, comforting even. He told her about the origin of his name and how his mama admonished him to live up to his namesake, Joseph-in-the-Bible.

Now, Joseph leaned over the long piece of cherry wood and with precision aim brought the routing plane down the side, careful to make the groove even. He thought of the poem by a writer named Cowper. She had read it to him on a few occasions, and from the first time he'd heard it, the chilling words had taken root in his brain, never to be forgotten.

No truer words had ever been penned about the despicable system of slaves and masters, to his way of thinking.

But some other words, peace-giving words, life-sustaining words now came to mind, and the poet's phrases paled in comparison.

Joseph-in-the-Bible had the right attitude through every trial, his mother had said over and over, and in the end, God honored him. *Son, hear me well. If you determine in your heart to be like that, God will honor you.*

He stopped routing and reached to tighten the woolen scarf about his neck. The nights were growing colder as the autumn season made its way toward winter pell-mell like a horse to a trough. Soon, Christmas would be here.

"Christmas," he said aloud. "A babe named Jesus. A woman named Mary. A man named Joseph. . .a carpenter." He brought the lantern closer. "Hmm, I never paid much attention to this Joseph. The other Joseph is the one my life be built around, the man I have always looked up to and tried to model."

He stood there marveling. "This other Joseph-in-the-Bible is a man to model too. The angel of the Lord appeared to Joseph in two, three dreams, and every time, the Bible say he do what he bidden."

He rubbed his jaw. "What a man to look up to. This Joseph followed the leading of the Lord instead of choosing his own way. And the Lord blessed him mightily." He knew that this Joseph, of all the people in the ages before and in the ages present and in the ages to come, had been chosen to be the Messiah's earthly father.

He picked up his routing plane, and as he shaped the second edge, then the third, then the fourth, his thoughts turned to Winkie.

Winkie with her quiet manner.

Winkie with her gentle ways.

Winkie with her busy hands.

Winkie, a mother as tender as ever he saw.

Winkie, a wife as affectionate as ever he'd laid eyes on.

His wife?

He shook himself. "Be it too soon to start thinking this way?"

"It's past time," Uncle Solomon would say.

Uncle Solomon, the head groomsman at Fletcher plantation, was well learned in the art of courtship, and many a man went to the elderly gentleman for advice on wooing a woman and winning a wife.

"It's all in how you talk to her," Uncle Solomon often said. "The rules of courtship say you got to put riddles to her. If a young miss give a man as good a answer as the question he put to her, then she be the one for him."

A warm feeling flooded Joseph's heart as he put the first coat of stain on little Starlight's chair. Was Starlight's mother the one for him? The woman to jump the broom with? Working the brush into each rung of the child-sized chair, being careful not to miss one spot of the intricate areas, he reflected on Uncle Solomon's riddles.

"Pretty miss, if there be a ravishing rose, how would you go about getting it, if you couldn't pick it, pull it, or pluck it?" the young man might ask.

"Kind sir, it would be borne on the blossoms of love," she might answer.

Every young man and woman of the peoples knew a heap of riddles. It was like a game to them, the circumlocution they went through to find out the intentions of a sparking miss or man.

Sometimes, if the woman couldn't answer the man's riddle, she might say, "Sir, you are a peach beyond my pear."

Then he might say, "Pretty miss, let me explain myself more thoroughly so the peach and pear can go in the cobbler together."

He chuckled out loud, musing over this ticklish business of courtship. When he proposed to Winkie, it would be in plain English. He would put the question to her in simplicity and in earnestness—this woman who had come to mean the world to him, this lady who had captured his heart. How could he live without her? He was besotted, for sure.

As if from out of nowhere, a tiny doubt crept into his mind. *She doesn't partake of your faith.*

"She will," he said in the quietness of the late hour. "As soon as she gets more customers who come to her directly, her money worries will ease up, and she'll commence going to church with me."

With force of will, he drove the doubt away, deciding in his heart the course of action he would take.

"On Christmas Day, I'm going to give her my gift. Then I'm going to declare my love. Then I'm going to ask my winsome Winkie to be my wife."

Chapter 6

Three weeks before Christmas, Joseph sat in the balcony of the downtown church in Charleston.

"Turn to Second Corinthians," the minister intoned from his oak pulpit on the raised platform. "Our topic today is 'Be Ye Not Unequally Yoked.'"

The minister picked up his Bible. "Let us read from 2 Corinthians 6:14. Altogether now, 'Be ye not unequally yoked together with unbelievers: for what fellowship hath righteousness with unrighteousness?'"

The minister continued reading, but Joseph didn't hear another word he said. It was as if he'd been kicked in the stomach by a stallion. *Unequally yoked. Unequally yoked. Unequally yoked.* The sacred words pounded in his brain, then invaded his heart and gripped it with an iron hand.

If he and Winkie married, a wall would always be between them because of the differences in their faith. It would be like mixing grease and water, something that never worked. How could he do a thing that directly opposed the instruction of the Scriptures?

But how can I live without her? his soul cried out. He leaned forward and grasped the pew in front of him, his spirit vexed.

How could he give up the woman he loved? He had searched for the right miss for years, and when he finally found her, was he going to have to let her go?

His heart as heavy as a rock, he knew with a certainty that Christmas would not be the day of joy he had envisioned all these months. It would be a day of funereal sorrow.

Christmas would be the day he and Winkie would part company.

The elderly gentleman seated next to him twisted in the pew and let out a long sigh, and Joseph was distracted from his contemplations.

"The Bible says a man must love his wife as Christ loved the church," the minister was saying. "That is a sacrificial love, a love that makes a man think first of the woman, above himself."

A sacrificial love? Joseph mused. A love that made a man think first of the woman, above himself? Those were his sentiments exactly.

Precious Winkie. Winsome Winkie. He knew with a surety that she loved him. It was something tucked deeply inside him, like a secret knowledge between them. If he broke off their relationship on Christmas, the most joyful day of the year, Winkie would be doubly hurt that he'd chosen to do his ill deed on that special day.

He fiddled with his coat buttons as he formulated his plan.

I'll wait a couple of weeks past Christmas to tell her the bad news. That be sacrificial love.

Chapter 7

"Can you believe Christmas Day is coming to a close?" Winkie said to Joseph just as the sun went down, the two of them sitting at the table, eating another slice of sweet potato pie before he had to leave.

All afternoon they had been together, and it was a Christmas Day she'd long remember, one filled with glee and gladness. . . .

And big eating, as Joseph called it, turkey and stuffing and all the trimmings. . .

And vibrant singing, accompanied by Joseph beating on a cook pot and Cassie clanging spoons together. . .

And silly merry-making, Joseph telling riddles and stories, Cassie bursting out in fits of giggles, even Winkie laughing till her sides hurt.

Joseph. Joseph. Joseph. He was what made the day special.

As she savored the last bite of her pie, her eyes scanned the room and came to rest on the gifts. . . .

The beautiful blanket chest Joseph lovingly made with his own hands, intricate carvings adorning the cherry wood surface. The child-sized oak rocker Cassie was sitting in now, her little head slumped over in sleep from sheer exhaustion. The suit of clothes Winkie'd made Joseph, neatly folded atop the chest, waiting to be taken home with him. The red-and-white-striped bags of candy he'd brought, enough to keep Cassie in delight for weeks.

"I said, can you believe Christmas Day is coming to a close? I wish we could wrap it up like a present and open it again, don't you?" She rose from the table and picked up the pie pan, Joseph saying not a word the whole time. "Joseph?" she asked. "Did you hear me?"

He inched his plate forward. "It be a most pleasant day, Winkie."

Across the room, she stacked dishes in the tin pan on the shelf. Why was Joseph so quiet? She'd never seen him like this. He seemed to be almost. . .brooding.

What was the matter? He'd been subdued all the livelong day. True, he was cheerful when he gave her and Cassie their gifts, though he was restrained, far different from his usual frolicsome ways. And yes, he was grateful for the suit of clothes she'd made him. But he didn't jump in the air and kick his heels when he saw it, as she'd expected—a silly antic that made her laugh every time.

She pondered on this matter. What was the reason for his reserve? She touched her temple. Of course. He was going to ask her to marry him any day now, that she was sure of, and he was deciding how to go about the details. First, he needed to secure permission from Mr. Fletcher. She could picture it in her mind now, Joseph standing before Mr. Fletcher.

"Sir," Joseph would probably say, "I wish to marry."

"And who is the woman?" Mr. Fletcher would respond.

"Winkie Williams. She was here on Independence Day at the invitation of your wife and Miss Willie. She be a fine, upright woman. She be a free woman, residing in Charleston, making her living as a hatmaker. Miss Willie and Mr. Richard can vouch for her. She used to live on Laurel Ridge, where Miss Willie grew up."

"Sundays with a wife will be enough to satisfy you?"

"Have to, is all I know. You already give me a pass for that day, so the way I see it, if you be so kind as to keep that up, that be the time I spend with my new wife and child."

Now, in her mind's eye, Winkie could envision Joseph smiling at the words "wife and child." Broadly. Winkie poured water in the tin pan, lathered the rag with a bar of lye soap, and washed the dishes. She could see Mr. Fletcher sitting at his massive mahogany desk, Joseph standing before him.

"Why, that'll be fine, Joseph," Mr. Fletcher would say. "I don't see any obstacles. You can spend Saturday night through Monday morning of every week with your new family, as long as you're back at work early Monday morning. You're most deserving of happiness. If this woman will bring you happiness, if this is what you truly want, then I'll not stand in the way of it. When will this event take place?"

All the tableware washed and rinsed, Winkie picked up the first plate on the stack and dried it, then the next, her face growing warm at the thought of Joseph. What would his kisses be like? She rubbed her arms, all pimply like gooseflesh. Joseph's kisses would be dulcet yet ravishing.

Smiling shyly, she could almost hear Joseph's eager response to his master, concerning when their wedding would occur. "As soon as possible, Mr. Fletcher. Just as soon as possible."

She stared into the looking glass tacked to the wall in front of her. My, she was glad Joseph couldn't hear what she was thinking. She glanced sheepishly at him across the room. She saw his broad shoulders, his dark eyes that nearly always danced, his neat, clean clothing. She thought about his fond devotion, his gentlemanly deportment, his jolly ways.

Yes, this was a Christmas Day she would never forget, she thought as she glanced again at the tall, handsome man sitting at her table. Her Heart Happy Joseph.

Something told her a momentous occasion was soon to occur.

Chapter 8

From the moment Joseph awoke, he knew this was the day he had to tell Winkie. Three weeks past Christmas, this Sabbath was mild, warm enough to be outside, at least long enough for him to deliver his dose of dread.

"I need to talk with you about an urgent matter," he told Winkie when he picked up Cassie for church that morning.

A couple hours later, as the three of them walked toward the outskirts of town, Winkie's basket of food on his arm, Cassie between them with hands held fast, a glorious thought hit him. If he could convince Winkie to accept the faith, then they would be compatible. Perhaps no one ever presented the gospel to her in the right way. He would explain it in plain language. He smiled, thinking of Uncle Solomon's silly courting riddles. He wouldn't dilly-dally. He would give her a direct opportunity to accept Christ, and she would do so eagerly.

After they ate, as little Starlight swung high in the air on a rope swing, Joseph and Winkie got comfortable on her colorful quilt.

He decided to start right in. "Winkie, I have a very important question to ask you."

"I've been expecting it." Her voice was low and sweet-sounding as she leaned into him, shoulder brushing shoulder.

"Has anyone ever explained the gospel to you?"

She looked dazed as she pulled away.

"You see, when Adam and Eve sinned, God provided a sacrifice for them. A blood sacrifice—an animal. We don't rightly know why God required a blood sacrifice for sin, but He did from the very beginning of mankind. All through the Old Covenant, man had to offer a sacrifice regularly. Then God sent Jesus, His only begotten Son, to become the last sacrifice so we would never have to offer another one again."

Impassioned by his love for the Lord, Joseph plunged on. "All we have to do is accept this sacrifice—Jesus Christ. I'm talking about a gift of salvation. All we have to do is say, 'Lord, I confess my sins and ask You to forgive me and cleanse me—'"

"Is this the urgent matter you needed to discuss?" Confusion filled her eyes as she edged to the other side of the quilt.

"Yes. You see, Christ died on the cross for us, and when we accept Him as Savior, He fills our lives with peace, and He gives direction, and He helps us, and He comforts—"

"Joseph, I don't understand. I–I thought. . ."

"I'm trying to explain."

For long minutes, they went back and forth, him almost preaching, her almost rebutting.

"I–I thought you brought me here to propose." A sob escaped her lips, but she swallowed hard, as if willing herself not to cry. "I love you with all my heart." She swallowed hard again. "You know what I've taken to calling you secretly? My Heart Happy Joseph. You make my heart sing and my spirit soar." Tears trickled down her cheeks. "I–I'm not very good with words, l-like you are, but I can quote Burns:

"Till a' the seas gang dry, my dear,
And the rocks melt wi' the sun:
Oh I will love thee still, my dear,
While the sands o' life shall run."

Joseph's heart wrenched in his chest, and it took everything within him to bridle his trembles. In a flash, he was at her side, and he pulled her close. It was growing cooler, but it was more than that. He wanted to hold her. "I went about this all wrong."

She looked up at him, questioning, dabbing at her tears.

"I need to start from the beginning. As I was making your blanket chest, that's when I knew I loved you; that's when I decided I'd ask you to marry me on Christmas Day."

"What stopped you?" she said quietly.

"One Sunday in church, the minister preached on being unequally yoked. That means not marrying someone outside the faith."

He could feel her stiffen, but he continued on, though he felt a lump forming in his throat that made him short of breath. "I–I thought I would die, Winkie, when those words sunk into my soul. Unequally yoked. I, too, love you. . .more than life itself."

Tears formed in his eyes, but he blinked them away. "When I heard his sermon, I knew I'd have to give you up if I was to follow the ways of the Scriptures."

"But that won't stand between us. The faith, you call it."

"Yes, it will." He said it emphatically, and she made no response. "I felt like I was stricken when I realized what I needed to do. I felt like I couldn't live anymore."

He continued on, telling her everything. Then he paused and held her in his arms, Starlight shrieking with joy high in the sky, the two of them not saying a word, just basking in each other's presence.

For now.

"May I ask you something else?" he said respectfully, and he could feel her nod as he held her in a loving embrace. "Won't you accept Christ as Lord and Savior and go to church with me?"

She drew a deep breath. "I've seen too much, felt too much, all of it pain, pain, pain." Her voice grew in intensity. "I hate the white man for what he did to our people."

"You love Miss Willie."

"She's different."

"The Bible says to love your enemies."

"And that's why I don't want anything to do with it," she spat out. Then the tears flowed again.

Joseph was grateful to the Lord for the calmness that overcame him. "Winkie, Honey," he said, taking her hand, stroking her work-worn fingers that he loved so dearly and would never touch again after today, "the Bible isn't a book of strung-together, no-account words. There be a reason for everything in it. It powerful, and it sharper than any two-edged sword, and it true, and it be food to our souls. If we partake, if we will heed its life-giving precepts, if we will sow to the things of the Lord, we will reap blessings too numerous to name."

"If that be so, then what blessings are you reaping?" She let out a snort of disgust. "What white man is doling out delights to you?"

"Oh, Baby." He thought his heart would break in two. Why couldn't she understand what he was trying to say, to offer her? Peace and love and joy.

"Our real struggle," he said, "isn't against a person. It be against the devil. The Holy Book say, 'For we wrestle not against flesh and blood, but against principalities, against powers, against the rulers of the darkness of this world, against spiritual wickedness in high places.' Don't you see?"

"No, I don't," she said, her jaw tensed.

With forced stamina, he resisted the urge to lean down and kiss her good-bye, knowing what he was about to say would sever all ties between them.

He cleared his throat. "You're free, but you're not free."

She pulled away from him, sitting erect, her eyes flashing fire.

"You're bound by bitterness," he said.

Her eyes narrowed to tiny slits.

"The Bible says in John 8:36, 'If the Son therefore shall make you free, ye shall be free indeed.' "

She jumped up. "Come on, Cassie." She jerked on the edge of the quilt, like she was going to start folding it with him sitting on it. "I'm ready to go. Been ready."

He rose to his feet. How would she take the last thing he had to tell her? The edict he had to deliver? The words that stuck in his throat like a bullet in a rusty gun? Finally, he said with a quiet strength, "When you let the Son make you free—not some piece of paper—you be free indeed."

"I don't ever want to lay eyes on you again, Mr. Joseph Moore, you white-lover, you."

Chapter 9

Bundled against the winter weather, Joseph stood on the street corner, watching little Starlight walk toward Winkie's shop. Every Sabbath, he discreetly delivered her home, remembering Winkie's parting words with a sorrow unto death: "I don't ever want to lay eyes on you again, Mr. Joseph Moore, you white-lover, you."

He would respect her wishes. That much, he could do. Several times, he had been tempted to revive the relationship, but so far, he'd resisted.

He shivered in the cold wind, stamped his feet, blew into his clasped palms.

Just because Winkie won't go to church doesn't mean anything, a voice whispered in his heart. *She be a good woman, a lady who loves you. She'll make a fine wife to you and a tender mother to the children born to you.*

"She be a good woman, all right," he whispered. "She said she'd love me till the seas go dry and the rocks melt in the sun." He blinked hard as his eyes misted over, and it wasn't from the cold. He took a step toward Winkie's shop.

"No," he cried out, stopping dead in his tracks. "I can't do this." He swallowed deeply. Into his mind popped the words

Joseph-in-the-Bible had said: "How then can I do this great wickedness, and sin against God?"

Seeing Starlight safely inside the door of the shop, Joseph walked toward home with a firm resolve. "I'm going to follow the Lord's plan from now on. I've tried mine long enough."

His own way hadn't worked. First, on the night he'd carved the top of Winkie's blanket chest, he'd made plans to propose to her despite the doubt God sent his way. *She doesn't partake of your spiritual life,* the voice of the Lord had warned.

Then he'd tried to force her into accepting the gospel.

Joseph walked hurriedly down the street. A few minutes ago, he had followed the example of Joseph-in-the-Bible of the Old Covenant, and that had warded off the temptation that was dangling in front of his eyes.

"Now I'm going to follow Joseph-in-the-Bible of the New Covenant." He would do as God bid him to, just as that Joseph had. "I will bend my will to the Lord."

With a vexation of soul at losing Winkie but with a confidence that God would see him through, Joseph tramped on.

Chapter 10

Winkie leaned over the hat in her hands, sewing with railway speed. Madam was expecting two bonnets the next day, and three of her own customers would be waiting at week's end to pick up their orders.

"Mama, look," Cassie called from where she sat on the rug, holding a book Miss Willie had given her. "See the pretty pictures?" She held it up for Winkie to see.

"Those are plumb delightful." A gentle breeze blew in the window, the curtains billowing slightly, then falling, then billowing, then falling.

"March is coming in backward," Winkie said. "It's a lamb this year. Ah, this air is plumb refreshing."

A whoosh made the curtains stand straight out, and Winkie's scraps went flying. "Well, here come the lion. Sugarbun, can you close the window a mite? We're going to blow to Kansas."

As Cassie bounded toward the window, then shut it, Winkie drew the needle in and out. *Funny. Last fall, I remember thinking, "Fall is in the air, but it's springtime in my heart." Today, spring is in the air, but it's winter down inside.*

Funny? No, it wasn't funny at all. Never had she experienced such a cold, dank feeling. Desolate was a more fitting word. She was pining away for Joseph. Though he was out of her sight, he would never be out of her mind. Or her heart.

Heart Happy Joseph. He was the only man who could set her feet to dancing and her face to smiling. But not anymore. These days, she rarely smiled. Counting her ills was what she did the livelong day. It all but consumed her waking moments and many of the ones she should've been sleeping.

Her mother was right. Life wasn't fair. Work was hard. There was never no letup. And her man, her Heart Happy Joseph? He had been taken away from her just like her Sweet Love Roscoe.

It was more than flesh and blood could bear, yet she couldn't cry out as she sat there sewing. She would alarm Cassie. Instead she clamped her teeth shut and kept sewing at her stitching.

"When Mr. Joseph coming to eat with us again?" Cassie asked brightly.

"Why are you always asking that?" she snapped. "I told you a hundred times. Never. N-e-v-e-r."

Cassie threw her arms around Winkie, as if she was undaunted by the outburst, as if she possessed some special something that could always bring a note of cheer to Winkie.

Winkie couldn't help smiling, and she thrust her sewing aside and gathered her baby on her lap.

"Sugarbun, Sugarbun," Winkie singsonged, "Mama's darling sweet, you thrill me dear, see here, see here—" She burst out laughing. "I can't think of anymore rhymes." For long moments, bright laughter—both Winkie's and Cassie's—filled the room.

Then Winkie sobered. "I—I don't know what I'd do. . ." She fiddled with Cassie's braids, then straightened Cassie's rumpled pinafore "If I didn't have you, Sugarbun."

Cassie kissed her once more, then jumped down and went back to her book.

Winkie bent over the bonnet. *Out of sight, out of mind,* her mother always said. Maybe she came to that conclusion because of the many relatives who were sold out from under her. Maybe something came over her heart, like a scab over a sore to shield it. Maybe that was her mother's protection from the wounds down inside her.

But Joseph had wounds too. Hadn't he told her he was sold from out of his mama's loving arms? Hadn't he told her about the hardships he'd endured? But he wasn't sad, like her mother always was. On the contrary, Joseph made happiness everywhere he went.

"Be gone, dull care," she whispered. "My brain be too tired to ponder this any longer."

"What you say, Mama?"

"Nothing, Child."

A tap sounded at the door.

"Help me straighten up, Cassie. Customer's come a-calling. Make haste." Winkie jumped to her feet and set the table in order while Cassie picked up her book and doll and her dried gourds with the beans in them.

Winkie brushed at the sides of her hair, then opened the door. Before her stood a fine Charleston lady. That wasn't unusual. What was unusual was the servant woman who accompanied her, tending the lady's two children in tow.

It was Auntie, a woman Winkie hadn't seen since early childhood. Dazed, yet aware of proper deportment, she greeted the fine Charleston lady, then fell onto Auntie's neck in such a tight embrace, Auntie let out a little squeal.

When Auntie explained to her missus who Winkie was, the lady graciously stood to the side, waiting for them to finish their affectionate exchanges.

As Winkie hugged Auntie's ample softness, she couldn't get enough of her. Finally, she pulled away, her eyes moist. She offered the lady a chair as she inquired about her name. Then she said, "Cassie, come, Child. Show these little girls your new book while Mama waits on Mrs. Butler."

An hour later, Winkie had four new hat orders. And because of the lady's kindness, she had the pleasant prospect of a visit from Auntie.

Soon.

Chapter 11

Weekly visits commenced with Auntie, and they were like sunshine to Winkie's soul. Sitting at the table, eating hot biscuits slathered with jam or apple slices dotted with cheese or some other such treat—Winkie quickly found out Ample Auntie liked her treats—they talked about everything and about nothing.

She-she talk, Auntie called it.

Auntie was the mother Winkie needed. She petted Winkie, called her endearing names, treated her with loving regard, demonstrated tender affection toward her.

"You need a mammy," Auntie said with a gap-toothed smile on the first visit, hugging Winkie to her. "You need a mammy worse than Mrs. Butler's kids."

"I do, Auntie, I do," Winkie said back, swallowing the lump in her throat.

"I be your mammy every time I come see you. I is a good comforter."

On the second visit, after Auntie's antics died down, Winkie found out she was one of them—a church-going faith person. Same as Joseph. But Auntie didn't go on and on about it, and Winkie was grateful.

On the third visit, after Auntie's antics died down, the talk turned to the subject Winkie most liked to discuss.

The people and their plight.

Winkie pulled down her book of poems and read aloud the one on the creased paper.

After the reading of it, Auntie harrumphed loudly as she sat in the straight-backed chair. Then she pushed her half-eaten shortcake to the center of the table. "Don't you know, Winkie?"

"Know what, Auntie?" Winkie sewed away. "That your missus liked my hats and told her friends about me?"

"Don't you know, Winkie?"

"You got a riddle for me?"

"No riddle at all. It be plain as the lips on your face."

"What that?"

"There be haughty white folks and haughty dark folks. There be nice-acting white folks and nice-acting dark folks."

Now Winkie was harrumphing. Just as loudly as Auntie did.

"It don't matter what color a heart is wrapped in," Auntie declared. "They're all the same underneath."

On the fourth visit, after Auntie's antics died down, Auntie, sewing as furiously as Winkie to help her out, said, "Pride don't wear a color, Winkie. And neither does hate nor meanness nor greed. And neither does kindness nor goodness nor uprightness."

Then she said, "You keep your nose clean—even if it takes both sleeves."

"Auntie!"

Auntie's dark eyes danced, but her voice was serious-sounding. "No matter what the rest of the world do, you make sure your attitude be right. That all we be responsible for in life. If we do that, God take care of us."

On the fifth visit, after Auntie's antics died down, she said, "Winkie, the day you was borned, your mama let me name you."

"Yes, Ma'am. She told me about it."

"I buried newborn twins the month before—"

"I didn't know that." Winkie set aside her sewing and touched Auntie on the forearm, trying to swallow the lump forming in her throat.

"She thought it would make me feel better if I could name you. You was the sweetest little baby, and as pretty as can be. You know what your full name is, don't you?"

"Yes, Ma'am. It's Periwinkle."

"You know why I named you that?"

"Because it's your favorite flower. That's what Mama always said."

"Well, that too. Do you know much about a periwinkle, Sweet One?"

"It be purplish-blue."

"I repeat. You know why I named you that?"

"No, Ma'am."

"You be finding your answer in a lexicon."

On the sixth visit, after Auntie's antics died down, she said, "You find out the meaning behind your name, Sweet One?"

"It be a riddle."

Auntie's round mahogany cheeks shook back and forth, back and forth, wobbling like jelly.

Studying Auntie's nuances, Winkie ate the last bite of peach pie on her plate. That was one more thing to love about Auntie, the way she went on, exaggerated-like.

"It be plain as the ears on your head."

"No, it isn't. Miss Willie be kind enough to look up 'periwinkle' in her lexicon, but weren't nothing there about a girl's name." From her pocket Winkie withdrew a scrap of paper. "She wrote the meaning down for me, and I've read it again and again, but it be a riddle."

"Read it to me now."

Winkie looked down at the paper. "It say a periwinkle be a ground cover known for it purplish-blue flowers."

"Uh-huh." Auntie was wagging her head.

"And it say it be a trailing herb."

"Uh-huh." She wagged it again.

"And it say it be the name of a color."

Head wagging once more.

"I can't make no sense of this silliness, Auntie."

"Go on."

"That all there be."

"You sure?" Auntie's eyes were round with wonder—and with playfulness.

"All right. One more. It say a periwinkle be a shrub what be a source of medicine—"

"That it," Auntie exclaimed, throwing both hands in the air, hallelujah-style.

Winkie said nothing, just drummed her fingers on the table. When would Auntie tell her?

"What a medicine be, Child?"

Winkie shrugged her shoulders.

Auntie leaned forward. "A medicine relieve pain and cures ills."

"So?"

Auntie repositioned the shawl about her shoulders, taking time to drape it in precise pleats. "The Good Book say God be the God of comfort. The reason He comfort us is so we can turn around and comfort others with the same kind we received."

Winkie folded her arms across her chest. She didn't want to hear this.

"When I named you, I looked into your big brown eyes, and I said, 'Periwinkle, one day you going to bring the healing touch of comfort to others.' Don't run from your destiny no longer, Child. The Lord has decreed it. I feel it in my soul."

Winkie stood up, walked to the shelf, and busied herself by peeling a big red apple.

"The Lord be right here in this room with arms widespread, wanting to comfort you. Let Him, do let Him, Sweet One. Open up the door of your heart. Just a crack. That all it take. He come in, and that peace that passes all understanding will flood your spirit and take away your pain."

Still Winkie didn't respond, just kept working on the apple until one long, unbroken peel hit the floor.

"From this day forth, I going to call you Periwinkle. You will live up to your name. Mark my words."

Chapter 12

All morning, Winkie made ready for Auntie's visit. She straightened the shop, made a ginger cake with vanilla sauce, hurried with her sewing so she could give her full attention to Auntie when she came.

As she worked, she pondered on Auntie's last visit, three weeks ago. Why hadn't she come last week or the week before? What kept her away? Was Auntie miffed because she didn't respond to her God talk and her comfort speech?

In the afternoon, as Cassie played with her shaking gourds on the big oval rug, Winkie sat near the window to get the best light, waiting for Auntie to come, busy at her never-ending sewing. She leaned down, bit the thread above the knot, broke it off, rethreaded her needle.

As a gentle breeze blew in, she sniffed the room made sweet with ginger and savored both scents, spice and spring. She looked at the table across the room, edified by the sight. A patchwork tablecloth made from hat scraps. A cake in a serving plate. A crockery bowl filled with vanilla sauce. An earthenware pitcher holding fresh buttermilk.

When she heard a step at the stoop, she pushed her sewing into a basket and rose from her chair.

Auntie waddled across the threshold, a spray of flowers in her arms. "For you, Sweet One." She thrust them at Winkie with energy. "My, something do smell good in here."

"Ginger cake." Winkie took a whiff of the colorful blossoms as she put them in a jar. "And now, flowers."

"Hmm, hmm, ginger cake. My favorite. We in for a treat this hour. I couldn't get here sooner. Mrs. Butler's had me a-hopping lately, what with all her company a-coming and a-going and all the extra childrens to tend to."

Winkie stood at the table, adding water to the daisies and delphiniums, pansies and petunias—wild jasmine perfuming the bunch, even some periwinkles mixed in. "Thank you, Auntie, for the flowers." *And thank you for not being ired at me.* She placed the jar of blossoms in the center of the table. "They'll add pleasure to our eating, for sure."

"April showers bring May flowers. Now, will you do something for me, Periwinkle?"

"You know I will."

Auntie held up a Bible. "Will you read me a few verses after we sup? Mrs. Butler gave me this a long time ago, yet I never heard it read from before."

A half hour later, though Winkie offered a myriad of excuses, she found herself reading aloud to Auntie from portions of the Book of John as Auntie called them out.

"John 14:27."

Winkie flipped through the pages and found the spot. " 'Peace I leave with you, My peace I give unto you: not as the world giveth, give I unto you. Let not your heart be troubled, neither let it be afraid.' "

"Those be Jesus' words."

On and on they went, Auntie calling out selections, Winkie

finding them and reading, Auntie adding a bit of instruction here and there.

"John 8:36," Auntie said.

Winkie flipped to the verse, scanned it, felt like her heart would surely stop its beating. This was the verse Joseph had quoted to her at The Parting.

"Why you quit?" Auntie said. "This be a tonic to my soul."

Winkie felt her face grow hot, remembering the sharp interchange between her and Joseph on that dreadful day. "I–I—"

"Read on. These words ease my being—" Auntie patted her round midsection. "Better than tansy mixed in honey."

Winkie swallowed hard. "Haven't we read long enough?"

"Please? Just this last verse?"

She nodded. How could she deny Auntie? Auntie was her tonic, her easement from the bitter brews of life.

"While I be thinking on it, I aim to leave the Good Book with you—"

"Oh, no. That not be necessary." She didn't want to hurt Auntie's feelings, but she had no use for the Bible, felt right bristly that Auntie would do such as that.

"It don't do me no good, seeing as how I can't decipher a word. But you, you learned how. And you better give God the glory for it. He sent you a special blessing in the form of a mistress who taught you to read."

Winkie had never thought about God being the One who'd worked that out, and it set her to thinking, deeplike.

"Now, read that last verse. John 8:36."

She stared at the words on the page, feeling shaky inside. " 'If the S–Son therefore sh–shall make you fr–free, ye shall be free indeed.' "

"I got a powerful potion to say to you, Sweet One."

"What's that, Auntie?"

"I'm not free, but I'm free."

Winkie chewed on her bottom lip. How could this be? Not free but free—the opposite of what Joseph talked about. "You're free, but you're not free," Joseph had said to her.

"I'm not free, but I'm free," Auntie repeated, leaning forward, her voice all seriousness. "Christ Jesus set me free from the chains of sin, and in their place, He give me peace, joy, and love."

Winkie looked down at her lap, her hands making hard fists, her mind studying on Auntie's words.

"Yes, I'm free indeed." Auntie smiled. Broadly. "Periwinkle, one day you going to be able to say that too. Mark my words."

Chapter 13

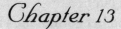

The Good Book sat on the shelf high on the wall, beside the stacks of colorful fabrics and hat trims. One day went by, then another, then another, Winkie never touching it a time.

On the fourth day, Winkie looked up at it, thinking it must have drawing powers. Seemed like every time she passed the shelf, the Good Book called out to her, making her shiver with every footfall.

That night, she couldn't sleep, and it wasn't because of Cassie's vigorous kicking. Even a pillow stuffed between them didn't bring Winkie the slumber she craved. Slowly she sat up in bed focused on the shaft of moonlight coming through the curtains, saw where the moonbeam ended.

The Good Book.

She felt herself shaking, heard her teeth chattering, touched her heart where it hammered against her chest. In a flash, she burrowed under the covers and snuggled close to Cassie. As she lay there, her heart still beating wildly, the verse she read to Auntie came floating through her mind, and she repeated what she could remember: "Something about giving us peace so that our hearts won't be troubled or afraid."

That be Jesus talking, Auntie had said.

"Jesus?" Glancing up at the Good Book bathed in the moonlight, Winkie pulled up her grit and stood. Like a miracle, her heart was strangely quieted, her soul wrapped in a cocoon of peace.

"Jesus?" she repeated. Her feet floated to the shelf, her fingers glided upward. With a flick of her wrist, she took down the Good Book, lit a candle on the table, sat on the straight-backed chair, and opened the Bible with steady hands, glad, so glad the Lord had kept her awake.

Like a starved person pouncing on a plate of victuals, she devoured the Good Book. She began with the Book of John and read every word. She flipped to the Book of Romans, doing the same.

Romans one. Romans two. Romans three. Romans four. Romans five.

"Romans 5:6," she said. " 'For when we were yet without strength, in due time Christ died for the ungodly.' "

She cleared her throat. " 'For scarcely for a righteous man will one die: yet peradventure for a good man some would even dare to die.' "

She pulled the candle closer. " 'But God commendeth his love toward us, in that, while we were yet sinners, Christ died for us.' "

Her heart was hammering again, only it wasn't from trepidation. It was from revelation.

"Sweet Love Roscoe," she whispered, feeling all a-twitter with new knowledge, "in a way, you died for me, a woman who loved you so. Yet it says Christ died for those who didn't even love Him. How could someone do something like that?"

The magnitude of Christ's love hit her like a shaft of sunlight, and she slipped to her knees in the dim candleglow. "Lord, can

You forgive me?" she cried. "I be one of those who didn't care a thing for You, yet You died for me to take away my sins before I even asked."

She brushed away her tears. "Lord, I be sorry for being insensitive to what You did on Calvary. You provided salvation, and I accept that now. Set me free from the chains of sin, like You did for Auntie."

It is done, the Lord assured. *I have paid the price for your liberty.*

"I'm free, Lord, truly free," she exclaimed, then lowered her voice so she wouldn't waken Cassie. "I promise to live for You the rest of my days and to proclaim Your glory to all I meet."

A peace sweeter than a honeycomb seeped over her being, from the top of her head to the tips of her toes, and she knelt there for eons, crying tears of joy, pouring forth words of love for her Savior.

Finally, Winkie quieted, basking in the Lord's presence. When she arose, her knees were stiff from kneeling on the hard wooden floor, for how long she didn't know. Then she saw the fingers of dawn peeking through the curtains.

"Ain't gonna' study war no more," she sang softly as she walked toward the bed. "Ain't gonna' study war no more, ain't gonna' study war no more-ore-ore. Ain't gonna' study war no more, ain't gonna' study war no more, ain't gonna' study war no more."

With eyes brimming with joy tears, she crawled in beside Cassie for a little shut-eye. As she settled beneath the bedclothes, into her mind came Auntie's words: *Periwinkle, one day you going to bring the healing touch of comfort to others.*

"Lord," she whispered, wiping yet more tears away, "this be Periwinkle talking. I promise to comfort those that need comforting wherewith You have comforted me."

Chapter 14

"Y ou think I ought to go find Joseph and tell him I made it right with my maker?" Periwinkle asked Auntie on the second visit after her Day of Liberty.

Auntie's brows drew together in contemplation. "Why not give it a few weeks, Sweet One? Let the Lord work it out for you. I know He going to."

"Yes, Ma'am."

"Meantime, you keep reading the Good Book and get yourself rooted and grounded in the things of the Lord."

"I am, Auntie, I am. I be eating it up."

Auntie wagged her head, saying "Um hmm" over and over. Then she paused. "The Bible say, 'They that hunger and thirst after righteousness shall be filled.'" She licked her lips. "Now, have you got a dab more of them spiced apples and that clotted cream?"

On a bright June morning as Periwinkle took the pan of biscuits off the outdoor fire and put them on a plate, she saw her neighbor, Mercy Jones, across the alleyway.

"How goes it?" she called, friendlylike, wrapping the plate

of biscuits with a checkered cloth.

"Misery, pure misery." Mercy, a freewoman and clothes washer who had previously avoided Periwinkle, walked toward her, wringing the last drops of water out of a towel. From the bunglesomeness of it, Periwinkle judged the towel held a gang of collars and wristbands that belonged to some fine gentleman.

"Misery? How so?" Periwinkle put down the plate and turned her attention to her neighbor.

"My throat be purely plugged with terror. There's talk of war and such stuff all over. Every time I make my deliveries in town, that all I hear. Yesterday, Mrs. Davis—she be one of my customers—why, she told me about a war in this country before the turn of the century, she said, where guns was shot off and innocent people was killed right and left."

Mercy let out a little sob. "I be terrible scared, just terrible. I don't want no bullet to go through my skull. I have tried turning my shoes upside down every night for weeks now, and I even made the soles face the wall. But nothing helps. The talk gets worse every day. Oh, why can't I go on to Diddy-Wah-Diddy, where we going to dance on the streets, sing and eat chitlins and possum pie all the day long?"

Mercy was beside herself, groaning and moaning, and when she dropped the towel full of laundry, Periwinkle knew how deep her despair was. Water was too hard to come by to let clean clothes fall in the dirt.

It's time, Periwinkle, the Lord seemed to whisper. *This is your destiny.*

"Yes, Lord," she whispered back. With a gentle grip, she held Mercy's shoulders and looked into her eyes. "Mercy, the Good Book say, 'Let not your heart be troubled.' It also say, 'Thou wilt keep him in perfect peace, whose mind is stayed on Thee.'"

Periwinkle hugged Mercy to her in a sisterly embrace. "Oh, Mercy, Christ Jesus has set me free from the chains of sin, and in their place He give me peace, joy, and love. And He want to do the same for you, right here, right now. His peace will flood your soul like the waters that cover the sea if you trust in Him."

A quarter hour later, her biscuits cold but her steps light, Periwinkle went inside to wake Cassie.

"Yes, Lord," she said, looking heavenward, smiling and crying a joy tear at the same time, "I promise to comfort those that be in need of comforting wherewith You have comforted me."

Chapter 15

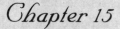

Periwinkle stood at the window at breaking of day and smiled. "Independence Day has dawned without a hint of rain in the cloudless sky." At her light footfall across the room, Cassie bounded out of bed.

"Parade day," Cassie said, jumping up and down, nightdress jiggling. "It's finally here. It's finally here."

"Yes, it's parade day, but that parade don't start for a good three, four hours, young lady. You better get some more shut-eye, or you be too tired to enjoy it."

"I can't, Mama, I can't."

For close to an hour, as Periwinkle worked on her hats, Cassie played with her collection of gourds and then with the doll Miss Willie gave her.

At last, Cassie curled up on the rug, fast asleep. As Periwinkle pinched a piece of fabric to form a green satin leaf, she thought about the pleasant prospects of the day. First, there would be the parade. Then there would be the picnic, what she promised Cassie, on the outskirts of town. In a few minutes, she would lay down her sewing and get the chicken to frying in the vat and the sweet potatoes to baking in the hot coals. Then it would be time to wrap and pack them, and then she would get Cassie up and dressed and herself dressed too. Then it would be time for them to head to town and commence some merrymaking.

I always thought Independence Day was better than Christmas, Miss Willie was known to say.

"Yes, me and Cassie both be looking forward to some gaiety today," Periwinkle whispered to herself.

She pulled her needle in and out of the rose-colored silk, turning the fabric just so, until a perfect rosette emerged. She remembered last Christmas and how she'd thought it was the best Christmas Day she'd ever had, except for wondering about Joseph's brooding silence. On that day, she thought Joseph was quiet because he was planning The Proposal.

A few weeks later, she'd learned the truth of the matter. He was planning The Parting.

"Oh, Joseph," she said, feeling all weepy inside, "I have sorely missed you." She bit off the thread and rethreaded her needle, her hands trembling. "My Heart Happy Joseph, the man who set my feet to dancing and my face to smiling, him who made my heart sing and my spirit soar, where art thou, as the poet said?"

She glanced up. "Lord, what be Your plans for my future? Do they include my Heart Happy Joseph? Will my heart sing and my spirit soar once again? Be it possible that I might get a glimpse of him today at the Independence Day parade?"

I have everything under control, Periwinkle, the Lord seemed to whisper. *Have faith.*

Chapter 16

Once again, as on the previous Independence Day, Joseph Moore stood amidst a sea of brown faces in the proper section of downtown Charleston, his arms folded across his barrel chest, anticipating with relish the parade that was about to commence.

He remembered last year's parade as if it had happened yesterday, a warm feeling flooding his heart. On last Independence Day, right here on the same corner, he'd met his winsome Winkie and her charming daughter, Starlight.

That afternoon, there had been a formal introduction at the Fletcher plantation. Their first meeting entranced him. Their second meeting thrilled him. As they shook hands under the arbor, her feet did a little dance in the dirt, and he thought his heart would burst from happiness.

He was so deep in thought, he almost jumped when he heard the loud notes of a lively patriotic song being played close by. To his left, just within his view, he saw a band marching down the street.

When only a few minutes had passed with his toe tapping to the beat of the rousing tune, the crowd closed in tighter, slaves and free people alike, all straining to get a glimpse and enjoy the frivolities of the day. He glanced around to see if he knew anyone, but the crowd kept jostling and shifting.

His mind studied on the events of the past year.

Getting to know Winkie.

Sharing meals together.

Enjoying outdoor picnics on the wayside.

Falling in love with her.

Carving her blanket chest.

Making plans for a future together.

And then. . .

The sermon. "Unequally yoked," the minister had called it. *Unequally yoked. Unequally yoked. Unequally yoked.* The first time Joseph had heard those fiercesome words as he sat in church, they had pounded in his brain, then invaded his heart and gripped it with an iron hand.

How could he live without her? his soul had cried out, his spirit vexed. How could he give up the woman he loved? He had searched for the right miss for years, and when he finally found her, he had to let her go.

Etched into his mind, never to be forgotten, were the immortal words Winkie had quoted the day of their parting:

> *"Till a' the seas gang dry, my dear,*
> *And the rocks melt wi' the sun:*
> *Oh I will love thee still, my dear,*
> *While the sands o' life shall run."*

Now, standing on the street corner listening to the patriotic tunes, his heart wrenched in his chest, and it took everything within him to bridle his trembles. How many times since their parting had he made his way to her, only to turn his steps around by sheer willpower—and God's power too? How many times had he thought of taking her into his arms and making her his wedded wife, to love and to cherish, forever and ever?

Trust and obey, the Lord seemed to say on each occasion. *Give Me time to work.*

"How long must I wait, Lord?" he mumbled, in anguish of soul.

"Mama, I can't see," said a child to his right. "Please pick me up one more time."

"You're too heavy, Sugarbun," said a woman's voice, low and melodious.

Instantly, he recognized the voice, and his breath caught in his throat.

"I be plumb give out from holding you."

Joseph glanced down and saw a little girl with a pleading expression on her face as she tugged on a woman's skirts. Then he looked directly at the woman, saw wide somber eyes, smooth-as-buttermilk brown skin, smart hat and gown, and he couldn't help smiling at the pleasant sight before him.

Winkie looked up into his eyes, not dipping her chin as was her custom, just staring straight at him, smiling so big, her teeth were near to falling out of her mouth.

His heart hammered in his chest as he noticed the tears in her eyes, and she drew near him and raised up on her toes, and he thought she was going to hug him, only she didn't, just leaned toward him, toward his neck, toward his ear, not touching him at all.

"My Heart Happy Joseph," she whispered so no one else could hear. "I'm free indeed."

If he hadn't been standing in a packed crowd, he would have leaped in the air and kicked his heels together. "You're free indeed, Winkie?" His heart was beating so hard, he felt dizzy for a moment. Dizzy with love.

"Liberty, sweet liberty," someone hollered out.

"Joseph, I know with a surety that Jesus paid the price for my liberty."

He understood exactly what this meant for her, as well as for them, and he reached into his pocket, withdrew his hand-kerchief, dabbed at her tears, holding his in check all the while. "Joy tears," he said softly as he kept dabbing, so overcome he could hardly speak.

"That be right."

"For more reasons than one?"

She nodded, smiling up at him through tear-glistened eyes.

"Oh, Baby." He hugged her to him amidst the jostling crowd, with Cassie sandwiched between them and embracing the both of them, expressing her joy in her own quiet way. How good Winkie felt in his arms.

"I'm sorry for the angry words I said to you—"

"Don't you worry your pretty head a minute more."

She sighed. "Wilderness wanderings come to an end. . ."

"Wedded bliss about to begin." He smiled.

She did a little two-step in his embrace, what had thrilled him when they were formally introduced, what thrilled him now.

"Kind honored miss," he said, holding her tightly, repeating one of Uncle Solomon's courting riddles, "will you condescend to encourage me to hope that I might, some glorious day in the future, walk by your side as a protector?"

"As soon as possible. Just as soon as possible."

After the parade, at the wayside picnic, she told Joseph about her new name, Periwinkle.

"That was my borned name," she said, "and that's the name I be living with from now on."

"You mean you had a name change?"

"You might say that."

"That be like Sarah in the Bible. Her name be Sarai, but when God gave the promise to her husband, Abraham, God changed her name to Sarah. It mean 'princess.'"

"That sound purely poetical. I going to read that story in Auntie's Bible when I get home."

"And when God changed her name, the Good Book say the Lord told Abraham that He would bless her and would give her a son by him." His eyebrows went up and down, his eyes danced beneath them, and his face wore a silly grin.

She laughed out loud at his antics, catching his meaning.

"Princess Periwinkle." He pecked her on the lips. "That be what I going to call you from now on."

As they made their way back to town in the late afternoon of Independence Day, Periwinkle saw a crowd gathering at a red-white-and-blue bunting-draped podium.

"Guess they going to make another speech or two," she said.

"And a few more songs, maybe?" Joseph gestured at the colorfully uniformed band behind the podium.

Through the throng they made their way, and from out of nowhere it seemed, a tall man—a plantation owner by the looks of his white linen suit and wide planter hat—bumped into Periwinkle, knocking her bonnet askew, then continued on his way as if he'd collided with nothing more than a gnat.

I love you, white man, you, she groused in her heart, trying to hide her grimace, *because the Bible tell me to. But I sure don't like you.*

"You look as if you stepped in a briar patch," Joseph said. "What you be thinking?" He stared at the man in the white linen suit walking briskly away, saw her adjusting her bonnet. "I think I know, Princess." He paused. "Baby, you got to love them."

"Oh, I will." *In the sweet bye and bye.* She squelched a chuckle.

"It be the right thing to do."

She nodded, and they continued walking, her holding his arm, Cassie at her side, thinking of Auntie's words.

"You keep your nose clean—even if it takes both sleeves," Auntie had said.

"Auntie!" Periwinkle had exclaimed.

Auntie's dark eyes had danced, but her voice was serious-sounding. "No matter what the rest of the world do, you make sure your attitude be right. That all we be responsible for in life. If we do that, God take care of us."

"You be right, Auntie," Periwinkle whispered as she walked beside Joseph.

"What you say?" he asked now.

"Nothing." *Lord, I choose to obey Your Word and live by Your commandments, if You give me the strength.*

That pleases Me, Daughter, the Lord said back.

"Come on, Princess. Quit dragging. We got wedding plans to make." Joseph's eyebrows went up and down, and his eyes danced beneath them, and his face wore that same silly grin.

"That so?" she said, dipping her chin.

"That so."

"Mama, look," Cassie spoke up, tugging on her mother's skirts.

"What, my mama-look baby?"

"I got something to ask you and Mr. Joseph."

Periwinkle stopped in her tracks, and Joseph did too, and they both looked down at Cassie, waiting for her question.

"Is the peach and the pear going in the cobbler together?" Cassie was smiling so big her teeth were near to falling out of her mouth.

Joseph laughed heartily, along with Periwinkle. "They sure is," he said. "They sure is."

"Liberty, sweet liberty," someone shouted.

Epilogue

1866

Yes, two days shaped my future, both of them having to do with liberty. The second one, I call my Day of Liberty. It was the day I realized I was free indeed, oh joyous thought, according to John 8:36: " 'If the Son therefore shall make you free, ye shall be free indeed.' "

Six years have passed since my Day of Liberty, and during those years, war came to our nation, pitting brother against brother with its terrible scourge of despair, disease, and death. Four long years of horrific tragedy passed, so tortuous I cannot put adequate words on it.

When it was going on, I often wondered if it was God's judgment against America for the sin of slavery, much as the poet Cowper suggested.

No one will ever know.

But I do know this. If I keep my nose clean, though it may take both sleeves, God'll take care of the rest.

That's come to be my philosophy in life.

And there's another thing I know, for sure. "For I know whom I have believed, and am persuaded that he is able to keep that which I have committed unto him against that day."

That's from 2 Timothy 1:12, another of the many verses I have committed to memory.

Joseph and I have found this verse to be true in our lives. God kept us during the war, and we came through unscathed, and Cassie too.

And along the way, God gave us a son.

His name is Joshua. It means "salvation."

—*Princess*

KRISTY DYKES

Kristy lives in sunny Florida with her hero husband Milton, and she's a native Floridian as are generations of her forbears. She's had hundreds of articles published in such publications as two *New York Times* subsidiaries, *Guidepost's Angels*, *Leadership*, etc. For one *Times* subsidiary, she wrote a weekly cooking column, "Kristy's Kitchen," which generated more reader mail than the Letters to the Editor page! This is her second Barbour anthology. Her first is *American Dream* (contains her historical novella, "I Take Thee, A Stranger"), still available. Kristy is also a public speaker, and one of her favorite topics is "How to Love Your Husband." Her goal in writing is to "make them laugh, make them cry, and make them wait" (a Charles Dickens's quote). In all her endeavors, her motto is, "Whatsoever thy hand findeth to do, do it with thy might" (Ecclesiastes 9:10). Kristy loves to hear from her readers. Write her at kristydykes@aol.com or in care of Barbour Publishing.

AMERICAN PIE

by Debby Mayne

Dedication

Thanks to Reverend Scott and Lori Welch
for their dedication to
the ministry of FreshStart.

Chapter 1

1890 Southern Mississippi

"Mm-mm, somethin' smells mighty fine, Miss Sophie." Sophia turned around and looked her mother's housekeeper, Dora, in the eye and smiled. "It better smell good. I've been workin' on it all morning. It's apple pie. Mama's recipe."

Dora stepped closer, clicking her tongue. "Apple pie. My goodness, Child. You gonna spoil that man and make him think he done died and gone to heaven."

"I wouldn't go that far, but I sure hope it tastes as good as it smells."

"Looks good too," Dora said. "But you didn't have to go to all that trouble for Mr. Jacobson. He's so sweet on you, you coulda made a mud pie, and he woulda bid his right arm on it."

"Maybe so," Sophia agreed, "but Mama wouldn't approve. She insisted I use this recipe." With a soft chuckle, she added, "You know how Mama is."

Dora shot Sophia a quick side-glance and shook her head.

"Think he might pop the question soon?" Dora asked as she stuck her finger into the mixing bowl, then pulled it out to taste it. "Mm-mm. That's some fine cookin'."

Sophia inhaled deeply, then slowly let out her breath. "Who knows," she said. "Men can be so thick-headed sometimes."

"Don't I know it." Dora shook her head as she chuckled and headed toward the kitchen door. "Just try not to trip when you're carryin' that thing across the church yard."

"I'll try not to," Sophia replied.

As soon as Dora left the kitchen, Sophia backed up and sank into one of the half dozen kitchen chairs that surrounded the large pine table. The last thing she wanted was to become William Jacobson's wife, but it appeared that they were meant to be together. Ever since they were children, their parents had been planning this wedding, hoping to bring the two families together. Mama had told her she'd never meet a finer man than William, which was probably true. But whenever Sophia was around him, she felt shackled, like she couldn't be herself. He was so quiet, she often thought of him as moody. However, he was a Christian man, and that was the single most important feature she must look for in a husband.

As far as Sophia was concerned, arranged marriages should be banned. While her parents said she didn't have to marry William, she knew they'd be deeply disappointed if she didn't. That is, if he ever got around to asking her.

Sophia was beginning to think he dreaded the thought of it as much as she did. *If that's the case,* she thought, *then it better not happen. No sense in two people being disappointed.*

"Sophia, better hurry up. The auction starts in an hour, and it's a good half-hour ride."

"Comin', Mama," Sophia said as she stood up. Better get there on time or the whole congregation would wonder what had gotten into her.

Sophia held the pie in her lap as her mother chattered non-stop all the way to the church. "Don't think for one minute you're the only girl there with a delicious pie, Sophia," she said. "You have to smile at William and let him know you're interested."

"I know, Mama."

"And you can't leave it up to him to do all the talkin' once he wins you in the auction."

"Once he wins my pie, Mama," Sophia corrected her.

"That's right. You have to let him know you like him without seeming too eager."

Sophia swallowed hard. Based on how it had started, this was going to be a very long day.

As they rode the rest of the way to the church, Sophia's mind wandered while her mother's incessant chatter droned on and on. Every year, each of the single, available women from the church baked a pie that was to be auctioned off at the Fourth of July celebration. Men—or suitors, to be exact—bid on whatever pie their favorite girl brought, as people standing around watching chuckled and made appropriate comments, encouraging them to start thinking about the rest of their lives. And some did. The Church on the Hill had a very high number of proposals on July Fourth, and weddings generally followed soon after. Most couples didn't want to wait too long once they'd decided they wanted to spend the rest of their lives together.

Sophia liked William Jacobson enough to consider him a very good friend. In fact, he was the person she chose to sit next to at potluck dinners and during fellowship gatherings—any place where she needed to keep quiet. But marriage? William's solemn manner and brooding disposition would surely depress her if she had to face him every day for the rest of her life.

"Okay, Sophia, hop down and get on over there. Looks like the rest of the girls have found their spots."

She glanced over at the long row of tables that had been set out on the church lawn. Young women—some her age but most a year or two younger—were standing behind their creations, chattering and giggling to each other. This all seemed so silly to Sophia.

"Hey, Sophia," her best friend, Gina, called. "Over here."

At least there was one person who understood her. "Coming," she called as she glanced around to see if Mama was looking, then hiked her dress and ran, precariously carrying the pie in one hand.

"Look at all the men," Gina said. "Looks like they're all hungry too."

"Men are always hungry," Sophia said with a snort. "But I guess this is for a good cause."

"That's right; don't forget about the cause."

Gina and Sophia had already agreed that if this auction didn't bring in a huge amount of money for the orphanage the church helped support, they'd never in a million years agree to be part of it.

"Is Richard here yet?" Sophia asked.

"I don't think so. He's almost always late for everything. That's why I told the pastor I wanted to go last. Richard would just die if someone else bid on my pie and he wasn't even around to outbid him."

"At least you know you love him," Sophia reminded her.

"You poor dear," Gina offered sympathetically. "I know you like William, but you should never have to marry him if he's not the man you love with all your heart."

"I just wonder if such a man exists. Maybe I should just do

what Mama and Daddy want me to do and get on with life."

"You always do what they want you to do. I would have given a few people a piece of my mind by now, if I were in your shoes."

Gina probably would too. She often accused Sophia of trying too hard to make everyone around her happy when she was suffering greatly. Sophia just didn't like to disappoint those she loved, so she'd always gone along with whatever her parents wanted. Why should she stop now?

Reverend Breckenridge tipped his hat as he walked by the end of the long row of tables. "Mornin', ladies."

"G'mornin', Reverend," Gina said. "Looks like we have quite a turnout on this lovely day."

"It's mighty hot already," he said with a chuckle. "I hope everyone stays long enough to bid on all these pies."

"I'm sure they will." Gina had picked up a church fan and begun waving it at her face.

The minute Reverend Breckenridge turned his back and walked away, Sophia laughed. "I don't know how you do it, Gina, but you can talk to anyone about anything."

Gina grinned back at her. "Not really. I just don't have a fear of anyone here, but put me in front of a group of school-teachers and my tongue freezes."

Sophia remembered when they were young girls, talking about what they wanted to be when they grew up, her best friend said she wanted to be a schoolteacher. "They get to boss every-one around all the time, and everyone thinks they're smart."

"That's hardly a reason to become one," Sophia had argued.

"It's good enough for me."

But Gina hadn't become a schoolteacher, and Sophia hadn't been married right out of school like she'd thought. Both of them still lived at home with their parents, helping their mothers run their households and trying to figure out what the Lord had in store for them.

"Maybe we'll never figure it out," Gina had said the week before the auction. "Look," she now whispered, her voice tinged with excitement. "That man over there. I've never seen him before."

Sophia glanced over in the direction Gina was nodding. "I think I might have seen him in church last Sunday. Isn't he one of the new men on the lumberyard?"

"Oh, that's right. Andy Sawyer said they hired some more men to supervise on the yard. He's probably one of them."

"He sure is handsome," Sophia noticed.

Gina leaned back and gave Sophia one of her practiced schoolteacher looks. "Now don't go gettin' any ideas about this man, or you might cause William to faint dead away."

Sophia waved her hand from the wrist. "Don't be silly. William couldn't care less if I think some other man's handsome."

"Maybe so, but there's rumor going around that William's looking at building a house on the back of his family's property," Gina said in her all-knowing way. "And you know what that means." She gently placed her hand on Sophia's arm. "Brace yourself for the proposal."

With a long sigh, Sophia wiped her forehead with her handkerchief. "I don't know anything about it."

Gina turned her attention to the woman who'd come up on the other side of her and set her pie on the table. While they discussed recipes, Sophia fought back the urge to take her pie and run as far away as she could. This whole pie auction was wrong for her. All her life, other people had decided what she should do and where she should be. She'd gone along with whatever they wanted because she didn't want to upset her mama and daddy.

William was a very sweet man, but she never felt anything when he'd kissed her—either time. Both kisses had been short and sweet, but nothing had happened. No sparks. No music in her heart. No racing pulse. Nothing. Surely the Lord would want her to feel something.

Sophia didn't expect too much from life, but she wanted a husband who could give her something to look forward to each day when he came home from work. She knew that if she loved her husband as much as her mama loved her daddy, she'd want to cook and decorate, doing all the things to make her home a comfortable place for the man who headed her household. With William, she'd wonder what sadness he would bring home.

Although William was sweet, he was sad all the time. He rarely smiled, but Sophia understood why. His family had relied so heavily on him since he'd been big enough to help out in his father's store, he'd never been allowed the opportunity to be a happy-go-lucky child.

"He's responsible," Mama had said when she started talking to Sophia about her future. "You want a responsible husband."

Yes, that's exactly what she wanted, but not William. All she wanted from William was friendship, but that didn't appear to be what she'd get.

Sophia knew, long before the pie auction started, that William would most likely be the only man bidding on her pie. He'd get the opportunity to have lunch with her, and they'd slice the pie for dessert. He'd take the rest of it home, and everyone would say what a wonderful wife she'd make because she could cook. It was all so predictable. Why couldn't Sophia have the freedom to fall in love with someone of her choosing? And why couldn't she have more excitement and fun in her life?

She shut her eyes for a short prayer before the ceremony began. *Lord, I'm here to serve You, and I want to do Your will. Please give me peace and joy as I do Your work. Amen.*

When she opened her eyes, Sophia saw that the reverend had gone up to the podium that had been set up on the small wooden stage. His voice was strong, so he didn't need the megaphone he'd pulled out. But he used it anyway.

"Before we start the auction for these delicious pies, I'd like to hear from some of you what this Fourth of July celebration means to you."

At first, no one volunteered, so Reverend Breckenridge called on one of the elderly men in the front row to speak first. The gray-bearded man hobbled up to the podium with his cane, then looked around at the crowd and grinned. "We are all here to give thanks to the Lord for placing us in this fine country where we are free to worship Him without fear." He opened his mouth like he had something else to say, then he held his hands up, shaking his head. "That's all. Amen."

A few people laughed out loud, but most hid smiles behind their hands as they tried to be polite. He might have had few words to say, but Sophia felt like they were words filled with truth.

"Amen," she whispered as he walked back to his wife, who was smiling with pride at her husband.

Several more men stood and talked about how the Fourth of July would always be significant because of freedom and liberty. They each related their own experiences, telling how they'd been able to choose their paths in life. "Without freedom, I'd never have the acres of farmland and my beautiful bride," another elderly gentleman said. His wife of nearly fifty years blushed and reached for him as he joined her. They'd been married the longest of any couple there. Sophia saw the love and tenderness they shared, and she wondered if she'd ever have a relationship like that with a man.

Then, to everyone's surprise, the new man Sophia had noticed earlier stepped up to the podium. Everyone hushed as he looked around at all the staring eyes.

Suddenly, his voice boomed through the megaphone. " 'For all have sinned, and come short of the glory of God; being justified freely by His grace through the redemption that is in Christ Jesus,' Romans 3:23-24." He cleared his throat before he continued. "The only freedom we have, folks, is through Him, our Lord Jesus Christ, and I for one give thanks to Him every day for what He did for me. No country, no free land, no government can take away my relationship with my Lord. He will always be with me. Amen."

After that powerful speech, no one dared come forth to add their thoughts of freedom. He'd said it all.

Sophia felt an odd tingling sensation in her stomach, almost like butterflies were fluttering their wings against her ribs. She watched the man as he made his way back to where he'd been standing, less than twenty feet from her end of the pie table. She wasn't sure of his name, but she intended to find out.

William appeared from out of nowhere. "Hi, Sophia. Your pie looks mighty good."

Her lips were still dry from the effects of the stranger. She turned to William and forced a smile. "Why thank you, William."

He looked down at his feet, then back toward her, although not directly at her. That had always annoyed Sophia, the fact that he rarely met her gaze. Her mother had said that was because he was shy, which sounded silly to Sophia. But

Mama was probably right as usual.

"I'll see you in a little while," William said as he backed away from Sophia. "Your pie will be one of the last to be auctioned." Then he was gone. He didn't even have the good graces to say good-bye.

When Reverend Breckenridge moved back to his position behind the podium, speculation ran through the congregation. He said a prayer, reiterating what the stranger had already said. Then he said, "Let the auction begin."

The first was a cherry pie baked by Lucy Morris. Two men bid for the pie, but from the very beginning there was no doubt who'd win. Her brother's best friend had already expressed his intentions, and Lucy was thrilled to walk away from the pie table arm-in-arm with him.

Sophia felt the tension build in her chest as the pies and single ladies disappeared with their bidders. When it was her turn, she had to force herself to smile and not run away. Mama and Daddy would be furious with her if she didn't go through with this. She shut her eyes and begged the Lord to not have William propose on this day.

William placed the first offer, which was a very paltry amount. Sophia was embarrassed, but she knew William didn't have very much money. She started to pick up her pie and head over to him when another bid came in, this one doubling William's offer.

Everyone in the crowd turned and stared as the bidder stepped forward. It was the stranger who'd shushed everyone with his comments on freedom! Sophia felt her face grow hot as the bidding war began.

William had already bid dangerously high for his salary. Sophia felt sorry for him and found herself calculating how she'd offer to reimburse him for that stranger's stupidity. Didn't he know this wasn't done?

Finally, when the stranger bid a sum that had people gasping, William faded back into the crowd.

"Sold!" the reverend called out. "Miss Mayhew, you may take your pie over to the payment table and join Mr. Ellis for a picnic lunch. Enjoy your pie. I'm sure it's worth every penny."

Sophia's knees grew weak as she did as she was told. Every eye was focused on her, making her feel like crawling into a hole. But she had to keep walking toward the man who'd bid on her pie, past William, past Mama and Daddy, past all the leering people who knew this was significant. What would she do now?

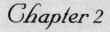

Chapter 2

That pie looks scrumptious," the stranger Reverend Breckenridge had called Mr. Ellis said. "I can hardly wait to cut into it."

"Who are you?" Sophia asked since he didn't appear anxious to introduce himself.

He grinned. "I'm Hank Ellis. I thought you might know my name. Sorry for my rudeness."

Sophia felt ashamed of herself for being so abrupt. "I'm sorry too," she said. "I'm Sophia Mayhew."

"Yes, I know. In fact I've known who you were for quite some time now."

"You have?" she asked, her voice a much higher pitch than normal. She lifted her free hand to cover her mouth as she cleared her throat. "How?"

"I've been watching you for several weeks, and I asked some of the other church members."

Sophia studied his face for a few seconds. "You've been going to church here for several weeks?"

"Yes," he replied with a deep, hearty chuckle. "I'm afraid I'm one of those people who likes to sit on the back pew. But I do listen to everything the reverend says, and I read my Bible every day." He lifted his right hand. "I promise."

She laughed with him. "You don't have to go that far. I believe you."

Hank took the pie in one hand and offered his other arm for her to take. "Shall we?"

"Yes," she said as she glanced nervously over her shoulder at all the people behind them. Just as she'd thought, everyone was still staring at them. Well, let them stare. Maybe they'd learn something.

"How's that oak tree over there?" he asked. "I see someone has put a settee beneath it, just for us."

Sophia's heart fluttered as she looked at Hank Ellis's profile. He was a handsome man, and he smiled a lot. She liked that.

"I hope you don't mind if we eat right away," he said. "I'm starving."

Sophia didn't want to admit that when she took his arm, her appetite had vanished. Her stomach was filled with those butterflies. With a shrug, she replied, "I ate a big breakfast this morning, right before we came here. But go ahead and get something for yourself."

"I'll be right back," he said as he backed away from her, leaving her sitting beneath the oak tree with her pie. "Don't go anywhere."

She lifted her hand and waved her fingers, smiling. "I'll be right here when you get back."

Hank almost ran smack dab into the reverend before he turned around and caught himself. Sophia watched him apologize, walk briskly toward the picnic table filled with food brought by the married women, then appear once again with his plate piled high. He didn't waste any time coming back to her.

"I thought you might want a little nourishment, so I

brought enough for both of us." He tilted his head forward and looked at her teasingly from beneath hooded eyes. "That is, if you don't mind sharing a plate."

Sophia had never been asked to share a plate with a man before, and this sounded quite adventurous. "I don't mind at all," she replied.

Although she wasn't the least bit hungry, Sophia picked at the items she could lift with her fingers. This was more fun than she'd ever had with a man before. In fact, other than William, this was the only man she'd ever been alone with.

"I hope you aren't too upset about me bidding on you so unexpectedly," Hank said between bites. "I was afraid I might lose you to that other gentleman who seemed determined to win your pie."

Sophia nibbled on a slice of bread she'd lifted from his plate. "William is an old friend of the family."

"Is that all? I sort of got the impression there might be more to it."

"Well, maybe, but not for me."

"So you're saying you're a single woman with no attachments?" he asked.

With a slight hesitation, Sophia nodded. Her face felt flaming hot. She'd never been so bold in her life, but he'd asked a question, and it would be rude not to answer it. She wanted to get to know Hank Ellis.

Hank leaned over and brushed a stray hair from Sophia's cheek, then lifted her chin with his fingertips, turning her toward him. "No need to feel embarrassed, Sophia. I only wanted to make sure I'm not interfering in something you already have going with another man."

"You're not," Sophia managed to say, her voice softer than

she could ever remember it being.

He smiled, lifted his arms to the sky, and said, "Hallelujah!"

Sophia had never seen William express himself so openly or with so much enthusiasm, making the difference between the two men so great there was no comparison.

"Want to know what I find so appealing about you, Sophia—besides the beautiful honey-blond hair and those large brown eyes of yours?"

She looked at him and waited. No words came to mind. Even if they had, her voice had gotten lost somewhere in her astonishment.

"You wear your heart on your sleeve and your thoughts in your eyes."

Leaning forward, Sophia scrunched up her forehead and managed a weak, "What do you mean by that?"

He belted out another hearty laugh, something she could easily get used to. "I can tell you care deeply for others, and you have a strong emotional side to your being."

"Doesn't everyone?"

"Oh, no," he replied. "If they did, this world would be a much better place. As for your eyes, I can look into them and see to the depths of your soul."

"Then maybe I should shut them."

Hank reached for her cheek and touched it softly before pulling back. "Your skin is like peaches and cream, so soft and touchable."

Sophia wanted him to keep on telling her more of what he liked about her, but she didn't dare ask. "Thank you, Mr. Ellis."

"You must call me Hank if we're going to continue seeing one another."

She smiled back at him. "Hank."

"That's right. Now, my dear Sophia, let's cut into this delicious-looking pie and enjoy the fruits of your labor."

With every bite, Hank Ellis smiled and offered his gratitude for her culinary skills. He told her more than once how much he enjoyed fresh apple pie and said he'd love to see what else she could do in the kitchen.

Sophia knew that others were staring, but she didn't care. All that mattered to her was how she felt with this man—the only one who'd ever made her feel so exciting, so beautiful, so vibrant and alive. All the Williams in the world couldn't measure up to Hank Ellis.

Hank knew that Sophia was holding something back, but he wasn't about to press her for more details. He already felt as though he'd expected too much from her. In fact, he was surprised at how open and willing she'd been to talk with him.

He also felt the scorching heat from the stares of that man called William. It was painfully obvious that the man held a torch for this woman. No wonder. She was a raving beauty, and she was sweet. The fact that she could bake was a bonus that delighted him to no end.

Hank could imagine himself falling in love with Sophia Mayhew, Lord willing. But he knew he needed to tread lightly, or he'd risk dividing loyalties within the church. He'd seen it happen before over matters of much less consequence than this. One of his earliest memories had been of a man turning his back on the church after his daughter had been inadvertently overlooked during a church pageant. That one simple oversight had caused people to take sides, and the church temporarily lost half its flock. The pews were bare for several weeks until the pastor managed to soothe the hurt feelings. After seeing the hurt caused by that situation, Hank wasn't about to knowingly cause similar strife in another church.

As he and Sophia ate their pie, he asked her questions about her family. She was somewhat guarded, but he could tell she was interested in him by the way she looked at him. Her direct eye contact showed an openness and a willingness to share.

When she turned her back to check on her family, he looked up and mouthed, "Thank You, Lord."

"Well," she said as she abruptly stood up. "I hate to eat and run, but I really must go. It's getting late, and my parents are starting to give me anxious looks."

Hank tilted his head back and laughed. "I understand, Sophia. When may I see you again?"

Her face turned bright crimson once again, and he felt his heart melt with joy over seeing such honest emotion. She wasn't guarded in the least, which he appreciated. This would be a woman he could share his heart with and not have to worry that she'd trample it.

"I'm not sure," she said after hesitating briefly.

"Sophia, I'm sorry for being so direct if it makes you uncomfortable," he said as he stood beside her. "But I have a good feeling about us, and I'd like to pursue a relationship to see if we might have something in common."

"Oh, that's quite all right," she said in haste. "I just don't know how long it'll take me to. . ." Her voice trailed off as she glanced behind her once again. With concern etched on her face, she looked back at him. "I really need to go now."

Hank decided not to push too hard, or he feared he'd lose her altogether. So he nodded. "Then be on your way. I look forward to seeing you in church on Sunday."

"Good-bye," she said as she hurried away, leaving him standing alone beneath the oak tree.

Hank would rather have walked her over to her parents, but he wasn't sure that would be the wise thing to do under these circumstances. It was clear that they were concerned about their daughter. Besides, he needed to learn what their relationship was with that William fellow who kept casting jealous glances his way.

Once Hank was certain Sophia and her parents were gone, he strolled over to Reverend Breckenridge and placed his hand on the man's shoulder. "May I have a word with you, Reverend?"

"Why, certainly," the reverend replied. "I'll be right there. Give me just a minute with these folks."

Hank politely stepped back and waited, his hands in his pockets as he watched the rest of the people who remained behind, lingering over their desserts and having good, old-fashioned fellowship. This was a sight Hank had been looking for all his adult life. His church back in Alabama had grown so large that most members of the congregation didn't say more than a few polite words to each other. Since moving to Mississippi, Hank had tried to find a way to do the Lord's work when he wasn't at the lumberyard. The Church on the Hill seemed to be the perfect place for him to establish his spiritual roots. This was more of a church family, one he could grow with and be nourished in the Word.

Finally, when Reverend Breckenridge came to him, some of Hank's urgency had faded. He had all the time in the world to win Sophia's heart. But he knew he needed to have some background information on William.

"It's nice having you join us, Mr. Ellis," Reverend Breckenridge said.

"It's nice to be here. I've really enjoyed the celebration."

"I see you've met Sophia Mayhew." The reverend had gotten right to the point, which was something Hank admired. No beating around the bush.

"Yes, she's a delightful girl."

"That she is," Reverend Breckenridge agreed. "I've always enjoyed the Mayhews. Very loyal to the church, that family."

"Have they been coming to church here long?" Hank asked. He wanted to know how long Sophia had been a Christian, and this was the best way he could think of to ask.

Nodding, the reverend replied, "Since a couple of years before Sophia was born. Her father's family lived on a farm about fifty miles from here. When her parents married, they saved their money and bought a place on the river."

"Are they farmers?" Hank asked.

"Yes, they grow sugarcane and corn."

"We have something in common, then," Hank said with pleasure. "My family farms cotton and corn back in Alabama."

Reverend Breckenridge thrust his hands into his pockets and rocked back on his heels as he studied Hank. "Are you looking for something to have in common with Sophia, Boy?"

So, the reverend was smart as well as blessed spiritually. With a friendly laugh, Hank nodded. "I suppose I am. And to hear that my quest is being rewarded in such a way is music to my ears."

"Sophia is a very sweet girl who is always willing to serve the Lord through good works. She reads her Bible, and she seems to have a fair understanding of the gospel."

"More good news," Hank said. "I don't know how much more perfect that girl can get."

"Oh, she's not perfect by any means," Reverend Breckenridge said.

Hank frowned. He didn't want to hear anything bad about the woman he planned to court, especially from the pastor of her church.

"Granted, this isn't exactly a flaw, but it's something you need to watch out for."

"And what is this we're talking about?" Hank asked.

"Her family is quite close to the Jacobson family, one of the oldest and most established families in these parts."

"Jacobson?" Hank asked. "Do I need to know these people?"

"Trust me, Boy, if you don't know them already, you will soon. William Jacobson is the young man who kept an eye on you and Sophia."

Hank nodded. "Ah, now I understand."

"Most people have assumed for years that William and Sophia would court for a few years and become engaged. To my knowledge it hasn't happened yet. To be honest with you, I'm a little surprised."

"Surprised?" Hank asked as his heart ached. He didn't realize it was this serious between the woman he was terribly infatuated with and that man with the dirty looks.

"So far, I don't believe William has proposed, and from the way Sophia was talking to you, I'm not sure she'd accept if he did propose."

"So you think I might have a chance?" Hank asked.

Reverend Breckenridge placed his hand gently on Hank's shoulder as Hank had noticed him do to others with whom he spoke. "Yes, it appears that you do have a chance, but be advised to be very careful in how you go about wooing this young lady."

"Oh, I will," Hank said gladly. "I'll be very careful. But I want you to be the first to know that I don't give up easily once I set my mind to something."

The reverend chuckled. "I can see that in you."

Hank chatted with Reverend Breckenridge about upcoming church events for the next several minutes, but his mind wasn't on their discussion. All he could think about was how he could court Sophia without causing a stir within the church.

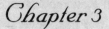

Chapter 3

H ow did Mr. Jacobson like your pie?" Dora asked as Sophia entered the kitchen.

"Mr. Jacobson didn't taste my pie."

Sticking her fist on her hip, Dora leaned forward. "What do you mean, he didn't taste your pie? You did go to the pie auction at the church, didn't you?"

"Yes, of course I did, but Mr. Jacobson wasn't able to out-bid the other man." Sophia had to bite the insides of her cheeks to keep from smiling. The joy in her heart made her want to jump and shout, but she refrained.

Dora lifted one eyebrow as a smile twitched the corners of her lips. "So, you seein' another man now?"

"Yes," Sophia said before she thought. Then she corrected herself. "No, I'm not seeing another man. It's just that—"

She cut herself off in midsentence, not sure what it was be-tween her and Hank Ellis. Although she found him terribly at-tractive and fun to be with, she wasn't sure that the reason he bid on her pie was because he didn't know about William's claim to her.

Sophia felt her chest tighten. Ever since she'd been old enough to consider marriage, her parents—and everyone else in the community for that matter—had pushed her toward William. And as much as she cared for William Jacobson, that feeling she always dreamed of when being with the man God had intended for her wasn't there. Her heart never once skipped a beat, and she didn't have a burning desire to see him again when they were apart. In fact, she dreaded the next time he'd call on her. The only time she enjoyed being with him was in church, and that was because she was expected to remain silent.

"Tell me, Child, who is this man?" Dora asked, still staring at her.

Sophia swallowed hard and shook her head. "He's from Alabama."

"Oh, I see. Alabama. I got people there."

"His name's Hank Ellis," Sophia went on.

Dora's smile widened. "You like this man, don't you, Miss Sophie?"

Once again, Sophia's face felt hot. She couldn't help but smile back at Dora. "He's very nice."

"Is he handsome?"

"Oh, yes," Sophia replied. Then she began to tell Dora how Hank looked, and without missing a beat, she went on and on about her conversation with him. By the time she came to a stopping point, she was out of breath.

"How's Mr. Jacobson feel about all this?" Dora asked.

"I don't think he much likes it."

"I s'pect not." Dora chuckled. "Hurts a man like Mr. Jacobson to see somethin' like what you done."

"What'd I do?" Sophia asked, suddenly confused. She couldn't remember doing anything to hurt William.

"You was havin' fun with that new man."

"Yes, but—"

Dora shook her head and clicked her tongue. "No man wants his lady to laugh at another man's jokes."

"Oh, I see." Actually, Sophia didn't see, but she knew William's ego was pretty powerful. And those stares he gave her and Hank were pretty telling of his feelings.

"Don't worry about it, Miss Sophie," Dora said. "He'll get over it. Just make sure you don't burn any bridges. If you start courtin' this new man, Mr. Jacobson's not likely to want you back."

Dora turned to face the wood-burning oven, which she opened. "Mm, mm, that sweet 'tater pie sure do smell good."

"Yes, it does," Sophia agreed, her mind already off and wandering again.

Sophia left the kitchen with its spicy nutmeg and cinnamon scents lingering in her hair. She needed to go upstairs to her room to think. Although she knew how she felt when she was around Hank Ellis, it was only the first time they'd been together. Maybe that feeling she had was one of newness and discovery. Perhaps it would fade over time, and she'd have the same feelings for Hank that she had for William.

"I need to talk to you, Sophia," her mother said from behind the wall in the parlor.

"Not now, Mama. I have a lot to do this evenin'. Maybe after dinner."

"No, Sophia, now." Mama's voice sounded firm, so Sophia stopped in her tracks.

She blew out a sigh. "Okay, Mama, but I'm tired, and I need to get my clothes ready for tomorrow."

Noting her mother's tone, Sophia sat on the edge of the sofa, while her mother sat across from her in the rocker. *This should be quite a lecture*, Sophia thought, bracing herself for what was sure to come.

"Who was that young man who bought your pie?" Mama said, getting right to the point.

"Hank Ellis," Sophia replied. She bit her lip to keep from sounding too eager about Hank. Surely, Mama wouldn't approve of him for the simple fact that he wasn't William.

"Where does he come from?"

"Alabama. His family farms cotton and corn."

Mama paused for a few seconds before continuing her interrogation. "Is he a Christian?"

"I assume so, Mama. He goes to church, and he reads his Bible."

"Plenty of people go to church, yet we don't know what's in their hearts," Mama said. "We must be careful of those who have unsavory motives."

"Unsavory motives?" Sophia repeated. "What do you mean by that, Mama?"

Another long silence. "Be very careful of this man, Sophia. And don't ever forget that William loves you and most likely wants to marry you."

"But what if I don't want to marry him?" Sophia asked her mother for the first time.

"Sophia! How can you say that after spending only an afternoon with this stranger? You and William have known each other practically all your lives. He's kind and gentle, and he comes from a very good family. We know nothing of this Ellis family." She paused to look at Sophia with tenderness. "What you're feeling now is a fascination with someone you don't know."

"You're right, Mama," Sophia said as she sank back on the sofa, knowing it was futile to argue.

"William should be here in about an hour," Mama continued.

"Go on upstairs and freshen up. I expect you to be on your best behavior in his presence, and there will be absolutely no talk of this Hank Ellis."

"Yes, Mama."

Sophia stood and did as she was told. She knew her mother wanted what was right for her. Besides, she was probably right. William had been steadfast and true for years. Hank was exciting simply because he was new.

Oh, but how she wished William didn't have to come for dinner—not after such a perfect afternoon. Sophia wished she had at least the remainder of the day to dwell on hers and Hank's conversation. She'd enjoyed every moment of banter, with more laughter than she'd shared with anyone in her life. Talking with Hank lifted her heart and made her want to sing. Now she had to get herself ready to spend time with William, which meant preparing for the song in her heart to dissolve.

As she was putting the final touches on her hair, Sophia heard a commotion downstairs. She stopped and leaned toward the door so she could hear better. The voice that floated up wasn't that of William, but of Hank. A smile instantly crept onto her lips, and her heart began to pound.

She took off running down the stairs, still trying to fasten the clip in the back of her hair. Hank was standing at the foot of the stairs, looking up and grinning right back at her.

"You left this," he said, holding out the pie tin. "I wanted to return it."

"My, that was fast," Sophia said. "You could have kept it until you finished the pie."

He looked down at his feet sheepishly. "I already finished it, Sophia."

She tilted her head back and laughed, with her mother

looking on in dismay. "Sophia, I'll have to insist you take your guest into the parlor. We're expecting our invited company to arrive any minute now."

Sophia had never heard her mother take on such a tone. It was one of open hostility and anger. When she glanced at Hank, she saw he'd noticed it too.

"No, Ma'am," he said to her mother, tipping his head in a friendly gesture. "I only wanted to drop off the pie tin. I must be getting back to the boardinghouse. Tomorrow starts awfully early at the lumberyard."

Sophia's mother's eyebrows were raised as she nodded. "Thank you, Mr. Ellis. We certainly appreciate your consideration." She sounded very formal and much too polite.

Just as Hank turned to leave, Sophia took a chance and ran after him. "Wait," she said. "I'll walk you to your horse."

"That won't be necessary, Sophia," he replied with a glance toward her mother. "I shall see you in church on Sunday."

Sophia shrank back and nodded. "Okay, then. Good-bye, Hank."

Once Hank was outside, he put on his hat and waved in one fluid motion. "It's been a pleasure meeting you, Ma'am," he said to her mother.

"Nice to have met you too, Mr. Ellis. We'll most likely be seeing more of you." She lifted her chin as she added, "In church, of course."

Although it was a minor omission, Sophia noticed her mother didn't offer the usual, "Do come back." Instead, she'd given him the cold shoulder in her own polite way.

Long after her mother went inside, Sophia remained on the front porch, watching the cloud of dust kicked up by Hank's horse as it galloped away. She felt as though she must do something to see him again. But what? She didn't want to deceive Mama and Daddy. They loved her and only wanted what was best for her.

Several minutes later, she heard the shuffle of her mother standing at the door. "I suggest you stop pining for something you know nothing about and concentrate on making all this up to William."

"Make what up to William, Mama?" she asked.

"He was none too happy about all that carryin' on you and Mr. Ellis did in the church yard this afternoon."

"We weren't carryin' on. We were just talking," Sophia objected.

"I heard you laughing all the way across the yard, Sophia. How do you think that makes William feel?"

Sophia hung her head. She had no idea how that had made William feel, but she knew how Hank made her feel. But Mama was right about not knowing Hank well enough to get all worked up over him. Perhaps he was lonely and wanted feminine companionship, and she'd been the girl he'd picked because he wasn't aware of William. Now that he knew, he might not be so eager to court her, in spite of what he'd said.

Once Hank was completely out of sight, Sophia went inside. She headed straight for the kitchen, where she found Dora pulling biscuits out of the oven.

"Need some help, Dora?" she asked.

"If you can hand me that jar of butter over there, I'd be most grateful," Dora said stiffly. Sophia knew something was up with her.

"What's the matter, Dora?" Sophia asked.

"Nothin'." She banged the tray of biscuits onto the trivets on the counter before turning to face Sophia. "Your mama just gave me a tongue-lashin'.'"

"She what?"

"You heard me. She tol' me to mind my own business about Mr. Jacobson."

Sophia leaned back and studied the woman standing before her. Dora had become her best friend, since she'd practically raised her.

"What'd she say, Dora?" Sophia asked.

"It don't matter now, Sophie. All I know's I can't tell you to follow your heart. Your mama reminded me how much Mr. Jacobson appreciates my biscuits and fried chicken."

In spite of her frustration, Sophia laughed. Mama sure did know how to get her point across without having to come right out and be direct.

"Let's get the dining room set up before Mr. Jacobson arrives. He's likely to be starvin' since he didn't eat at the church."

"There was plenty of food," Sophia said. "If he didn't eat, it's his own fault, and it serves him right if he's hungry."

"That's what I told your mama, but she just gave me one of her looks."

Sophia knew that look. In fact, she'd seen it a few minutes ago when Hank came.

By the time William arrived, Sophia and Dora had set the table and all the food was on platters, ready to be served. There was enough food to feed twice the number of people who were there.

"Looks mighty tasty, Miz Mayhew," William said. "Tell Dora how much I appreciate her goin' to all this trouble."

"I'm right here, Mr. Jacobson," Dora said from the kitchen door. "I hope you enjoy it."

Sophia settled back in her chair and nibbled on small bites

of the food she'd put on her plate. She couldn't remember a time when conversation had been so strained.

What bothered her the most was that all this bother was over William being outbid by Hank. Sophia knew she should be flattered, and she was to some degree, but she wished she didn't have to feel as if every single move she made was being watched. If it weren't for some unspoken agreement between her and William, Sophia was certain no one would be making such a fuss.

It was Sophia's father who brought up the subject of the lumberyard. Sophia's mama shot him that look, but he wasn't paying a bit of attention.

"Did you know that nice young supervisor at the lumberyard is regularly attending our church?" he asked.

"Why yes, I was aware of that," William said. "In fact, he's the man who bid on Sophia's pie."

"Oh," her father said, his fork inches from his mouth. He put his fork down, coughed into his napkin, then shook his head. "I didn't realize that was the man."

Sophia's mother tried her best to change the subject and bring on a more palatable discussion, but the damage had been done, and William was back to his moping self. Sophia wondered if he knew how unattractive he was when he frowned.

After dessert, which had been barely touched, William folded his napkin and placed it beside his plate. "I really must run now. Papa is expecting me to help him set lines in the pond tomorrow. We have to clean out the adult bream so the fingerlings can get food."

"If you have extra, we sure do love fried bream, Son," Sophia's daddy said. "I'll be glad to swap you some corn in exchange for a mess of fish."

"I'll tell Papa," William said with his usual somber expression. "No doubt he'll send me over with some."

Everyone stood up and walked William to the door. Sophia's father tried to chat with him, but William wasn't in the mood for small talk. That was just fine, since Sophia wasn't in the mood to be around William with him acting this way.

Once they were back inside the house, Sophia's mother turned and looked at her. She shook her head, then headed upstairs. Daddy, on the other hand, wanted to talk.

"So how do you like that new fella?"

"I beg your pardon, Daddy?" Sophia asked. Her father had always been more open and direct than her mother, but this still caught her off guard.

"That man from the lumberyard. The one who outbid William for your pie. What is he like?"

Sophia started to relax but then caught herself. She knew how her parents felt about William. "He's very nice, Daddy."

Her father nodded and rubbed his neck. "I'm glad, Sweetheart, but don't forget your relationship with William. There's talk that he's getting close to proposing."

Letting out another of her sighs that were coming with greater frequency, Sophia forced a smile. "So I've heard."

All night, Sophia lay in bed, pondering her dilemma. William was the man she'd been informally promised to, but Hank was the man who made her heart flutter. She kept going over what everyone wanted to remind her of. William was always there, and he was reliable. Hank was someone she knew very little about. It wasn't hard to figure out why everyone was so concerned. People knew William and loved him. Hank was the new man in the community who might one day up and take a notion to leave.

Sophia got very little rest that night, but she managed to awaken at the crack of dawn. She hurried and put on her clothes so she could meet Dora in the kitchen to help with breakfast, one of her favorite events of the day.

"Miss Sophie, you won't believe what everyone's sayin'," Dora said as she handed Sophia the pan for eggs.

"What, Dora?"

"That new man, Mr. Ellis, has plans for you."

"Plans for me?" Sophia said, her voice squeaking with excitement. "What kind of plans?"

"Well," Dora began as she thrust out a hip and shoved her fist on it. She looked away as she thought, then turned back to Sophia. "He told the reverend that he planned to give Mr. Jacobson a little competition."

In spite of how Sophia knew her parents would take this news, she grinned. It felt mighty good to have Hank willing to take such a big risk, just because he wanted to be with her.

"How did he respond?" Sophia asked. "Do you know?"

Dora shrugged. "From the way my daughter made it sound, he didn't seem to mind."

Cleo, Dora's daughter, was Reverend Breckenridge's housekeeper, so she often had the inside story of whatever was going on at the church. Most times, Dora didn't discuss matters her daughter told her, but Sophia guessed the older woman had made an exception this time because she knew the topic was important to Sophia.

"I wish everyone else had the same feelings," Sophia said.

"Only thing the reverend is worried about is how everyone else in the church will take this."

"Everyone else?" Sophia said. "Why would everyone else have a reaction?"

"You know how people are, Sophie. They make it their business to mind yours."

"But this is the church, Dora." Sophia carried a platter of biscuits to the rough-hewn pine table and sat down.

"People's people," Dora said with a shrug. "Don't matter whether they're Christians or not, they still talk."

As Sophia nibbled on a biscuit, she knew that Dora spoke the truth. Not only did she have to worry about upsetting her parents and William, she had the entire congregation to be concerned about. They all loved William, and most of them would stand behind him, no matter what.

"What should I do, Dora?" Sophia asked. "I like William. I truly do."

"But do you love him?" Dora asked.

"I'm not sure, but I don't think so." She sniffled. "Mama says I'll learn to love him over time."

Dora clucked. "Miss Sophie, it ain't none of my business, but I do know your face lights up whenever you mention Mr. Ellis's name."

"He's so fun and filled with joy," Sophia moaned. "Why couldn't William be more like that?"

"Some folks is just serious. Nothing you can do about that."

"I know, but I don't want to be serious all the time. God has blessed us with the ability to experience laughter, and I want to do it as much as possible."

"Then do what's on your heart, Miss Sophie," Dora advised. "Just be prepared to face everyone who don't agree with what you think you want."

Chapter 4

S ophia leaned back and thought about Dora's words: "Do what's on your heart."

Those were powerful words, and Sophia wasn't sure if she could follow that advice. William's feelings were at stake, and she wasn't about to hurt the man her parents favored. Doing something so outrageous would surely upset more than a few people.

As she thought about the situation, she realized there was William, Mama, Daddy, William's parents. Then there was the woman who always grinned when she spotted William and Sophia standing next to each other. Besides that, many people from the church had let it be known they wanted an invitation to the wedding when it happened, not if.

"Miss Sophie," Dora said, startling Sophia from her thoughts. "You come help me stir these grits while I pick the bacon out of the pan."

Sophia was thankful for the interruption, since her thoughts had begun to depress her. She was terribly confused about what was the right thing to do. Would a good, Christ-loving woman so much as entertain thoughts of taking up with a virtual stranger when the man she'd known all her life was standing, watching?

"Don't you worry no more, Miss Sophie," Dora said as she took the wooden spoon out of Sophia's hand. "Let the good Lord do things in His own time; that's what I always say. And I dare say that's good advice."

"Yes," Sophia agreed. "I dare say it too. I'll pray about it and let Him take over."

A shuffling sound at the kitchen door got Sophia's attention. It was Mama.

"Mornin', Miz Mayhew," Dora said as she nudged Sophia out of the way. "Mistah Mayhew on his way?"

"Why yes, Dora, he's coming down directly. C'mon, Sophia, join me in the dining room to wait for your daddy."

"Okay, Mama." Sophia followed her mama into the dining room. Silence fell between them for a long moment.

Sophia's mother pulled out her chair but remained standing behind it, waiting for her husband to join them for a blessing before the family sat down to eat. She glanced at Dora as she came through the doors with a couple platters balanced on her arms and shook her head. "Dora, I overheard you telling Sophia to let the good Lord do things in His own time. You weren't referring to something personal, now were you?"

Dora glanced at Sophia, then back at her employer. "Yes, Ma'am, it was very personal."

Sophia let out a long breath. She never would have expected Dora to lie for her, and thank the Lord she hadn't. It truly was a personal matter—one she didn't feel like discussing with Mama. Not yet, anyway.

When Sophia's daddy came to the table, his eyes gleamed with excitement. "What's goin' on, Daddy?" Sophia asked. "You look like a squirmin' snake on a hot summer day."

Grinning from ear to ear, he reached out and patted Sophia

on the shoulder. "Our daughter sure is intuitive, Maggie. I do have some good news."

"Good news?" Sophia's mother asked, lifting one eyebrow inquisitively.

"Very good news, in fact. We have thirty men from the church coming over to finish working on the barn on Saturday." He turned to Dora as she came through the door to the dining room. "You hear that, Dora? We'll need plenty of food to feed an army of hungry men on Saturday."

Dora glanced at Sophia before turning to him and nodding. "Yes, Suh, I'll make sure there's plenty."

"And tell your folks they're welcome to join us," he added. "Every man should come to work, and the women can join us for a feast."

"I'll tell 'em, Mistah Mayhew. I'm sure they'll all want to be here."

Sophia's daddy turned back to her and her mama. "I want to make sure all the men have plenty to eat. If you speak to any of the women folk, let them know they're welcome to come."

"I have a social with some of the ladies tomorrow afternoon," Sophia's mama said. "Why don't you come along, Sophia? You're getting to the age when you'll need to know what's going on in our group."

In other words, Sophia thought, *marrying age.*

Sophia couldn't think of anything more boring than her mama's social club, but she nodded. "Okay, Mama, but I don't like sewing, so don't expect me to bring any."

Her mama tilted her head back and laughed. "Did we raise a tomboy, Edward?"

"I certainly hope not," Daddy replied.

"Whatever I am, I certainly won't be one who makes my own clothes."

"At least you're a good cook." Sophia's daddy shoveled a forkful of food into his mouth, then wiped his chin with his napkin as he stood up. "Gotta run, Sugah," he said as he leaned over and kissed her mama. "Try and stay out of trouble, Sophia."

"Yes, Daddy."

Why her daddy ever said that, she'd never know. Sophia never got into trouble. She had always been the most compliant child she'd ever known, but her parents were the kindest and most loving, so she figured they got what they deserved—a good, obedient daughter.

"You might want to bring some of those blueberry muffins Dora taught you to make, Sophia," her mama said, interrupting Sophia's thoughts. "I'm sure the other ladies would appreciate that."

"I'll bake them first thing after breakfast in the morning," Sophia said. "That way they'll be fresh and warm."

"Mm-mm. I can just taste them now." Her mama closed her eyes and grinned with her mouth closed, looking like she'd had a taste of heaven.

As soon as her mama left the dining room, Sophia lingered behind to help Dora clean up after breakfast. She wasn't about to leave with this big of a mess. Besides, she felt like talking to the wise elderly woman who knew practically everything going on in the community.

"I heard you tell your mama you'd go with her to her social tomorrow, Miss Sophie."

Dora hadn't wasted a single moment before speaking out and letting herself be heard. That's another thing Sophia loved about her.

"Yes, I'm going. Any idea what I should talk about?"

"Oh, Honey, I'm sure they'll give you plenty to talk about with all the questions they're sure to ask. You'll wish you could just curl up in a corner and be quiet before the morning's over."

Sophia let out a sigh. "You're probably right, Dora. How should I answer their questions?" She knew she didn't have to mention that all the questions were likely to be about William.

Dora stopped, put down the dish she'd picked up, stuck her fist on her hip, and bit her bottom lip as she thought. Then she turned to Sophia. "Just answer them honestly. Don't tell too much, and be sure to watch out for trick questions."

"Trick questions?"

"Those women are smart, and I'm sure they've been listenin' to all the talk that's been goin' on since Mr. Ellis bid on your apple pie. They'll find a way to set you up, Miss Sophie, so you better watch yourself."

"Oh," Sophia said as she gathered up the silverware. "Keep my answers short and don't tell them anything they don't ask, right, Dora?"

"That's right, Miss Sophie. You might even think of a question or two to ask them." Grinning she added, "Most folks love to yap about themselves. That'll get their mind off your business."

"Good idea."

After they cleared away the breakfast dishes, Sophia headed back to her room. The kitchen was hot, and she needed to freshen up before she went into town. Her mother had left her some money to pick up a few things at the general merchandise store. They were almost out of flour, and she needed some for the muffins in the morning.

The horse and buggy were ready for her when she went out on the front lawn. Other than the fact that Sophia didn't love the man her parents wanted her to marry, she felt that she was a very fortunate woman to have all the blessings God had given her. She never went without anything she needed, and her parents made certain she had most of what she wanted. If only she could figure out a way to prevent William from proposing, Sophia knew she'd be the happiest woman on earth.

She was halfway to town when she spotted the single horse and rider in the distance. Slowing down, she crinkled her forehead. Not many people came this way at this time of day. She wondered who in the world it could be.

The moment she was able to make out the form of the rider, Sophia felt excitement spread from her mind to her heart. It was Hank. He was coming to visit her. Nothing could have flattered her more.

Then she realized she was being silly. Hank could have been going to any number of places, including the farm on the other side of the Mayhews'. And even if he were going to her place, perhaps it was to see Daddy.

"Whoa," he said as he brought his horse to a standstill beside Sophia's buggy. Tipping his hat, he nodded. "Sophia, it's so nice to see you out and about."

"Good to see you too, Hank."

"I'm glad you feel that way, Sophia, because I was coming to visit you."

Sophia was so flustered she couldn't speak. His quick, frank comment had caught her completely by surprise. "I, uh, I have to go into town for a few things. Would you care to join me?"

"That's an excellent idea. I'll just ride alongside, and we can chat when we get there."

Her hands shook as she held onto the reins. It took every-thing Sophia had to control her horse, but she knew she must not get too worked up over a simple social call from this very handsome gentleman who just happened to overbid on her pie. That thought caused a positively giddy feeling to wash over her.

When they arrived in town, Hank took care of her horse while she gathered her purse and parasol from the buggy. When she had gathered all her belongings, he offered his arm. Reluctantly, she took it.

"Oh, my," Mrs. Crandall from the church said as she passed them on the street. Sophia heard her whisper to her husband, "Did you see the Mayhew girl with that strange man? She's been promised to the Jacobson boy. I wonder if her folks know."

"Better keep that to yourself, Viola," her husband said. "You have no idea what's going on with those people."

Sophia tensed. Although they were whispering, it was painfully obvious to her that they wanted her to hear.

"I suppose I better keep some distance between us," Hank finally said as he gently pulled her arm from his. "I wouldn't want to be the talk of the town when I've barely warmed my room at the boardinghouse."

"That's most likely a good idea," Sophia agreed.

Hank walked with her as she shopped, and he carried her purchases to the buggy. Afterward, he turned to her and softly said, "I told you, Sophia, that I think we would be wonderful together, if I can ever get past your protective father." He offered a contrite grin. "Not that I don't respect your father."

Shaking her head in understanding, Sophia said, "You'll have to excuse Daddy. He's not used to all the goings-on with gentlemen callers and my pies being auctioned at church."

Leaning back and belting out a deep belly laugh, Hank replied, "I can certainly understand. If I had a daughter as beautiful and talented as you, I'd keep her under lock and key."

"He hasn't exactly done that," Sophia said softly.

"No, but he only lets you out of his sight when you're with William Jacobson."

"But—"

Hank reached out and gently touched his finger to her lips. "You mustn't feel that you have to explain, Sophia. I under-stand—at least I think I do. What I have to do is overcome that one big obstacle, William."

"Yes," Sophia said, her head held down, "I'm afraid so."

"Don't fear anything, my dear. If you and I are meant to be, then the Lord will pave my way. I have the utmost confidence in His ability to bring two searching hearts together."

"Yes, I believe you're probably right."

"Just tell me one thing, Sophia."

She turned and looked him in the eye, something she real-ized was a mistake the moment she saw the depth and inten-sity of their blueness. Her heart raced. "What's that, Hank?"

"Do you love William?"

"No, don't be silly. Although I am very fond of him, I only want to be his friend. You must believe that."

"Oh, I do. And since you have convinced me of your inten-tions toward him, I want you to know I plan to pursue you with all my abilities."

Sophia felt the heat as it crept up her neck and onto her face. "That's very sweet of you, Hank."

He laughed. "Sweet isn't the word I'd use, but I'll take it from you right now. Be warned that I can be very persistent."

They'd reached her buggy and paused to continue talking while people passed by, pretending not to stare. For once, Sophia wished she didn't know so many people.

Hank reached out and touched her chin, gently guiding it

so she was looking him in the eye. "Don't worry about what everyone thinks, Sophia."

"I can't help it," she admitted. "Most of them have known me all my life."

"They know William too, right?"

She nodded. The look on his face was one of understanding and kindness, not anger as she might have expected from someone else.

"You said you aren't engaged to William. Does this still hold true?"

"Oh yes, that's absolutely the truth."

"Then don't worry. You haven't promised your hand in marriage to another man, so you're free to be with me. We're doing nothing wrong, Sophia, so let yourself have fun."

In her head she knew he was right, and her heart was with Hank. But that didn't stop the guilt of letting her parents down as well as disappointing all the wonderful people from the church.

"I'll be working with everyone from the church on Saturday, so you'll see me then," he said.

"Saturday?"

"Your father's barn, remember?"

"Oh, that's right. My father told us about it at breakfast this morning. William will be there too."

"Yes, I know, Sophia," he said as he continued smiling at her. "And I promise I won't cause a scene, even if I feel like it."

Sophia frowned at him. "Causing a scene wouldn't be a very good idea at all, Hank." She remembered the scene he'd caused at the church Fourth of July celebration when he'd bid such an exorbitant amount on her pie. Even though he hadn't intended to upset people, she knew that he had. Hopefully, that wouldn't happen on Saturday. But she didn't dare say anything about it.

"See you on Saturday?" he asked.

Sophia nodded but didn't say a word as she got into her buggy with Hank's help.

"Have a safe ride home," he told her as she pulled away.

"You too, Hank," she whispered so softly she doubted he'd heard her.

All the way home, Sophia played over in her mind how it felt to be with Hank. It seemed so right, yet she knew how her family felt about William. Why did being with a man have to be so complicated?

Carrying the provisions into her house, Sophia was deep in thought about how she'd handle being around both William and Hank at the same time. She almost slammed into her mother, who was walking out the door right when she stepped up and across the threshold.

"Sophia, I'm shocked at your behavior this morning," Mama said without so much as a greeting.

"My behavior?" Sophia asked. She was confused. What had she done?

"Mrs. Crandall stopped by to let me know she'd seen you in town. Why didn't you tell me you were meeting Mr. Ellis? Do you have something to hide?"

Sophia's hand flew to her mouth as she found herself speechless. She knew Mrs. Crandall would talk, but she had no idea it would happen this quickly.

From the look on her mama's face, Sophia knew she had some explaining to do. She wasn't sure if what actually happened would be sufficient to satisfy her mother, based on the angry glare in her eyes.

Chapter 5

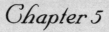

Sophia knew better than to lie. Not only would she not be able to sleep at night, she knew the Lord would accept nothing but the truth from her lips.

"Yes, Mama," she said as she hung her head. "I did see Hank Ellis."

"Why didn't you tell me you were meeting him?" Mama asked, her face registering pain and disappointment.

"It wasn't planned. He just happened to be riding out to see us, and we met on the road. Then he escorted me to town."

Silence fell over Sophia and her mama. If this was any indication of how things would be if she continued to see Hank, Sophia wondered if it was worth it. But when his face appeared in her mind, she knew it was well worth whatever it took because of the joy he brought her.

When her mama finally spoke, it wasn't with anger as Sophia had feared. It was with a weariness that was almost as bad.

"I only hope William doesn't catch wind of this. He will be so hurt if he finds out you've been meeting that stranger, Mr. Ellis, behind his back."

"He's not a stranger, Mama," Sophia reminded her.

"Maybe not a total stranger, but we don't know anything

about him or his family."

Sophia had never defied her mother, but she felt the urge to stand up for the man her heart longed to see again. "I do know he's a Christian."

"How do you know?" her mama asked.

"He told me."

"Plenty of people walk around talking about their faith, Sophia. But we know William and that his faith is true. We've watched him grow up in the church, and we see him in action. His faith in the Lord is very real, day in and day out."

"Yes, I realize that, but I don't love William."

"Love will come in time." Sophia watched her mama's face change shape as she remembered something, most likely her courtship with Sophia's daddy.

Although no one had ever told Sophia, she suspected her parents' relationship had begun much the same as hers and William's. Their parents had known each other all their lives, and when her mama and daddy were teenagers, they'd attended the same church functions together. Based on how her mama reacted to Sophia's voiced concern about the lack of spark she felt toward William, she figured her parents had "grown to love each other" just as her mother had said would happen between her and William.

For years, that had been enough for Sophia. At least, it was enough until she'd met Hank. But now that she'd experienced that excitement and joy that she knew was possible between a man and a woman, she didn't want to settle for less.

"Run on to your room, Sophia," her mama finally said after they'd both pondered the circumstances of the day. "You need to think about what you're doing, and I'll speak to your daddy."

"Okay, Mama," Sophia said as she turned and did as she

was told. She welcomed the opportunity to be alone with her thoughts, which would no doubt be about Hank.

Over the course of the next couple days, several visitors stopped by the house to report on what they'd seen in town— Sophia and Hank talking intimately beside her buggy. Sophia was amazed at how people could speak of something they knew nothing about.

Dora had been right about the social. The ladies were very smart, and they knew just the right questions to ask, nearly throwing Sophia into a dither as she tried to avoid discussing how she felt whenever she was around Hank. Fortunately, she'd managed to turn things around once she remembered Dora's advice to start asking questions of the ladies. They absolutely loved talking about themselves. She knew this would only work for so long before they were on to her scheme.

Sophia wished Daddy would say something to clear the air, but he didn't. He remained silent, but he often looked at her with a curious expression, one that Sophia had never seen on his face before. She wondered what was on his mind.

Meals were strained, but nothing was mentioned of her encounter with Hank. If her parents would say something, Sophia could at least explain what had happened to both of them at one time. She thought of simply blurting out the story, but she decided it would be best if one of her parents brought up the subject. And they didn't until Saturday morning.

Sophia was startled when her daddy walked into the kitchen as she and Dora prepared breakfast for the crew that was due to arrive soon to help work on the barn. "Good mornin', Daddy," she said over her shoulder as she rolled out another sheet of biscuit dough.

"Hey, Sugah," he said as he bent over and kissed her cheek.

"May I have a word with you before the men and their families start arriving?"

"Sure, Daddy, have a seat. I'll be right there."

Dora nudged her out of the way as she gave her a knowing look. "Go on, Miss Sophie. Talk to your daddy. I'll finish up here."

As Sophia sat down across from her daddy, she had a sinking feeling she was about to hear something she wouldn't like. "Yes, Daddy, what did you want to discuss this morning?"

"You and William," he replied. "And Mr. Ellis."

From the tone of his voice and how differently he'd addressed the two suitors, Sophia knew exactly how her daddy felt about both of them. She sighed.

"I understand you've been taking up with that new young man," he began. "I'm not so sure that's such a good idea."

Sophia sat and listened, wishing she could argue and tell her daddy how she felt, but she suspected he wouldn't pay much attention.

"As you know, everyone is expecting William to propose to you soon, and I'd hate for you to ruin the opportunity to take such a well-suited husband for yourself."

Now she had to say something. "But Daddy, I'm not so sure I want to marry William."

"Don't say such a thing, Sophia. William Jacobson is a fine young man, and he'd make an excellent husband for you. He knows how to run his family farm, and he loves the Lord."

"Yes, I know, but I don't feel. . .well, I don't have those feelings for him." There. She'd said it.

"Those feelings," her daddy began, "can get you into an awful lot of trouble, Sophia. People have been talking, and no one knows anything about this Mr. Ellis except that he's from Alabama and he works in the lumberyard."

"Daddy, he's a Christian man who makes me laugh." Sophia wasn't able to put all her other thoughts and feelings into words, so she knew her argument sounded mighty weak.

"Making you laugh is the last thing a husband needs to concern himself with, Sophia. You must look at the overall man. A good husband is someone who will provide well for you, uplift you spiritually, and be a good daddy to your children."

"Yes, I know, Daddy."

"Apparently you don't know as well as you think you do. I want you to stop this nonsense and concentrate on you and William."

His tone was strong and filled with conviction. Sophia bit back the words that threatened to pour from her lips. She didn't dare say the things that came to mind, so she remained silent.

"The men and their families are starting to arrive," her mama said from the kitchen door.

Sophia was startled by her mama's voice. She quickly stood up, straightened her apron, and resumed her position beside Dora as her daddy left the kitchen out the back door to greet his workers.

"Oh, Dora, what am I to do?" Sophia cried as soon as they were alone in the kitchen. "Daddy doesn't seem to understand about my feelings toward William and Hank."

"Yes, Miss Sophie, I heard every word. Don't do a thing. The Lord will take care of everything in His own time. Be the sweet young woman you always are, and I'll pray for you."

Sophia reached out and covered Dora's hand with her own. "Thanks, Dora. I love you."

Dora reached up and rubbed her nose with the back of her wrist as she sniffled. "I love you too, Miss Sophie. Now run along and carry some of them trays out to the workers. They need to eat something before they get started on the barn."

Sophia did as she was told, but she didn't like having to face her daddy and possibly William. Fortunately that problem was avoided because Mama was waiting by the table set up for the food.

"I trust you'll behave yourself, Sophia?" Mama said as she took the food from Sophia.

"Of course, Mama," she replied without looking her mama in the eye. It wasn't that she planned to misbehave; rather she wasn't about to be rude to Hank if he should strike up a conversation with her.

The sound of horses came up the dusty road, capturing both women's attention. It was Reverend Breckenridge and Hank Ellis. They'd come together, bringing a smile to Sophia's lips.

"Well, I'm not believin' this," Mama muttered. She fidgeted with her apron before turning back to Sophia. "Run on inside and get some preserves."

With a much lighter step, Sophia headed back to the kitchen, not wasting a single second. She grabbed a basket from the pantry, then pulled down half a dozen jars of preserves she'd put up weeks ago.

"They all here yet?" Dora hollered from behind.

"No, Dora, but they're gettin' here."

Sophia hurried back out with the preserves just in time to greet the reverend and Hank as they came to the table. She smiled at the older gentleman before turning to Hank.

"Hello, Mr. Ellis," she said in as formal of a tone as she could manage for the sake of her mother who was staring holes through her back.

He tipped his hat. "Sophia," he said softly, a mischievous smile teasing his lips. Then he turned to her mama. "Miz

Mayhew, it's a mighty nice mornin' to work on a barn. I'm happy your husband invited me."

Sophia's mother appeared not to know what to say. She glanced back and forth between the reverend and Hank, as she shifted from one foot to the other.

Reverend Breckenridge slapped Hank on the back and pulled him forward by the arm. "Grab a plate, Hank, and pile it high with biscuits. Sophia is handy in the kitchen. She learned from the best. Did I ever tell you about their housekeeper, Dora?"

"No, Sir, I don't believe you did," Hank replied, still smiling.

Sophia could tell her mama didn't want Hank lingering around her any longer than necessary, but she was too polite to say anything in front of the reverend. Hank was a genius to have thought of enlisting Reverend Breckenridge for a traveling partner.

Reverend Breckenridge motioned for everyone to bow their heads for the blessing. When he finished, he grabbed a biscuit, chomped down on it, and said, "Mm-mm, this is mighty fine cookin'. Biscuit melts in your mouth." He turned to Sophia and nodded. "You outdid yourself this time, Sophia."

"Aw, Reverend, biscuits are the easiest things in the world to make."

"I'm sure to someone as competent as you in the kitchen, they are," Hank said, "but if I were to attempt anything like this, we'd wind up with charcoal for breakfast."

Even Sophia's mama smiled at this comment. Hank had already begun working his charm on her, to Sophia's delight.

"We best get to work, Reverend," Hank said after devouring a half dozen biscuits and a couple slices of cured ham. "I aim to work until this job is finished."

"That's my boy," the reverend said as he and Hank walked toward the barn, where several men had already begun working.

"Mama, would you like for me to bring you something?" Sophia asked.

Her mama was still staring after the men. She slowly turned back to Sophia and shook her head. "No, Sophia, I don't think so, not right now. Maybe later."

Sophia grabbed the opportunity to run back inside to tell Dora about what had just transpired. Dora listened with obvious delight, her eyes glistening and her lips turning up at the corners.

When Sophia finished, Dora looked up and said, "Praise the Lord. He's already working on your mama's heart. Now let's see how your young man gets on with your daddy."

"Daddy's much more difficult, I'm afraid," Sophia said. "He doesn't take to charm quite like Mama and me."

"Child, the Lord don't need no charm to do His work. All He needs is your trust."

Sophia sighed. "Yes, you're right, Dora. I have to have faith that I'll be free to love whomever I want."

"Remember what those men at the church Fourth of July celebration said before the pie auction?" Dora said.

"Yes," Sophia replied. "One man in particular. Hank's speech was particularly moving."

"Why yes, it was. But they were all good because they spoke of freedom and how we can make choices in this great country."

Sophia noticed the mist in Dora's eyes. Dora's parents and grandparents had been slaves during the Civil War. Until their freedom, they'd had to worship behind closed doors and in the small field shack they'd used as a makeshift chapel. Now, they could worship openly in the church that had been built specifically for the freed slaves. However, they had to work hard to share the gospel, since many other former slaves had never heard the Word. Those who knew the Lord worked tirelessly, sharing their faith with others after putting in long days at jobs, often working for their former masters. This was a significant test of their faith, and Dora's people had passed with flying colors. Sophia envied the strength she saw in Dora and Hank.

Her own faith had been with her since birth. She'd never doubted the Lord's sovereignty, but she'd never had any reason to worry either. Dora, on the other hand, was a woman whose faith had brought her through all sorts of adversity.

Now Sophia found herself wondering about Hank's faith. Had he always been a Christian with parents who brought him to church faithfully and served the Lord with open hearts? Or had he come to faith later in life? Something about him was different, but she couldn't put her finger on it. She'd have to pay closer attention when he spoke and perhaps ask him if the opportunity presented itself.

Sophia continued cooking alongside Dora in the kitchen throughout the morning, cleaning up from breakfast and then starting the noon meal. All those men would be starving after working all day on that barn. From the looks of things, they'd be done before sundown, which would make her daddy awfully happy.

Ever since Reverend Breckenridge had come to pastor the Church on the Hill, people had started coming together to help each other in a way they hadn't in the past. Before he'd arrived, people offered their hands to each other, but it was never as organized as it was now.

Reverend Breckenridge had brought the men together, insisting they form what he called an "army of servants" who would do anything they needed to help one another. To everyone's amazement, this didn't require more work. The congregation grew closer, and the activities gave them the opportunity to strengthen their faith through fellowship and working toward a common goal.

As the sun moved to the top of the sky, the men began to come out of the barn, mostly for water. It was hot, and they were thirsty. Sophia was right there with pitchers of water and plenty of cups.

William came out of the barn wearing his usual somber expression. He walked directly over to Sophia and said, "I'll be in church early tomorrow morning."

"That's nice, William," Sophia replied without looking him in the eye. She knew he wanted her to say she'd get there early too, if that pleased him, but she didn't.

However, her daddy was right behind William. "I think it would be a mighty fine idea if we got there early too, Sophia."

"Whatever you say, Daddy."

Sophia turned to get more food, but her daddy reached out and grabbed her by the arm. "Why don't you and William have lunch together under the tree over there?" He pointed to the large oak tree on the edge of the lawn, away from the rest of the people.

William nodded, picked up his plate, and headed over in that direction. Sophia didn't have a chance to argue. He was gone before she could say anything.

"Let William know you're interested in him," her mama hissed from behind. "He's beginning to worry that you don't care about him. I can see it in his eyes."

"It's not that I don't care, Mama—"

"Go on before he thinks something's happened." Her mama nearly pushed her over, she shoved her so hard.

Chapter 6

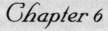

S ophia," William said as she approached where he was standing. "How have you been?"

"Just fine, William," she replied politely. "And you?"

"Can't complain. We have most of the work done on the barn. Just a few finishing touches and we'll have it in tip-top shape." No smile, just his low voice. Sophia glanced around, looking for Hank, then she turned back to William.

"That's good. You always were very handy."

Sophia was running out of things to say, and she hadn't been standing there for more than a minute or two. She couldn't help thinking that would never happen with Hank. They'd always have something to say, no matter how long they were together.

William shrugged as he squatted down on the ground. "Care to join me?"

"Uh, sure, William," she replied. "Let me go grab a blanket and a plate, and I'll be right back."

Sophia ran to the house, pulled a small blanket from the top shelf in the hall closet, then headed out the back door. She heard Dora's voice behind her.

"Be careful not to get Mr. Jacobson's hopes up, Miss Sophie. Let him down real easy."

She snickered. It wasn't William's hopes she was worried about. Her own were probably much higher than they should be considering how little she actually knew of Hank.

But she knew enough to feel positively giddy whenever he was nearby—something she'd never experienced before. The mere sight of his face brought a smile to her lips and her heart. Sophia craved being with him, but she knew it wasn't a good idea today. She needed to have her meal with William, if for no other reason but to make Mama and Daddy happy.

Doing her best not to look over at the working men as they crouched down beneath the shade trees in the yard, for fear she'd find herself exchanging a glance with Hank, Sophia put a spoonful from each bowl on her plate and crossed over to where William was still sitting.

"Sorry it took so long," she said. "I had to go inside for the blanket."

He shrugged. "That's quite all right. I didn't notice."

That was another problem, she realized. He barely noticed her.

She knew she needed to attempt to strike up a conversation, since William wasn't likely to. "Have you thought about joining the choir at church?"

"No," he replied. "Have you?"

Sophia tilted her head back and laughed. "Apparently you haven't heard me sing lately. I'm afraid the angels would cry if I joined the choir."

William didn't join her in laughter. He just turned to her and stared, his face solemn.

Didn't he ever smile? she wondered. *Was he always this serious?* She knew the answer to that, and it made her own cheerful mood drop.

It seemed to take forever to eat her meal, but she finally finished a respectable amount. "Well, I must run and see if Dora could use a hand in the kitchen."

William nodded. "I'll be seeing you around, Sophia."

Sophia grabbed her plate and forced herself to walk at an even pace back to the house. It wasn't an easy task since she felt like lifting her skirt and running.

"How is William?" Dora asked.

Sophia leaned her head forward and glared at Dora from beneath hooded eyes. They both broke into giggles.

"Shame on me," Sophia finally said when she caught her breath. "I can't help it, Dora. He's so quiet, and I don't have any idea what to say to him. He must think I'm a foolish girl."

"You are not a foolish girl," Dora told her firmly. "Just a spirited young woman who wants a little fun in her life."

"Well, maybe so, but I'm afraid I need to tame my spirit a little in order to keep peace around here."

Dora shook her head and clucked her tongue. Sophia knew she did this when she was thinking something she knew was better left unsaid.

Footsteps from behind startled her. She spun around and found herself facing Hank.

"Just wanted to pop in and thank the cooks. Y'all did a mighty fine job with that chicken."

"Miss Sophie did most of the work," Dora said, grinning at him. "She baked some pies too. I'll send her out directly when they're cooled. Y'all can take a little break in about an hour."

"I can hardly wait," Hank said. "Sophia, would you do me the honor of joining me for dessert?"

Sophia felt cornered. She wanted nothing more than to join Hank, but she knew she'd have the wrath of most of the congregation on her, so she felt compelled to turn him down.

"I'm sorry, Hank, but I—"

Hank didn't let her finish. "That's quite all right, Sophia. I understand. You mustn't upset William. And I wouldn't want you to. After all, he's been knowing your family for years."

Sophia stared at Hank. He grinned back at her, but she wasn't able to manage even a half smile.

He nodded. "See you around, Sophia. And Dora, you keep on doin' what you've been doing. The food is the best I think I've ever had." Then he was gone.

Sophia wasn't able to say a word after that. In fact, she was not sure why, but she went from a feeling of pure joy at seeing Hank's smiling face to wanting to cry in a matter of seconds.

The moment he was out of the kitchen, Dora turned to Sophia and clucked some more. When she finally spoke, she said, "Don't let that one get away, Miss Sophie. He's got that bounce in his step just like you. That man will make someone a fine husband."

Sophia had thought the exact same thing. Until now, she wasn't certain she should go against her parents' wishes to marry William. But there were a couple reasons she had to do something. First of all, William hadn't even proposed to her yet. And secondly, she didn't want to go through life with a glum husband who barely noticed her.

"Oh, Dora," Sophia said as she tossed her dish towel on the table and sank down in the chair. "What should I do?"

"Talk to the reverend. He'll know."

"You don't think he'll understand what I'm going through."

"Surely he will," Dora replied. "He's a wise man who knows the human heart. He might even talk to your daddy if he thinks it'll help."

"Perhaps I'll talk to him, if I can't figure out what else to do."

Dora cackled. "You don't like turning things over to someone else, do you, Miss Sophie?"

"What exactly do you mean by that, Dora?" Sophia glared at the housekeeper.

"Your hands are tied, there ain't nothin' you can do, but you still won't trust that everything will be just fine."

Sophia grunted. "The Lord gave me a mind to work things out, and I plan to do that."

"Then what you gonna do, Miss Sophie?"

"I, uh, I'm not sure yet, Dora. I'll let you know when I figure it out."

Dora turned away, still cackling.

Hank knew he needed to join the other men back in the barn before they began wondering where he'd wandered off to. But he felt drawn to the house where he knew Sophia was toiling with her mother's servant. Being with her seemed more important than anything else he could think of.

He could tell she was having a terrible time of dealing with her feelings for William. He saw in her eyes that she didn't love the man, and there was some doubt as to William's intentions toward her. Their parents had already decided Sophia's and William's fate, regardless of the younger people's feelings. Such a pity too, Hank thought, but there was nothing he could do about it.

Sadness filled his heart, something that rarely happened to Hank since he'd discovered the Lord. He'd gone to church most of his life, but until he allowed the Word to actually sink in, he never knew true joy. Since then, he'd started each day with a newness and overwhelming gladness that couldn't be stifled.

Reverend Breckenridge was waiting for him by the barn opening. "Been to see Sophia?" he asked.

Hank nodded. He wasn't sure what else he should say. The reverend already knew his feelings.

"You do understand this thing with William goes way back, right, Hank?"

"Of course I do, Reverend," Hank snapped. When he realized how harsh he'd sounded, he took a step back. "I'm sorry. I shouldn't have been so abrupt. It's just that—"

Reverend Breckenridge grinned, slapping Hank on the shoulder. "You're falling in love with another man's girl."

"Certainly appears that way."

"Then fight for her," Reverend Breckenridge said.

"Fight for her?" Surely, Hank hadn't heard right. He narrowed his eyes, looked the reverend in the eye, and said, "Could you please repeat that?"

Reverend Breckenridge opened his mouth to speak, but he quickly snapped it shut as he nodded toward the barn door. Hank turned around just in time to see Sophia enter the barn.

"Hank?" she said as she walked toward him, squinting.

"Yes, this is me, Sophia," Hank said. It took every ounce of willpower not to run to her and pull her into his arms. She looked so vulnerable walking slowly toward him. And oh, so beautiful.

"Good," she said, picking up her step and moving rapidly toward him. "I wanted to talk with you about something."

"Would you like to go outside?" he asked.

All hammers had stopped banging on the barn, and it was clear that every single man in the barn was listening to their conversation. That worried Hank.

"No, that's not necessary," she said.

"Okay, then what would you like to discuss?"

She smiled, her face glowing. He could tell she was nervous, but she was determined to say whatever it was she'd come to say.

"Us," she replied.

"Sophia, we'd better go outside," Hank said, taking her by the arm. "We don't need an audience."

She didn't resist. Instead, she literally leaned a little toward him, which made his heart race. He wished he could gently place his arm around her shoulders, but he doubted her father would approve.

Once they were outside, Sophia turned to him and said, "Hank, I don't know if I'm speaking out of my own foolishness, but I feel like you and I should get to know one another better."

"No, Sophia, it's not foolishness. I feel the same way. However, I don't want to do anything that will upset your family."

Reverend Breckenridge's advice came to mind. He'd fight, but not with recklessness. Instead, he'd woo Sophia Mayhew and earn the right to be with her. And he'd win her parents over in the process, no matter what he had to do. Hank knew they were good, God-fearing people who only wanted what was best for their daughter. And he knew he'd be the best man to make her happy.

"I don't really care anymore, Hank. All I know is that whenever I'm around you I'm happy and I feel free. It feels good to feel so free."

"Feeling free is good," Hank agreed. "But we need to keep our wits about us, or we won't feel so free."

He glanced up and saw that some of the men had followed them outside the barn and were staring. The few women who'd accompanied their husbands had also looked up from their needlework to see what was going on.

"Let us take this thing slow and steady, Sophia. I want to court you in the correct way and not ruffle too many feathers."

Sophia slouched back. "Yes, you're right, Hank. I don't want to upset anyone either."

"But we'll work together on this, Sophia."

One of the women had stood up and walked over to them. She tilted her head forward and scowled at Sophia. "I'll have a talk with your mama about your behavior, young lady. It's not becoming for a young woman to act in such an impudent manner."

Sophia started to argue, but Hank shook his head. He tipped his hat to the woman and smiled. "I really need to finish my work inside the barn, Sophia. I hope your mama is feeling better." Then he turned and went inside the barn.

"Is your mama not feeling well, Sophia?" he heard the woman ask.

Hank started to turn back around to take care of what he'd started, since he felt ashamed for leaving Sophia to pick up where he left off. But he spotted Dora standing by the kitchen door, waving him on. Dora was a good woman. He'd have to remember to thank her some day.

He let out the breath he'd been holding and picked up his hammer. The men had resumed their work, but he felt the tension all around him. No one except Reverend Breckenridge would look him in the eye. The reverend grinned and nodded but didn't say a word.

Chapter 7

Sophia was left speechless. She had no idea what to say to the woman.

Suddenly, Dora stuck her head out the kitchen door and hollered, "Miss Sophie, come quick. I need your help."

"I better run," she told the woman, then took off like a streak of lightning.

Relieved by Dora needing her, Sophia silently prayed that there wasn't a disaster in the kitchen. She was breathless when she got to the kitchen door.

"Yes, Dora, what do you need?"

"These pies are about ready to go out there. I reckon they've cooled enough to cut."

Sophia started to reprimand Dora for a false alarm, but then she realized what had happened. She smiled instead and gave Dora a hug. "Thanks for saving me from that awful woman, Dora."

"You better get used to people doing that, Miss Sophie. William's mighty popular around here, and people don't take kindly to another man coming in and taking what they think should belong to one of their people."

"I don't belong to anyone," Sophia reminded her. "Didn't

you listen to yourself when you were giving me that talk about freedom?"

"I didn't say you shouldn't be free to love any man you want to. I just said you better get used to people acting like that woman."

"Oh," Sophia said.

She knew Dora was right. Not only would she have to face people's questioning, she had her parents to deal with as well. And they would be the most difficult of all, considering how they'd been planning hers and William's wedding for years.

The pies were all still warm to touch, but the aroma of fresh baked apples, peaches, and pecans wafted up to tease her nostrils. Pecan pie was Sophia's favorite, but she didn't want to eat something that was intended for the men who'd come to help Daddy. She left the utensils beside the pies on the table, then went back inside.

When she turned to look out the window, the men had swarmed around the tables, each claiming one flavor of pie, then moving on to snatch a sliver of another. Her gaze rested on the good-looking Hank Ellis. He managed to keep his mood high, even though it was painfully obvious that most of the others around him were giving him the cold shoulder. At least Reverend Breckenridge was being friendly.

Maybe Dora was right. Reverend Breckenridge would understand, and he'd have the wisdom to know what to do in this sticky situation. She'd have to go to the church and chat with him sometime next week.

By nightfall, all the volunteers had gone home, leaving Sophia to face Mama and Daddy alone. Not even Dora stayed behind. She had her own family to take care of.

"Sophia," Daddy said as he leaned back in his chair, his feet up on the tiny footstool with the needlepoint tapestry top Mama had made for him. "We need to talk. Sit down."

She crossed the room and did as she was told, choosing the straight-back wooden chair over the soft, stuffed sofa. "Yes, Daddy?"

"What's all that carryin' on with the new man all about?" He stopped and glared at Sophia.

"I wasn't carryin' on, Daddy. I was just talking to him."

"Talking to him is the same thing. Do you want people to talk, Sophia?"

She shrugged. At the moment, she didn't really care if people talked or what they did, for that matter. She was tired of feeling so constrained. There were times she felt as though she were in prison. But she didn't dare say that, or Daddy wouldn't let her out of his sight for days, maybe even weeks.

"Let them talk, Daddy," she said with a shaky voice.

"That's not a good attitude. We have a church family, and they are concerned about your welfare. I want you to come to your senses and pay more attention to William."

"I do pay attention to William, Daddy," she blurted out as she stood up. Pacing the floor, she continued, "It's William who acts like I don't exist."

"William loves you, Sophia."

"He certainly doesn't act like it."

Mama came into the room and stopped as she looked at her husband questioningly. "Have a seat. We were discussing her carryin' on with Mr. Ellis."

"I hope you told her to stop that nonsense."

"I certainly did," he replied. Then he turned back to Sophia. "From now on, you're to pay attention only to William Jacobson whenever you feel the need to flirt with a man."

She held her hands up in despair. "I wasn't flirting, Daddy. Don't you understand? William ignores me, Hank is nice to me, and everyone else in the church is mad at me. I can't win for losing."

"Don't take that tone with me, Sophia," Daddy growled at her. "Go to your room this instant. We'll see you in the morning for church."

Sophia stormed from the room, wishing someone would at least listen to her. But that was too much to hope for since they already had her future planned for her.

So much for freedom. In Sophia Mayhew's world, freedom didn't exist unless everyone in the church approved.

She found sleep in the wee hours of the morning. But when the sun rose, her eyes popped wide open. Dread washed over her as she remembered her daddy's words the night before. Without any enthusiasm, Sophia got up and dressed for church. She was in the midst of positioning her hat when Mama knocked at the door, then opened it.

"Good, you're almost ready," she said.

"Of course," Sophia said without looking her mama in the eye. "Why would you think otherwise?"

"Don't be sassy, Sophia. It doesn't become you. Now finish getting ready and come downstairs for breakfast. Your daddy wants to get there early."

Sophia knew why he wanted to get to church early. It was so she could spend some time with William before the services started.

No one in the family uttered more than a few words all the way to the Church on the Hill. Reverend Breckenridge stood outside greeting the early arrivals.

"Good mornin', Mayhew family," he bellowed. "So nice of

you to get here at this time. I love it when my flock is eager to hear my sermon."

"Mornin', Reverend," Sophia's daddy said. "Have you seen the Jacobsons?"

Reverend Breckenridge's smile dropped, but only for a moment. He glanced over at Sophia, then turned to her daddy, nodding. "Why yes, they arrived early too. I believe they're in the basement with the choir."

Sophia reluctantly started to follow her parents, but Reverend Breckenridge reached out and took her by the arm. "I'd like to have a few words with you if your folks don't mind."

Sophia's daddy turned and gave a curt nod. "Of course we don't mind, Reverend. Send her on down when you're done with her."

As soon as Sophia's parents were out of sight, the reverend gently placed his arm around Sophia's shoulder and pulled her to the side of the building. "Are you feeling well, Sophia?"

"I'm fine and dandy, Reverend," she said.

"No, you're not. I'm not blind. In fact, what I see is a woman who wants to be with one man, while the world expects otherwise."

"You noticed?" she said.

"Of course I noticed. In fact, everyone has noticed."

Her heart fell as she hung her head. "Yes, they have, haven't they."

"But don't you pay a bit of attention to all the gossip mongers. They don't have any idea what's in your heart."

She snapped her head up and looked him squarely in the eye. "Do you really think I should ignore them?"

"If you want happiness and love, you most likely will have to ignore plenty of people."

"But what about William? Mama and Daddy don't want me to make him angry. All I seem to do to William is upset him." She looked down again.

Reverend Breckenridge reached out and tilted her chin up so she was facing him. "Are you sure about that?"

Sophia held her hands out to her sides as she tried to explain. "He hardly even talks to me, and when he does, it's in short sentences that don't mean anything. I don't think I've even seen him smile more than once or twice since we were children."

The reverend belted out a belly laugh. "Darlin', you and William are still children to me. And your folks. But seriously, Sophia, you need to follow your heart. The Lord brought Hank Ellis to our neck of the woods for a reason, you know."

"Do you know?" Sophia asked. "Why the Lord brought Hank to us, that is?"

Reverend Breckenridge shrugged. "For all I know the only reason he's here is to work at the lumberyard. But perhaps the Lord brought him here for you."

"I never really thought about it that way," Sophia said as the feeling in her heart lifted. "But I still don't know what to do about William."

"Sophia, William is a grown man. He can take care of himself."

"I know, but Mama and Daddy—"

"Sshh. Let me handle them. I have a feeling they'll come around sooner or later."

"Sooner, I hope," Sophia said. "But later, I fear."

The reverend belted out another hearty chuckle that echoed between the church building and the trees. "We shall see. Let's pray about it."

He held both of her hands as he asked the Lord for guidance

in this matter of the heart. Then he prayed that they'd do His will. When it was over and they'd both said "Amen," Sophia reached out and hugged her pastor.

"Have I ever told you how much I appreciate you, Reverend?"

His lips quivered into a smile. "That makes everything I've said worthwhile, Sophia. I'll continue to pray for you. Oh, and don't forget to meet your parents in the church basement. I'm sure they're waitin' for you now."

"Of course," Sophia said. "I'll go right down there."

When she got to the bottom of the steps, William was waiting for her. "Your mama said you were talkin' to the reverend. Can we go outside for a few minutes, Sophia?"

"Uh, sure," she said as she glanced around to see who all was in the basement.

The choir members stood in the positions they'd take in the tiny loft behind the pulpit. Her mama and daddy were both watching as she turned back to William.

"Let's go," she finally said. She hadn't seen Hank, which was good.

Once outside, William asked her to walk over to the small courtyard where they held celebrations such as the Fourth of July pie auction. He led her to a bench that was nestled in the midst of several tall pines.

"What did you want to discuss, William?" she asked.

"How long have we known each other, Sophia?"

She was startled by his question. "That's silly. We've known each other for a very long time. Almost all our lives."

"That's right. And we both are very fond of each other."

"Yes, William," she replied. "We always have been."

Sophia sat and stared at William in horror as he stood up, glanced around, then got down on one knee. He took her hand in his and stared at it for a minute before he broke into a coughing fit. *What is going on?* she wondered. Her chest suddenly felt like it would cave in.

"William, what are you doing? You'll get your good Sunday trousers dirty if you don't get up."

"Sophia," he said slowly, not looking her directly in the eye. "Will you be my wife?"

Sophia was so startled by his question, she was speech-less. When she opened her mouth to speak, no words came out.

"Sophia, did you hear me?" he asked, no emotion showing whatsoever.

"I believe I heard you ask me to be your wife." She felt like jumping up and running away screaming, but she didn't dare.

"That's right," he said, "I did."

Sophia stood up and turned to William, who still didn't seem to want to look at her. Pointing to the bench, she said, "Sit, William. I have a question for you."

"What?" he asked as he complied.

If it was this easy to get him to obey, Sophia thought, per-haps she should consider accepting his proposal. But no, that's not what she wanted, and she now knew he didn't want it ei-ther. William didn't love her. That much was obvious.

"Why are you asking me to be your wife, William?" she asked in a tone that reminded her of their schoolteacher back when they were children.

"Because I want to marry you?" he said questioningly.

"Do you really?"

"Of course I do, Sophia. Why else would I ask you?" He averted his gaze.

"Look at me, William," she demanded. "Look me in the eye and tell me you want to marry me. To spend the rest of your life with me. To have children with me. To always be there through thick and thin with me."

He looked at her, then turned away. "I can't," he finally said.

"Just as I thought. Neither of us wants to marry the other, but we're acting like this on account of our parents, who want the best for both of us." Suddenly a thought occurred to her. "Are you in love with someone else, William?"

His face turned the brightest shade of red Sophia had ever seen. "Maybe, but I'm not sure how she feels about me."

"William!" Sophia said with more excitement than she'd felt since first meeting Hank. "This is grand! We have to tell our folks."

"No, I think that's a bad idea. They want you and me to marry each other, not someone else." The sadness in his voice made Sophia want to reach out and hug him. But she didn't dare. He would most likely get the wrong idea.

"We have to do something."

"Look, Sophia, I don't think there's anything we can do. They have their minds made up."

Sophia straightened and stamped her foot. "That's just too bad. We have to let them know we should be free to love whoever we feel like loving."

"Whomever," he corrected.

"Okay, whomever. C'mon, William. We'll tell them now."

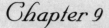

Chapter 9

T
he first person they saw when they walked through the back door of the church was Hank, to Sophia's dismay. He stopped, took a step back, and surveyed them both, glancing back and forth between them as if assessing the situation.

"Mornin', Hank," Sophia said. She tugged on William's arm and pulled him away. "C'mon, William."

For the first time since she'd met him, Hank remained speechless. She feared he had the wrong idea, but there would be time for correcting that later. For now, she had to straighten out a few very important details of hers and William's lives.

Her mama and daddy were still in the basement waiting for her. When they saw her holding onto William's arm, both of them beamed with happiness.

"So you finally came to your senses," Daddy said. "I couldn't be happier."

"Yes, Daddy, we did come to our senses. William and I have something to tell you as soon as we get his parents down here." Turning to William, she said, "Any idea where they might be?"

William pointed to the corner of the room where several women were setting up refreshments. "My mother is with those women. She'll know where my father is."

Sophia let go of his arm and crossed the room to the re-freshment ladies. As soon as she got Mrs. Jacobson, she sent William off to find his father.

"Looks like our children have finally gotten together," her daddy said to William's mother, who was beaming.

Sophia wondered if any of them would still be smiling once they heard what she and William had to say. She stood in one spot, tapping her foot with her arms crossed over her chest. Her thoughts wandered while she waited. If William hadn't been so shy about voicing his feelings to his parents, none of this would have to happen. But because he was timid and quiet, she had to be the forceful one, taking the lead to let everyone know she and William both wanted freedom in their choices.

To Sophia's surprise, both Reverend Breckenridge and Hank were with William and his father when he returned. Hank looked like he didn't want to be there, but the reverend had a knowing smile plastered on his face. Sophia had a sneak-ing suspicion that he'd had a hand in this whole thing.

"You have something you'd like to tell us?" William's father asked. "Some good news, I hope?"

William turned to Sophia as if looking to her to start. She opened her mouth but was quieted when he spoke up.

"Father," he began, then cleared his throat. "Mother, Mr. and Mrs. Mayhew, Sophia and I decided we wish to remain friends. However, we don't feel that we're suited for each other in marriage."

"What?" Sophia's mama cried.

"Son," William's father said as he took a step toward Will-iam. "Perhaps we need to discuss this, man to man, without anyone else present."

"I know this came as quite a shock to you," Sophia hastily intervened, "but William and I have already discussed it at length. He proposed marriage to me, I suspect to be polite and do the honorable thing, but I knew his heart wasn't in it. We were both relieved when I turned him down."

The two sets of parents looked confused.

"Remember when men stood up on July Fourth and talked about the freedom we have in this country?" Sophia asked. "William and I want the same freedom. We want to choose our life partners without interference from our wonderful, loving, well-meaning parents."

"But Sophia," Mama said in a squeaky voice, "we wanted to make certain you had a Christian husband."

"I want that too," Sophia agreed, "but there are other Christian men besides William."

Reverend Breckenridge stepped forward and bellowed, "Congratulations, Mr. and Mrs. Jacobson and Mr. and Mrs. Mayhew, your children have finally grown up. This is a glorious day!"

All eyes turned to him. He nodded toward Hank.

"I suppose I don't need to let you know that I, for one, am very relieved," Hank said. After a nervous moment of silence, everyone chuckled.

Sophia turned to William. "Is there anything you'd like to tell us, William?"

His face turned red again, but he shook his head. "Not at the moment."

Hank reached for Sophia's hand and lifted it. "I have something to share," he said.

Reverend Breckenridge nodded. "Go ahead, Lad."

"From this moment on, I wish to pursue this woman in a

courtship that I pray is happy, fun, and without too many distractions." He turned to Sophia's parents. "And I'd like your blessing."

"Go ahead and give it to him," Reverend Breckenridge said to them. "He's a persistent young man, so you might as well save yourselves some trouble."

They both finally nodded but continued their stunned silence. William's parents also appeared to be in shock.

The two families, as well as Hank, sat together in church and listened to the sermon with interest. Reverend Breckenridge spoke of both the seriousness and the joys of relationships between men and women, pausing to let the meaning of his words sink in. Sophia felt as though he was speaking directly to her, so she listened with rapt attention.

After the service was over, the congregation stood up, shook hands, then headed for the door. This particular Sunday, no picnic was scheduled. Some people went down to the church basement for quick refreshments before departing, while others left the church.

Sophia had no idea what was in store for her, but at least she now had the freedom she'd wanted since becoming an adult. Her parents had accepted the news, but they still didn't have much to say about what had transpired. She suspected they had quite a bit to think about and discuss between themselves before she heard their feelings on the subject.

As they stood outside the church, saying their good-byes, her daddy surprised her and turned to Hank. "Young man, if you're not doing anything later on this afternoon, we'd be honored if you'd stop by so we could get to know you."

A look of joyful surprise crossed Hank's face as he nodded and said, "Yes, Sir. What time should I be there?"

Everyone laughed at his eagerness. Sophia's heart was so filled with happiness she thought it might burst.

Two months later, Hank and Sophia sat in the tree swing on the front lawn of her family farm. He lifted her hand to his lips and gently kissed the back of it.

"Sophia, I don't have to tell you how I feel about you. It must be pretty obvious by the way I act."

"Yes, Hank, it's pretty obvious." She giggled, covering her mouth with her white-gloved hand. Hank beamed from the inside out to see her so happy. "But I would like to hear it just the same."

"All right then," he said as he stood up and looked her in the eye before getting down on one knee. Her face registered a combination of the surprise and pleasure he felt every time he was with her. "Miss Sophia Mayhew, I love you with all my heart. I would go to the ends of the earth to make you happy. My sole wish is to look into your eyes and see the same love I have for you reflected in them."

"Oh, Hank, I do love you," she said breathlessly.

"Good," he said as he covered her hand with both of his. "At least you won't think me the complete idiot for what I'm about to ask."

"Yes, Hank?" she said with childlike impatience.

He touched his forehead to her hand, then looked back into her eyes. "Sophia, I pray that this is not too soon to ask you to marry me, to love me forever, and to share our faith in our Lord as husband and wife."

Sophia threw her arms around Hank's neck and pulled him back into the swing. "I thought you'd never ask."

"Then please loosen your grip. You wouldn't want to strangle your future husband," he said as he resumed his position in the swing beside Sophia.

They both burst into laughter.

"When did you want to have the wedding?" she asked. Before he had a chance to reply, she went on. "We need to let your parents know so they can be here. Is there anyone else?"

Hank raised both hands to the sky. "I want to let the world know, and they're all invited, every last person and creature God has created!"

"Then we might want to have the wedding outside," Sophia said with a chuckle. "All God's creatures won't fit in that little Church on the Hill."

"We can have it anywhere, any time your heart desires," Hank said, "as long as you promise to love me to the end."

"I have an idea," Sophia said. "Why don't we have it on the church lawn where we first met, and we can plan it for the Fourth of July, right after the pie auction."

"Excellent idea," he replied, "with one exception."

She cast a look at him with the prettiest frown he'd ever seen. "An exception?"

"Yes," he replied. "We shall have it before the pie auction. I don't know if I can wait any longer."

Hank's heart swelled with more joy than any one man deserved as Sophia hugged him once again. He looked up and quietly said, "Thank You, Lord."

Still holding onto Hank, Sophia added, "Amen."

DEBBY MAYNE

Debby has been a freelance writer for as long as she can remember, starting with short slice-of-life stories in small newspapers, then moving on to parenting articles for regional
publications and fiction stories for women and girls. She has
been involved in all aspects of publishing from the creative
side, to editing a national health publication, to freelance
proofreading for several book publishers. Her belief that all
blessings come from the Lord has given her great comfort during trying times and gratitude for when she is rewarded for her
efforts. She lives on the west coast of Florida with her husband
and two daughters.

LILLY'S PIRATE

by Paige Winship Dooly

Dedication

To my husband, Troy, for taking on more household and childcare duties while I wrote. And to my children, Josh, JT, Dalton, Tessa, and Cassidy, for being patient during my hours at the computer. Also to my parents, Myron and Sharon, and in-laws, Don and Lora, for their encouragement. Most of all, I dedicate this story to my ninety-six-year-old grandmother, Mary Ellen, who is my constant inspiration. Though nothing like the character in my book, my grandmother has a spunk and a love for the Lord that inspires us. I love you all!

Acknowledgments

Thanks to Pamela G., Tamela H. M., and Debby M. for their support, critiques, and advice on this story. A heartfelt thanks goes out to my sister, Shelly, and brother-in-law, James, for their suggestions that got me going. And a special thanks to my brother, Kent, who encourages everyone to keep their focus on the Lord.

"Stand fast therefore in the liberty
wherewith Christ hath made us free,
and be not entangled again with the yoke of bondage."
GALATIANS 5:1

Chapter 1

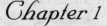

1900 Pirate's Point, Florida

Lillian Appleby stared out the window, lost in thought while voices droned in the background. She caught herself dreaming of the freedom that beckoned from outside and forced her wayward thoughts back to the meeting. It was April, and the Pirate's Point Women's League Fourth of July Planning Committee meeting was well underway. Unfortunately, the committee at this point had far more words in its name than specific plans.

Mabel Pinkerton wanted a parade. Lilly pointed out that in order to have a parade, you needed a lot of people and a band— neither of which the coastal town of Pirate's Point, Florida, could boast.

Clara Ledbetter wanted to talk about her ailments, which would be fine any other time, but the planning meeting hardly seemed the place to ramble on about poor health.

Lilly's patience was frayed. Not one of her opinions or suggestions was acknowledged, and she wondered why she wasted her time on such a beautiful day. Frustrated, she ran her hands through her hair, frowning when a blond strand flipped across her forehead. She blew it back, knowing the motion made it worse, but at this point she didn't really care.

At the first hint of silence, Lilly jumped to her feet. "Ladies, please. Listen a moment, and think about what I'm trying to say. Our town is too small. If we have a parade, there will be no one in town left to watch it. Now I ask you again— what would be the purpose of undertaking such a venture if there are no spectators?"

She drew in a breath, only to have her ninety-five-year-old grandmother, Sophia, interrupt. "If we're going to march in a parade, we're gonna need flags! Parades always have flags." Lilly sighed. The need for flags had been her grandmother's only repeated declaration since the meeting began.

"I don't know how I'm supposed to wave a flag with my rheumatism flaring up again," Clara said with a nod, finding yet another ailment to mention. "Can we march slowly? I don't have much tolerance for heat. It's going to be a hot one this summer, I dare say. My body always knows."

Lilly wondered how Clara could nod so vigorously when she'd already bemoaned the fact that the arthritis in her neck made it impossible to move her head.

"I think we need to plan for our annual picnic and then set off a few fireworks as usual," Lilly pleaded, hoping to finalize arrangements and end this first meeting. They could plan what to bring and how much food would be needed at the next meeting. "We can have singing and recitations as always—and of course the food contests."

Lilly's grandmother sighed. "I really wanted to carry a flag when we marched in that parade."

"Nana, I don't think it would be possible for you to march anyway," Lilly chided gently. "We can arrange for you to carry a flag, though. I don't see that to be a problem."

Sophia smiled with pleasure. The other women were staring at Lilly with what she hoped was acquiescence, but those hopes where dashed with Mabel's next words.

"How do you suppose we should go about setting up a parade?"

While the women murmured their thoughts to each other, Lilly snatched up her satchel and slipped out the back door of the room. If she stayed, she would surely lose her temper.

Outside, the slight breeze cooled her overheated body as she walked into the fresh air. The brilliant blue sky buoyed her spirits. Crossing the street, she hurried around the small general store, heading south to the beach.

From habit, she walked toward her favorite hideaway, stopping only to remove her stockings and boots.

Her father would have a fit if he knew one of his daughters was showing her ankles while out in public, but who would ever see her? This path was never used. The townspeople seemed to prefer the more accessible trail to the west. Besides, her long skirt hung to the ground, and she only needed to hold it up a bit so as not to trip.

Lilly slowed her pace and enjoyed the tropical sounds around her. The breeze rustled the magnolias, and the sea oats reached out to tickle her ankles. Her bare feet sank into powder white sand, and Lilly sighed with relief. Ahead, she could hear the surf gently breaking on the shore.

Seagulls called out as they played in the wind, oblivious to Lilly's approach. She reached the edge of the path, stopping in awe as she always did when first glimpsing the emerald green waters of the gulf.

Gently, she placed the satchel in the sand and removed her

latest novel, a story full of pirates, exotic places, and romance. If only Lilly could be so unencumbered—maybe meet a pirate who would whisk her away to freedom and adventure. Instead, after this brief reprieve, she'd need to walk back to escort her grandmother home from the meeting.

Lilly loved her family but sometimes resented their expectations. Not only did she have Nana to lead around, but also her twin sister, Annabelle.

Thrown from a horse two years ago, Annabelle had lived with constant pain. When Annabelle's doctor said he could do nothing more for her, their parents purchased a special tonic from a pharmacy in the next town. Though the tonic relieved the pain, Annabelle had severe mood swings that made everyone think she was losing her mind, and Lilly, as her twin, was the one who coped with the brunt of the behavior.

She knew people gossiped behind her back about her eccentric grandmother and quirky sister. To compensate, Lilly had excelled in academics and joined every committee, hoping to overcome other people's judgment. She was tired of trying to please everyone. It never worked.

Lilly's thoughts returned to the present, and she smiled when she caught sight of two dolphins leaping in the waves. Ah, to be like that! No routine. No chores. No expectations.

She dropped onto the sand and opened her book, determined to lose herself in her favorite pastime of reading. Immediately caught up in the intrigue, she became entranced by the story of a lonely woman captured by renegade pirates.

Chills ran down her back when the heroine was taken prisoner aboard the massive pirate vessel. When the story became a bit too intense for such a lonely location, Lilly nervously gathered her things, preparing to leave. She would read the next scenes in the security of her home.

"Some adventurer that makes me." Lilly smiled at her own cowardliness.

Suddenly she noticed that the dolphins were quiet. She walked to the water's edge, shading her eyes to look for them. Lazy from the heat, feeling a bit groggy, Lilly lifted her skirts and waded into the cool water, hoping it would revive her for the long walk home.

Small shells washed around her feet. She gasped when an unexpected wave splashed against her knees.

"Great, now my dress is wet," she muttered aloud, wondering how she'd explain that to her parents. She hoped it would dry before she reached home.

A loud splash distracted her, and she laughed with delight when her dolphin friends returned. They played dolphin tag in the waves, and Lilly wished she could swim out and join them. The larger dolphin did a perfect flip midair, which the smaller dolphin tried to imitate, splashing on its back when it didn't quite complete the stunt.

"It's okay, Baby," Lilly called out. "A bit more practice and you'll be flipping every bit as well as your mother."

Shading her eyes once more, she lamented her forgetfulness that allowed her to leave her hat at home. Though a face tinged with pink would be a dead giveaway that she'd skipped the meeting that afternoon, she was more frustrated because her vision was hampered by the bright sun reflecting off the water.

Lilly squinted as something on the horizon caught her eye. A schooner! The ship was beautiful as it sailed into view, exactly like the one in the pirate story she'd been reading. Though not an unusual sight—merchants shipped their wares from Pensacola through these waters quite often—this craft seemed different.

The schooner set anchor offshore, and Lilly scanned the beach, noticing for the first time a small rowboat pulled up at the far end. Hair stuck up on the back of her neck when she realized she wasn't alone. This was not the first time her penchant for adventure had placed her in a predicament. She'd isolated herself from help when she'd carelessly sat down to read without bothering to check out her surroundings.

"Hello."

The voice from behind made her jump, spin around, lose her balance, and fall into the surf. Her startled scream ended abruptly, cut off by a mouthful of saltwater. Strong hands grasped her upper arms, pulling her to her feet while she sputtered and coughed. Hair dripped around her face as she peered at her rescuer, but the sun was behind him and prevented a clear view.

"You're bleeding."

The deep voice was calm but concerned.

"I'm f-f-fine," Lilly stuttered, shivering from both the cold water and the scare. She touched her forehead where she'd scraped it on the sand during her tumble in the waves. Groaning inwardly, she realized how undignified she must have looked rolling head over heels, her ankles and bare feet all over the place for anyone to see.

"I'm so sorry. I didn't mean to startle you. You looked worried, and I thought I could help." The stranger wrapped a blanket around Lilly, which warmed her slightly and shielded her from the breeze.

She covertly glanced down, making sure her toes were hidden. She felt so exposed.

"Awwk. Pretty girl. Awwk." A voice from somewhere behind the man called out the words.

"I beg your pardon?" Lilly asked, her face flushing with embarrassment. Pretty was the last thing that could be said about her at the moment.

The seawater mostly drained from her eyes, Lilly pushed her soggy hair back, enabling her to see the man who'd helped her first into the water and then back out.

She gasped. Her rescuer was a pirate! From the shoulder-length black hair, to the sparkling blue eyes, right down to the large bird perched upon his shoulder, he looked exactly like he'd walked out of her novel. He was so handsome, Lilly felt herself begin to swoon.

"Meet Peter. He escaped from the boat," the handsome pirate explained as he steadied her. "I named him after the impulsive disciple in the Bible."

Lilly hoped he attributed her dizziness to the fact she had flipped into the water. Realizing her mouth still gaped open with shock, she clamped it shut, not wanting to look simple.

Like simple would matter after that clumsy plunge, she thought.

"I'm dizzy from the fall," she muttered inanely, not wanting him to know he made her weak in the knees.

Her pirate smirked, then glanced at the ship. His face darkened. "I'm sorry. I must go. Again I ask that you please forgive me. Are you sure you'll be all right?"

Stunned, Lilly nodded, forgetting how to speak as her pirate smiled, gently took her hand, and lifted it to his lips for a brief kiss. He then loped off, stopping to pick up a book that resembled a Bible before rowing away in the small boat toward the ship.

Still speechless, Lilly stared after him and realized she didn't even know his name.

Suddenly aware of the time, she ran up the beach, taking

the path away from town, knowing it was too late to escort her grandmother home. Someone else would surely have seen to that by now. Besides, she wasn't about to let the ladies of the Pirate's Point Women's League Fourth of July Planning Committee see her in this disheveled state.

Her father waited on the porch as Lilly approached. He crossed his arms over his chest when he caught sight of her. She watched his anger wane when he saw her condition.

Once inside, she explained about the pirate and her rescue. Her parents exchanged worried glances.

"Mother, if you'd only seen him! He was so handsome and polite. He pulled me out of the waves, then his bird talked to me, and he picked up what looked like a Bible and rowed off across the sea."

"Lilly, please sit still while I tend to this wound," her mother commanded, gentle fingers probing the aching area. "Land sakes, I don't know how you managed to do this in a tumble through the waves."

Lilly ignored her, wanting to share more about the pirate. "Mother. . . "

"Here, put these dry clothes on, and I'll help you into bed."

"I don't need to lie down," Lilly protested. "I want you to meet my pirate. Maybe his ship is still out there."

"Lilly, Dear. You've hit your head. I think you need a little rest," her mother said in a patient voice usually reserved for the younger children.

"But my pirate!" Lilly wailed. "He'll be gone. I never even thanked him."

"Oh, my." Lilly's mother put a hand to her chest. "She's gone daft like Annabelle."

"Nonsense," her father answered. "She's only hit her head.

She'll be fine by morning. I've told you to stop letting her read those fanciful romances. She has her head in the clouds enough as it is."

He turned to Lilly. "Now, Lillian, I've warned you about that overactive imagination. I think we all know that pirates no longer exist. This is the twentieth century, not the uncivilized days of the high seas."

He walked to her door, glancing back to add, "Tomorrow we'll have no more talk of pirates, do you understand?"

"Yes, Father," Lilly said softly. They thought she was like Annabelle, not able to grasp reality. She wouldn't give them reason to think such a thing again. Now that she thought more about it, she also was beginning to doubt what she saw. Maybe she'd fallen asleep on the beach and dreamed the whole thing. Or worse yet, maybe she *was* becoming like her twin, and the insanity was rubbing off.

Chapter 2

Lilly wasn't allowed to visit town for almost a week, and even then she could only go if accompanied by her slow-moving grandmother.

Now it was Friday, and the walk she'd gone on had taken three times longer than it should have. Lilly felt her patience being severely tested. Stopping for what felt like the hundredth time, she waited for her grandmother to shuffle alongside her.

"Nana, I do wish you'd speed up just a bit." Lilly's words were impatient even to her own ears.

"Honey, I'm sure I would if this old rheumatism would stop bothering me," the older woman stated, reaching Lilly's side and continuing on.

Lilly hid a smile. "Nana. You know you don't have rheumatism. That's Clara's ailment. It's those boots you insist on wearing. I think Grandpa would understand if you wore your own instead of his."

Nana turned her nose up into the air. "Shows what you know. Your grandfather told me himself he wanted me to wear these boots."

The woman never lost pace. She continued to shuffle the

whole time she talked, with Lilly falling into step beside her.

These were the moments when Lilly felt at a loss. Her grandmother was constantly mixing up reality with dreams, or things she'd read, or things she'd heard—like Clara's rheumatism. Nana had come across the boots in the barn weeks earlier and had worn them every waking moment since.

"I think you dreamed that Grandfather said that, Nana. He can't talk to you now. He's waiting in heaven, remember?"

"He told me before he passed on," her grandmother insisted stubbornly, and Lilly let the topic drop. She wasn't having any more success than her father in convincing Nana it had been a dream.

"When do I get my flag?" Nana asked, changing the subject.

"Right now," Lilly said, relieved to speak of something other than the boots. In buying the flag, she would bring peace to the entire family. Grandmother had gone on for a week about how she had to have that flag.

Lilly waved and greeted a neighbor who held the door to the general store open for them. Lilly went on inside, talking over her shoulder to her grandmother, who again lagged behind. "We'll get that flag first thing, then choose the other items on Mother's list."

Lilly received the usual, peculiar glances from fellow shoppers as she walked down the rough planks toward the counter at the rear. She was accustomed to their curious looks. Whenever she brought her grandmother or Annabelle into town, people stared.

Lilly thought she heard something about "just like Annabelle" as she passed by. Oh well. Nothing new there. People always were amazed at how much alike the twins looked. Only after Annabelle's accident and personality change had the majority of the comments stopped.

The thought made Lilly sad, and she forced her mind to concentrate on her shopping.

"I suppose the flags are behind the counter. We'll just ask." Lilly proceeded down the aisle, smiling at Mrs. McCarthy as she approached.

The woman looked concerned. "Lilly? Can I help you?"

"Yes. We'd like a flag, as well as a few other items here on this list." Lilly handed over the slip of paper. "We'll just browse as you get the things together."

Mrs. McCarthy glanced over at her husband, who shrugged.

"Is something wrong?" Lilly asked.

"I'm just wondering why you keep saying 'we' when you're alone, Dear. Are you feeling all right?"

Lilly looked over her shoulder for her grandmother. Other than the couple of shoppers who'd looked at her strangely, the large room was empty. No wonder she'd received such odd looks. She'd been chatting away to thin air.

"Oh, no!" Lilly cried, dashing toward the door. "I'll be back. I've lost my grandmother!"

Nana couldn't have gone far. Perhaps those boots were a blessing after all. Rushing outside, Lilly glanced both ways up and down the boardwalk, finally spotting the older woman ahead, well past the store.

Hurrying to catch up, Lilly again lost sight of her grandmother as she wove her way between people, finally stopping when she noticed that several men stood outside the saloon peering over the doors. Lilly hesitated. Not seeing her grandmother anywhere up ahead, she joined the men and peeked inside. The idea of her grandmother entering such a place was preposterous, but sure enough, as her eyes adjusted, Lilly saw Nana sitting inside.

Having never been inside such a disreputable place, Lilly didn't know what to expect, but she did know she had to go in after her grandmother. Pushing open the swinging doors, she braced herself for the evil about to affront her. Loud music clanged from a piano in the far corner, but Lilly couldn't see it due to the dim light of the room. She waited a few moments for her eyes to adjust and made a mental note to speak with her father. He was sure to change his mind about Lilly needing an escort after his own mother did something like this!

Lilly moved farther into the room, trying to ignore the interested stares. So much for Grandmother keeping her out of trouble. She soon spotted Nana sitting with two of the most notorious men in the bar, known for their raucous fights and drunken misconduct.

Though terrified, Lilly would have laughed in any other setting at their expressions of bewilderment as they looked at her grandmother, who was earnestly chatting away at the two men. Lilly pushed her way through the crowded room to intervene.

"Grandmother!" she hissed, ready to throttle the elderly woman. "Come here. We need to get back to the store."

"Oh, Honey, come meet my new friends, Ned and Stan," Nana encouraged, oblivious to Lilly's discomfort.

Lilly didn't know what else to do, other than force her weak limbs to walk closer to her renegade grandmother. The name "Nana" and Lilly's image of her grandmother might never reconcile again. The very word presented a mental picture of the God-fearing, cookie-baking woman of Lilly's past who didn't remotely resemble the woman before her, sitting in a saloon, fraternizing with convicts.

The men clumsily stood to their feet, swaying as they

bowed. Their movements were rusty, and Lilly figured it had probably been years since they'd faced a decent woman.

"Ma'am," one of the men stuttered as his slovenly partner snickered and belched, then looked around in confusion to see where the sound had come from.

Repulsed by the odor, Lilly felt her face twist into a pickle-eating expression. She decided to hold her breath until they could get out of there.

"Please just. . .just sit," she insisted, waving the men back to their chairs while taking her grandmother by the arm. "We need to go."

"Privy is out back, through that door." The man Nana had called Ned pointed in three different directions as he obviously tried to remember where the door was.

"Privy?" Lilly was baffled before realizing he'd misunderstood her statement. Heat flooded her face. "I didn't mean. . . What I was saying. . ."

She looked helplessly at her grandmother, who just stared at her blankly.

"We need to leave."

"But I was telling them about my dancing days!" Nana cried, holding tightly to the bottom of the chair so Lilly couldn't pry her loose.

"There weren't any dancing days," Lilly huffed, continuing to tug as she spoke and finally grabbing her grandmother under the arms.

Bewildered, Nana glanced at the pictures of saloon girls on the walls.

"There weren't?" she asked sadly, abruptly letting go of the seat and causing Lilly to stumble back.

Lilly cringed as strong arms steadied her from behind,

much like at the beach days before.

Her voice softened. "No, Nana. You're thinking of the newspaper article I read you yesterday about the ballet dancers in New York."

"Oh. I suppose you're right. I'm sorry to have wasted your time," she told the men as she finally allowed Lilly to help her to her feet. "Now don't forget about church Sunday! You promised!"

The men mumbled incomprehensible replies, and Lilly took advantage of the moment to make her exit.

She turned, propelling Nana to the doors as fast as she could, only to be blocked by the human barrier that moments ago had stopped her fall.

Laughing blue eyes met hers as she stared up into the handsome face of her pirate.

She swooned.

His hands went to her shoulders, sending shivers down her arms. If he didn't let go immediately, she was going to melt into an embarrassing puddle on the floor. Then again, even if he *did* let go, she'd melt into an embarrassing puddle on the floor. Her leg bones had simply disappeared. Apparently, even breathing the fumes from a place such as this meddled with a person's equilibrium.

"Let me guess. Still dizzy from that fall, huh?" His words were for her ears only, his voice husky. The man was so tall. So solid. So masculine. She stared at the black buttons of his shirt, wondering why she found it so hard to breathe.

The world tilted, and Lilly looked up.

He grinned, and she fainted into his arms.

Lilly lay flat on her back as the shapes above her wavered into faces. Mrs. McCarthy, Grandmother, Doc, and. . .the pirate. She smiled, still woozy, then fainted once again.

Lilly was having a really nice dream until someone shook her, calling out her name. She fought to hold on to the image, but then the terrible odor of ammonia filled her nostrils. Coughing, she sat upright, rubbing her nose to chase away the awful smell.

"Ah, you join us once again!" Doc said with a smile as he replaced the lid on the smelling salts he held. "You had us worried, young lady."

Lilly looked around, uncertain of where she was. It took her a moment to figure out she was in Doc's office.

"What happened?" Her mind was muddled, giving her new insight into how her grandmother must feel most of the time.

Doc smiled. "You fainted."

"How did I get here?" she wondered aloud, trying to fit the missing pieces together.

"You were brought in by. . .hmmm." Doc glanced at Lilly's grandmother "What was it she called him again?"

" 'Her pirate,' I do believe," Nana supplied helpfully.

Of all times for her mind to be clear, this had to be the moment, Lilly thought, mortified. She fell back into the pillows, willing herself to faint again. It didn't work. She peeked out from under one eyelid to see them both still standing before her, smiling their smug little smiles. The wretched day continued, moment by humiliating moment.

"And look! Here he is now! Your pirate is back," Doc exclaimed as if Lilly could possibly be happy to see the man.

Right now, the only way she'd be happy to see him would be if he were walking the plank. Disappearing from her life. Sailing off into oblivion. Forever.

Lilly prayed this was all a bad dream.

She forced herself to sit up and tried to climb off the table without making eye contact with the. . .pirate.

"I think I'll go home now," she stated, ruing her shaky voice.

The pirate chuckled. "Not so fast. I'll be driving you home in the carriage I just retrieved. You've been out cold."

Lilly ignored him. "Doc? Where are my boots?"

"Don't have 'em anymore," he said, nodding toward the mysterious man. "He took 'em when he left to fetch the carriage."

Lilly closed her eyes, shaking her head in disbelief. "You took my shoes? Why would you do such a thing?"

"Because I've already noticed how stubborn you can be. I didn't want you to get the mistaken notion you could walk home if you came to before I arrived back with the carriage," he explained, his smile matching Doc's and Nana's. "I'm taking you, like it or not."

"I'll walk home in my stockings before I ride with you." Lilly just wanted away from the man. He must think her such a fool.

"Here, take my boots," Nana offered generously, lifting her skirt to expose the huge objects. "I'm riding with him."

"Nana, please, drop your skirt!" Lilly buried her face in her hands. Her next words were muffled. "Fine. Let's just go."

Lilly started to stand, but the man swept her up into his arms. "Don't faint," he whispered. "Everyone is watching."

She was too angry to faint this time. Had she really asked for this? The pirates in her novels were romantic, the heroines dreamy. She hadn't been specific enough in her prayers. She wanted a do-over, to clarify her request. God had sent the wrong pirate. This man was arrogant and obnoxious, *not* the sweet hero she longed for.

Carrying her outside, he settled her on the middle of the carriage bench, then helped her grandmother up onto the outer part, forcing Lilly to be pressed against him when he climbed up beside her.

"Tell me where to go," he said, waiting patiently for her directions as if this were just an ordinary day.

"I'd like to, but that wouldn't be very Christian of me." Lilly pretended to misunderstand.

"Lillian!" Nana admonished. "Young lady, you give him directions right now."

Again, her grandmother had to be lucid when Lilly's manners were at their worst.

"Fine. I want you to go to the beach. Climb into your little rowboat, and sail off into the sunset." Lilly kept her eyes focused straight ahead. "There, you have your directions, and I even tried to be nice while giving them."

He tilted his head to peer at her. "I've upset you."

The purposeful understatement hit its mark and almost made Lilly laugh.

"Apparently so," she replied dryly, still not wanting to look at him. He was so close, she could feel his hair blow against her cheek. Her voice dripped sarcasm. "You're very quick."

He leaned closer. "Is that any way to speak to your pirate?"

Touché! He was good. He didn't back down like her two youngest brothers.

Lilly feigned indifference, peering intently at the clouds. "I don't know what you're talking about."

She knew her traitorous face flamed, advertising the fact that she did indeed know exactly what he meant. "I hit my head recently, remember? I'm not accountable for anything I've said."

She stood and tried to move away.

"I want to change seats. I get nauseous in the middle. Grandmother, please scoot over."

The older woman now seemed distant, and Lilly eyed her suspiciously. It was uncanny how Nana's mind seemed to suddenly come and go at will.

A strong arm tugged Lilly back into place. "No standing while the carriage is in motion. You might fall and hit your head—again."

"We aren't moving," Lilly stated, ignoring him and still trying to move past her grandmother.

Reins snapped and the carriage jerked, bringing Lilly down onto the pirate's lap.

"Or this would be fine, if you'd rather," he said happily. "Though you might create a stir here in town if you don't slide over onto the seat. Then again, it won't be the first time you've drawn attention today."

Lilly felt her cheeks flush and did as she was told, sure he could hear her heart beating over the horses' loud hooves. He was still too close. His arm was pressed against hers, making her feel all mushy when she wanted to be strong.

He turned the carriage in the direction of her home.

"Why did you ask me for directions if you already knew where we were going?" she said in exasperation.

"I wanted to hear what you'd say. You're cute when you're angry." He smiled as she crossed her arms. "Doc gave me directions, just in case. Said he'd known you since you were born and that you tend to have an attitude when cornered. That you could also be a mite stubborn when you want to be. And that you—"

"I get the idea," Lilly interrupted, wondering if Doc *also* gave a copy of her medical documents to this man for his perusal while they passed time waiting for her to wake up.

"I don't know what Doc was thinking, sending us off with a man like you. Some concern he has for our well-being."

"A man like me? What's that supposed to mean?"

"The saloon. Don't deny you were there. I remember that part vividly."

"You were in the saloon too. Maybe I'm the one who's unsafe. I went in to visit my friend. He works there."

"I see," Lilly said, her tone implying she didn't see at all.

"I was there to invite him to church on Sunday."

"Church. That's a good one," she replied, then bit back her retort as his words sunk through her muddled brain. There was only one church in town. If he were going to be there, she'd have to face him again.

"Church? You mean like the one we just passed? Or do you mean some other church, like in a town far away from here?"

"The very one we just passed. Would you like me to pick you up Sunday morning? I can swing by on my way."

"No. Actually, I think I'm going to be sick this week," Lilly announced.

"That's fine. Miss Sophia? What time did you say you wanted me to pick you up for services on Sunday?"

He had the audacity to wink at Lilly as her grandmother answered.

Lilly didn't like pirates anymore.

At long last they arrived at her home. He reached out to tenderly touch her chin, forcing her to look into the most heart-melting eyes she'd ever seen. Leaning so close she could feel his breath, he whispered, "I loved the way you called me your pirate just before you fainted, but if you don't mind, I'd prefer that you call me Caden in public."

The dizziness was back. She might have fainted again had she not seen the glint of mischief in Caden's eyes as her head tilted back. Through sheer will and a healthy dose of indignation, she fought back unconsciousness, shoved away from Caden, and hopped down from the carriage.

Chapter 3

C aden watched Lilly move past her grandmother and hop to the ground. Unfortunately, she was still a bit unstable, and he winced as she fell forward, flat on her face.

Jumping down and hurrying around the carriage to help her, he stopped short when she glared up at him.

"Don't say a thing," she bit out.

He couldn't help himself. "Don't you just hate it when that happens?"

"Right, you fall off the wagon every day."

Caden glared. "I said I was only at the saloon to see my friend. I wasn't—"

He went silent as he saw the corner of her mouth tip up into a smile. "I was referring to my fall off the carriage, nothing else."

"Oh." Caden deserved that. He'd been goading her since they'd met, but something in her brought out his ornery side. It had been a long time since he'd relaxed and had fun.

Of course, he'd always liked a challenge, and Lilly was the first woman who hadn't tripped all over herself trying to get his attention. Well, she did trip a lot, but it was from evading him rather than trying to get near him. Her attitude was refreshing.

"Let me help you inside," Caden offered, holding his hand out to her.

Lilly pointedly ignored him and stood on her own. She dusted at her skirt for a moment, then shrugged. "You've only seen me at my worst. What's a bit of dust now?"

Caden's heart went out to her. If she could only see how endearing she looked: her hair once again in disarray, clothes covered with dust, and smudges of dirt on her left cheek.

Yet it was the expression in her soft green eyes that really drew him. They were troubled, a noticeable contrast to her quick wit and sharp tongue.

Caden wanted to know what caused her anxiety, and he wanted to fix it for her. Perhaps it was the situation concerning her obviously senile grandmother. The woman would be a great responsibility, but Lilly loved her, and Caden admired her for that.

The front door of the house opened, and several small children ran outside.

"Lilly's home! Lilly's home!" The smallest girl chanted. She squealed as Lilly swept her up into her arms and held her close. Lilly's countenance glowed as she flashed her first genuine smile.

"How's my Molly," she crooned, burying her face in the little girl's raven curls for a kiss.

"I'm fine. I missed you."

Lilly laughed, setting her down to hug the next little girl. "I've only been gone a few hours. Right, Gertie?"

Gertie nodded shyly, staring at Caden.

Two little boys covertly jostled each other for a hug from Lilly, apparently not wanting to appear childish in front of

Caden. They looked him over with blatant curiosity.

"My little brothers and sisters," Lilly explained after all the hugs were given. "Molly, Gertie, Jack, and Henry."

She touched each on the head as she stated the names. All but Molly had golden hair like Lilly.

"Where's Father and Mother?" she asked the oldest boy, Henry.

"Had to go get Annabelle's tonic." He rolled his eyes.

"Then they won't be back until tomorrow. No wonder you're so happy to see me." The strain was back on Lilly's face. "Guess Sarah was in charge?"

The second youngest, Gertie, grabbed Lilly's hand.

"Yes. Pwomise you'll stay home now." She had an adorable lisp.

"I'm here to stay."

"Is this everybody?" Caden asked, half teasing. There was enough of an age difference between Lilly and Henry that there could be others.

"I have another sister and two more brothers. They're probably over at the mill, covering for my father while he's not here. They work with him. Sam is fourteen, and Will is about to turn seventeen."

Caden noticed she didn't mention the sister. Would that be Sarah, the one the other children didn't want watching them? Or maybe Annabelle, the one who needed the tonic? Regardless, Lilly's hands were full. No wonder she was stretched to the breaking point.

"And your sister?" he asked.

Before she could answer, a melodious voice interrupted, calling to Lilly from the direction of the two-story house. Caden looked up to see who was there. Since porches ran the complete exterior of both levels, it took him a moment before he spotted a woman on the second floor, standing in the shadows.

Lilly gasped, and Caden turned, watching her face go white as a sheet.

"No," she whispered, so softly Caden almost didn't hear. "Please don't embarrass me. Not now."

"What is it, Lilly?" he asked, pushing a tendril of hair back from her face. Not understanding, he looked back up at the woman, wondering what it was about her that bothered Lilly so much.

"You need to leave. Please. I appreciate all that you've done for us, and someday maybe you'll see me in a normal situation. Well, I mean, normal for other people, not normal for me. . .I mean, never mind. Just go and forget we ever met."

Tears filled her eyes, and she quickly whirled her back to him. He was being dismissed.

Caden lifted Sophia down from the carriage. She brushed off his offer of assistance and shuffled after Lilly.

Caden wanted to stay, but he had an appointment in town with a friend and business partner, and he was already late. He grabbed the flag he'd purchased for Sophia but thought better of calling out to them, stashing it under the seat instead. He'd give it to her Sunday.

He watched Lilly hustle the children into the house, then glanced one last time at the woman on the upper porch. From what he could see, she was a mirror image of Lilly.

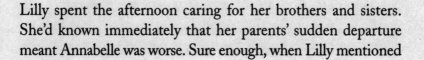

Lilly spent the afternoon caring for her brothers and sisters. She'd known immediately that her parents' sudden departure meant Annabelle was worse. Sure enough, when Lilly mentioned spending time with Caden at the beach, Annabelle had burst into tears and ranted about how everyone ignored her and no one wanted to spend time with her. Annabelle then locked herself into their bedroom, refusing all Lilly's entreaties to come out.

Now that the children were tucked in bed for the night, Lilly entered the kitchen, where Sarah was cleaning up from dinner.

"Sarah, I'm walking down to the mill. I'll be back before dark. Will you be around for a bit?" Lilly waited, expecting Sarah to complain. She was a wonderful cook. She prepared meals for all the mill workers in addition to the Appleby family, but her nerves wore out quickly when dealing with the younger children.

"I'll be fine, Miss Lilly. Take your time. You need some rest," she encouraged, catching Lilly off guard.

Even Sarah could see her despair?

Her heart was heavy as she wandered down the worn dirt trail. She loved her brothers and sisters, her grandmother, and her parents. However, she felt trapped. She didn't want to feel this way, but it seemed her life would always be like this.

It was so rare that she had a moment alone, and lately she'd made a mess of each situation. She was embarrassed to think of the opinion Caden must have of her after two bumbled meetings. Yet both times, she'd felt freer than usual, like something big was finally about to happen in her life.

That feeling made coming home harder than ever, yet home was where she needed to be. If only she could feel peace. If only she could go out in public and not be embarrassed. The only way she'd ever escape would be to start fresh in another town, but she loved her family too much to ever do such a thing.

A noise in the trees distracted her from her musings. She turned and listened, hearing sobs coming from up the path. She knew it was Annabelle. Reality called.

"Anna?" she whispered, hoping to find her sister in a reasonable mood. "Where are you?"

The sobs increased. Lilly followed the sound. Annabelle was sitting against a tree, hugging her legs, knees drawn up against her chin. "Lilly, help me. What's going on? What's wrong with me?"

Tears filled Lilly's eyes. If she only knew the answer to that question, Lilly would willingly live her life as it was for the rest of her days.

"I don't know, Anna. I wish I did. Mother and Father went for some more tonic." She sat beside her twin, inches away physically, but worlds apart mentally.

"I need the tonic now. It makes me feel better. I can't wait." She was sweating profusely yet shivering. Lilly touched her forehead, but Annabelle didn't seem to be running a fever.

"I know. They'll be back tomorrow. I'm sorry, Anna."

Annabelle began to cry again, and Lilly pulled her close. They used to know each other's every thought, shared every experience. Now, this was as close as they got—Annabelle crying for her medicine and Lilly comforting her.

"I hate the horse that threw you, Anna. If only we could go back. If you didn't have the pain. . ." Lilly's voice drifted off as she realized her twin wasn't listening. She was in a different place in her mind. A place Lilly couldn't reach. Only the medicine would help.

Lilly began to pray, but she didn't expect any results. Her sister had been this way for almost two years and wasn't getting any better. For whatever reason, God wasn't listening to her prayers.

Two days later, Lilly fidgeted on a church bench, afraid Caden would walk in, yet just as afraid he wouldn't. Nana had admitted she and Caden had been teasing when they'd said Caden would be picking her up for church. Lilly didn't want to see him again, but since her father refused to let her stay home, she went to great lengths to look her best. If she had to face Caden, she'd face him clean and dry. No tumble in the surf. No tumble off the wagon. Just a pretty dress and a fresh face.

The pastor walked forward. Disappointed, she turned to the front of the church. The service was about to begin, and Caden hadn't appeared.

The rear door opened. Lilly glanced back, her eyes widening in shock when both Ned and Stan from the saloon walked in and nervously took a seat in the last row. Their suits looked ready to burst at the seams, but both men had made an effort to dress in their finest. Will tapped Lilly's shoulder, and they stifled laughs as their grandmother gleefully called out to the men by name and shuffled back to greet them.

Lilly glanced at Annabelle, sitting beside her quiet and distant, waiting for the sermon to start. She seemed more focused when the tonic kicked in. But in the days before her accident, she would have shared a laugh with Lilly and Will at Nana calling out to the town bad boys.

Lilly caught sight of her father's frown and knew she'd somehow be to blame for Grandmother's excursion into the saloon. He hadn't mentioned knowing about it yet, but after today she was sure he would hear something.

Pages rustled as people settled down with their Bibles. Lilly heard the door open once more. Caden entered, and she smiled as she caught his eye, but the smile froze in place when she saw Edith McCarthy hanging on his arm. They took a seat near the front, and Lilly's heart fell.

To top it off, Horace Bentley, the town postmaster, snuck in and settled next to Lilly. The man was nice, but Lilly wasn't attracted to him in the least. She scooted closer to Annabelle. Several of Lilly's neighbors smiled knowingly. By unanimous agreement, they had all picked Horace to be her beau. No one seemed interested in Lilly's opinion. Though she was already eighteen, she'd stay a spinster before she married him. Everyone seemed to think it was time for her to settle down, but Lilly had enough to do without worrying about a husband. The thought of Horace coming home to her each night made Lilly shiver with disgust.

He immediately put his arm around her, bending down to whisper an offer of his jacket. Repulsed, she said no, then quickly leaned away from the range of his arms to fuss with her boot. Her forehead connected with the pew as she did so with a resounding crack.

Horace grasped Lilly's shoulders and pulled her toward him, using the excuse to see her forehead to get close. She shook him off, jumped to her feet, and rushed out the door.

Caden longed to go after Lilly. He wanted to explain to her that sitting with Edith hadn't been his idea. Edith had latched onto him outside the building, where she'd waited for him after finding out from her father that he would be at the service. Caden was doing business with Mr. McCarthy as part of his cover and couldn't risk offending the McCarthy family at this point.

He tried to concentrate on the sermon, but the hurt and disappointment in Lilly's eyes distracted him from the words. He'd agreed to have dinner with the McCarthys, so he wouldn't even be able to talk to her after church. Caden bowed his head. He couldn't do anything for Lilly at the moment, but he knew Someone who could.

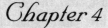

Chapter 4

Lilly eased back on the sand, feeling the heat of the sun penetrate her being. The past few weeks had dragged by, but she'd kept busy so she didn't have much time to waste thinking about her pirate.

Edith's pirate.

She was silly to think he'd be interested in her after she'd made a mess of so many meetings. By now she should be used to standing on the outside; but no matter how much she tried to convince herself she didn't care about Caden, in her heart she knew she'd been drawn to him from the first moment she'd seen him on this beach.

For one brief day, she'd believed her pirate had come to take her away, and she would relish that reprieve, short as it was, for her whole life. As for now, she'd have to be content to only read about adventure in her novels. She rolled over onto her stomach and picked up the latest romance.

Caden rowed toward shore. His heart skipped a beat when he saw a woman reading on the sand. It could only be Lilly. He'd looked for her every day, not wanting to drop by her home uninvited, and it was rare for him to find time away from the ship.

July was coming fast, and the operation would soon take over his every minute. He had to guard his time away as it was, not wanting to arouse suspicion.

His boat scraped sand, and Caden hopped out, pulling it farther up the shore. After reaching in to grab his Bible, he walked slowly toward Lilly, enjoying the private moment to observe her.

She lay on her stomach, arms braced on elbows, holding the book in front of her. One hand twirled the strand of hair that always seemed to escape, and every once in awhile her lips moved as she read. Her feet were again bare, crossed at the ankles, and she played in the sand with her toes. She was absolutely breathtaking.

Heat crept up Caden's face when he realized Lilly would not be happy to have her private moment invaded. He found himself wondering what it would be like to be Lilly's pirate for life. The thought was totally out of character for him and caught him off guard. She had an inner strength and zest for life that made him realize there was more to life than work—and it drew him to her.

Leaning down to place his Bible on the sand, he cleared his throat, letting her know he was there.

Lilly jumped a foot off the ground, then turned and slung her book at him. He caught it easily and flipped it over so he could see the cover.

Grinning, he read the title. "*The Pirate of Heartbreak*. Ah, are you reading about me?"

Lilly rolled her eyes, blushed, and reached for the novel.

Caden ignored her, flipping pages. He cleared his throat and began to read in a deep voice. "Woman, you do not understand the life I lead. I will only break your heart, as I have so many others."

His voice rose several octaves. "No! Bartholomew! You must take me with you or I shall die! Promise me your undying love, and whisk me away from here forever!"

Lilly's laughter filled the air as she futilely grabbed for her book. Caden held it high above her head. "Stop it. That's not in the story. I'd never read something silly like that."

Caden wanted to hear her laugh again. He walked backward, reading aloud as he moved. "Pull me into your warm embrace, Bartholomew, and I shall miss you no more! With me by your side, life will be just grand!"

Caden was rewarded by Lilly's chortles, but he didn't like the gleam in her eye. "What do you think, Lilly? Will his life be just grand?"

Lilly's smile was beautiful to behold. "There isn't a Bartholomew in my book. You're making it all up—and quite poorly, I might add."

She lunged for him. He stepped back, his knees connecting with his boat. In a fluid motion, Lilly grabbed her novel as he went down. He missed the rowboat's bench and ended up on the bottom of the small vessel, feet sticking up over the side.

Lilly took off across the beach and had a good lead before he finally made it to his feet and gave chase. He caught up with her at the tree line. Swinging her around, he stared into her startled eyes. The soft green matched the beautiful emerald waters behind him.

Both were out of breath as they stood there. He pressed closer, causing Lilly to back up. He smirked when she backed against a tree that prevented her escape. He always had been partial to magnolias. Arms braced against the tree on either side of her, he gave a lazy grin. "So, what about you, Lilly? Do you dream of your pirate's warm embrace?"

Lilly vowed not to collapse. Though her bones had let her down once again, she was not going to let this arrogant man see the amazing effect he had on her.

Time stood still. She noticed that Caden's eyelashes were long and black, and they framed smoldering blue eyes.

Smoldering? Where did that come from? She didn't find his eyes smoldering. They were more like, well, more like. . . She glanced up at him again. Oh yes, they were smoldering all right. Burning their way straight into her heart.

A soft sigh passed over her traitorous lips.

"I'll take that to be a yes," he whispered, his finger outlining her lower lip.

Caden looked every bit the pirate. He wore loose black pants that tied at the waist, and his black shirt was tucked in, billowing with the wind. His shirtsleeves were rolled up, exposing strong biceps. Added to his dark tan and long, jet-black hair, the look was of a very dangerous man.

Dangerous for Lilly's heart. She'd spent the past weeks trying to forget him, and now here he was, near enough to kiss.

Lilly flushed, not knowing where that thought had come from. Maybe she did read too many novels. Why would she be thinking about a kiss? A kiss was the last thing she wanted. After all, Caden was just playing with her; Edith was apparently the one he was interested in.

Caden was talking, but Lilly found it more fascinating to watch how his lips formed the words than to listen to what he was saying. For such a solid man, his lips looked so soft. It was absolutely amazing. And she'd never realized lips could move in such delightful ways.

Caden's chuckle brought her out of her reverie. "You haven't heard a word I've said. I do believe you are about to swoon. Is the pirate too close for comfort, my dear maiden?"

He moved nearer still, and Lilly found it hard to breathe. He'd called her dear. His dear. She knew he only used the endearment in a most arrogant way, but she liked how it sounded as it slid across his tongue. Rolled off his lips. Lingered in the air. She'd never heard such an engaging word.

His gentle fingers cupped her chin, tipping her head back. Caden stared into Lilly's eyes. "I like you, Lillian Appleby. I really do." His thumb caressed her cheek.

The words broke the moment, and she pulled away. He liked her! The rest had all been said in teasing, but that last statement, it was real. She'd never been so happy to be liked in her life. But it also scared her to death. What did "like" mean? What happened now? The carefree bantering would be over because she was. . .liked. This changed everything.

If he *liked* her, he might eventually move on to *really* like her. She didn't know how to act. Here was her moment and her pirate, and she was tongue-tied. Scared witless.

"I have to go," she stated, attempting to move past him.

Caden frowned. "Was it something I said?"

"Yes. No. I don't know. I just need to. . .I don't know. I don't know how to act now. You said you like me, and that changes everything."

Caden laughed. "It changes everything how? You act like Lilly. I act like Caden. Just be yourself."

Lilly sighed. "That's the problem. I don't know how to be myself. Everyone wants me to be something for them, and I've lost who I am. I'm Lilly the good daughter. Lilly the good granddaughter. Lilly the good student. Lilly the good citizen."

Caden tugged her down onto the sand. "I see exactly who you are. A beautiful woman who lives her life for others and dreams of living life for herself."

"That sounds selfish. But it's true."

"I wouldn't say selfish. But there is another aspect to consider when living your life."

Lilly waited. "And what would that be?"

"God. If you live your life for Him, all the other pieces just fall into place."

"You make it sound so simple. It isn't."

"It is. You pray and ask His direction before acting. If your life isn't pleasing to God, nothing else is going to make you happy. It's very simple."

"I prayed when my sister was hurt. She's still hurt. She has never been the same again. God ignored my prayers."

"Maybe God just has a different answer than the one you're looking for." Caden studied his hands, as if contemplating his next words carefully. "I saw your sister on Sunday. You're a lot alike."

"We are twins," she stated, her voice flat. "Of course we look alike."

"I don't mean physically. I mean emotionally."

"I don't understand," Lilly said warily. "I feel like a prisoner sometimes. Annabelle is free. No one expects anything of her because she's sick."

Caden leaned back to rest on one arm. Lilly watched the breeze toss his hair. A sand fly buzzed around her face, and she waved it away.

Grasping Lilly's hand in his, Caden waited for her to look up into his eyes before continuing. "No, Lilly, you're the one who's free. She's a prisoner of her own mind. Tell me about the tonic she's taking."

"I don't know the name. My parents get it from a pharmacy in Camp Walton. Why?"

"I think it might contain opium, which causes an addiction. Do you know what that means?"

"Not when you're talking about a tonic."

"A friend and I have been doing some research. Some tonics are made up of drugs that dull the pain or make it go away because the drugs alter the mind. Your sister has the classic symptoms of an addiction."

"What are you saying?" Lilly tried to follow his explanation. "Is this something we can fix?"

"It won't happen overnight, but yes, the addiction can be stopped, and Annabelle could be back to normal. Tell me about her accident."

Lilly took a deep breath. "We were riding out near the swamp when Annabelle's mount stepped over a rattler. The horse spooked, bucked, and Anna landed on her back. They thought it was broken at first. Later she suffered horrible spasms. When our parents went to town, they found a pharmacy that promised this tonic would stop all pain, and it did, but ever since, Annabelle has acted touched in the head."

"I need to see the tonic, and I need to meet Annabelle. I won't know for sure otherwise."

Lilly fiddled with a handful of sand, letting it slide between her fingers. "How do you know about Anna? You haven't met her."

Caden was silent, and Lilly glanced up at him.

He cleared his throat. "I spoke to her briefly after Sunday's service, and I asked Doc some questions."

He studied her. "This is important, Lilly, don't get angry."

Lilly pulled away.

"I'm not. I just get tired of everyone watching us, pointing at us, and whispering about us." She stood to leave, brushing the sand off her skirt. "I need to get home. I've enjoyed our talk. When do you want to meet Annabelle?"

Caden looked disappointed at her abrupt withdrawal.

She didn't want to leave. She wanted to sit on this beach with Caden and forget everything else in her life.

"Bring her by tomorrow. Same time. I'll try to be here. But no promises. I might not be able to get away."

Lilly frowned. "Away from what? Caden, what is it you do? You know so much about me, but I don't know anything about you."

Caden pulled back, as if by distancing himself physically, he could shut off her questions. "I work in shipping. We move up and down the coast, transferring cargo from town to town. I never know for sure where we'll be. Will you bring Annabelle, just in case?"

"I'll be here," Lilly promised, more curious than ever. He wasn't telling her the whole story. Her pirate was mysterious once again. He'd stripped away her defenses, but this little distance he'd placed between them put her back at ease.

"Remember what I told you. If you try to control your life, you'll never be any happier than when others try to control it. Don't shut out God, Lilly. Give Him a chance."

With that parting comment, he softly kissed her hand and walked down to his boat. He was strong, confident, and secure. Everything Lilly wasn't.

She watched him go, wanting more than ever to jump in beside him, lean on his strength, and row off into the sunset together. Instead, she gathered her things and headed for home.

Chapter 5

Heavy rain kept Lilly inside for the next two days. She missed Caden but knew he wouldn't be able to reach shore in this weather. She passed the time entertaining the children.

The activity didn't keep her mind off Caden. She found herself wondering about his occupation and why he became so vague when asked for details. She knew he was a godly man. Lilly was drawn to him, but he baffled her when it came to his private life. It was all rather puzzling, and she was determined to find out more.

Late that night, she peeked in on her sleeping siblings before heading down the stairs and out the side door. The rain had stopped. She walked over to the mill to check the buildings for signs of intruders. Normally, this wouldn't be necessary, but lately there had been several attempts by jealous competitors to set fire to the mill. Will motioned to her from behind a stack of finished lumber, putting his finger to his lips to silence her.

A movement near the main building caught Lilly's attention. She hesitated. Wanting to reach Will, yet needing her father, she couldn't afford to waste a minute in case of a fire. Will nodded to show he was aware of the unknown presence. Lilly ducked over to his side, and they both went around the corner together.

In the darkness they could see through the window without being seen themselves. Lilly's heart skipped a beat when she saw the flicker of a candle. The fire would send the mill into flames if the men had a chance to get it near the dry stacks of wood awaiting transport to Pensacola.

Will held up a rifle he'd been carrying, and Lilly covered her ears while he shot it into the air. The noise would bring their father and Sam. It also had the desired effect of sending the arsonists scrambling.

Lilly stayed put while Will chased them. But the men reached a small boat and disappeared out into the bayou before he could catch up.

Mr. Appleby arrived along with a group of hired hands, and he assigned guards to watch around the clock, allowing the family to return to bed.

Lilly couldn't sleep after all the excitement, so she sat in a rocking chair on the veranda outside her room, staring toward the mill. It concerned her that in a brief moment everything they had could be wiped out.

Will joined her. "You all right?"

Lilly nodded, not wanting Will to hear the worry in her voice.

"They won't be back tonight," he reassured, sitting in the matching wooden rocker beside her.

Lilly put one toe down, pressed against the plank floor, and set her chair in motion. "We could lose everything if they succeed."

"We'll keep guards around for now. No one will dare come

this close for awhile after word gets out about what happened tonight." Will chuckled in the darkness. "By the time the story quits circulating, instead of me shooting a rifle into the air, it will come back that a band of armed guards smattered the area with gunfire."

Lilly had to grin at the truth in the statement. Stories grew quickly around Pirate's Point. She'd seen it happen many times in her life.

"Lilly, we'll be fine even if they do succeed in burning a building. We can always rebuild. Don't borrow trouble."

"It takes time to rebuild," Lilly countered.

"We have a garden that covers ten acres," Will stated dryly. "I don't think we'll starve. We have the animals too. We'll be fine. Now come on, it's late and we need to retire." He stood and ruffled Lilly's hair, acting like an older brother rather than a younger one. Walking through the outer door into the room he shared with Sam, Will left Lilly alone.

The night was humid, with a symphony of bullfrogs' croaks carrying through the slight breeze. Mosquitoes buzzed around Lilly, worse than ever now that it had rained. She needed to move indoors, but fear kept her outside.

Caden's words came back to Lilly while she sat unofficially on guard. The bayou accessing the mill was available to anyone, and with all the wood around, a fire would be fast and furious. Lilly could sit up and worry all night, or she could turn it over to God and trust Him to watch over things. She felt tired.

Haltingly, she bowed her head and prayed. She believed in God but had a hard time putting her complete trust in Him. Tonight she felt she didn't have a choice. She was tired of trying to be in control. Rising to her feet, Lilly dragged her weary body inside. Careful not to wake Annabelle, she slid into her bed.

The next morning, Lilly walked into town, not wanting to battle the mud with the carriage. She preferred to walk anyway, enjoying the time spent alone. Without Nana or Annabelle along, she would be able to check around about Caden.

Her upbeat mood was refreshing after a serene night's sleep. Nothing further seemed amiss at the mill. Maybe Caden had something in his theory of letting God be in charge. She'd have to ask him more about it.

Lilly was the only patron when she entered the store. Edith spoke with her mother near the back. Lilly stayed up front near the door while mother and daughter set up a new display. She pretended to browse while she listened.

"Mother, if I marry Caden, this will be the perfect print for a dress," Edith gushed, holding up a new bolt of fabric.

Lilly cringed, once again feeling silly for thinking Caden could be interested in her. She bumped the table behind her, and several cans fell to the floor.

Edith laughed, the annoying sound abruptly cut off when Mrs. McCarthy reprimanded her daughter.

"Nonsense, Child! What is all this marriage talk? You're much too young to worry about such things. The man won't be in town much longer. And I sure haven't heard a proposal."

"Not yet, Mama, but he'll ask me soon." Edith made a point of looking over at Lilly, her smile smug.

Though her heart broke into a million pieces at the announcement, Lilly couldn't resist entering the conversation. "So, congratulations are in order? I didn't even realize you were spending time with Caden."

Edith glanced at her mother before answering. "Oh, yes,

he's here all the time."

Mrs. McCarthy peered over her glasses at her daughter. "He comes here to talk business with your father. I won't have you spreading rumors, Edith, insinuating something that isn't true."

"You'll see." Edith's face reddened in anger, and she stalked into the storeroom.

"Don't worry about her," Mrs. McCarthy said. "Caden will be gone after the first week of July. He agreed to haul supplies for us until then but said after that he'd no longer be available. Edith is infatuated and expects to sail off with him."

Lilly froze, stunned. She hadn't thought about Caden leaving Pirate's Point, and she wondered how much of what Edith believed could be true. Perhaps Mrs. McCarthy didn't know, and Edith and Caden really did have a relationship. Maybe he'd been misleading Lilly all along.

Lilly's heart told her otherwise, her newfound contentment a soothing balm. Caden had no reason to deceive her, and his character spoke of strength and trust, not of his being a ladies' man. He'd teased her on the beach, yet he hadn't acted on the emotions.

But would he really leave town so soon? How could she ever stand her life again after meeting Caden if he walked away?

Lilly needed some answers. She walked down to the beach, determined to find out more about him if she had to go out to his ship herself. Though still afraid that he did have feelings for Edith, she had to know what was going on for sure.

Her heart skipped a beat when she passed through the grove of trees and saw Caden lying back in the sand. He was reading his Bible in their spot from the other day. Surely that meant something.

His lazy grin made her heart beat faster. She walked over and dropped down beside him.

"I hoped you'd show up." Caden placed a marker in the Bible and closed it. "I just finished. Good timing."

He studied her, making her squirm. "Have you thought any more about what I told you the other day?"

Lilly's smile was genuine. "I have. I even tried out your advice last night."

Caden raised his eyebrows in surprise. "I'm pleased to hear that. What happened?"

"We've had problems at the mill lately. Competition's fierce, and there have been attempts to burn down our operation to put us out of business."

Caden looked concerned. "And last night they tried again?"

"I walked down to check on things and. . ."

Caden sat upright, his eyes darkening. "You were alone? What were you thinking? If someone is that dangerous to your family's business, do you think they'd hesitate to harm you if you got in their way?"

"Caden, I was with Will. But I can't live in fear. You said yourself there is a time for trying to do things on our own and a time for turning it over to God. And that's what I did. I thought you'd be happy to hear it."

"I am. But that doesn't mean you have to put yourself in harm's way."

Lilly ignored him. "I sat outside, keeping watch, but finally I realized I couldn't control this by myself. It was bigger than me. I prayed, then went inside and slept like a baby."

"Lilly, I don't want you hurt. From now on let your father or brothers or hired hands do the checking. Promise me."

His possessiveness and concern flattered Lilly. "Don't

worry. My father has already covered that. He put full security on the mill indefinitely. I'll be fine."

Caden visibly relaxed. "I've been thinking about some things you said the other day. You said you felt the townspeople judged you because of Miss Sophia and Annabelle, right?"

Lilly scowled. "Yes. But I'm used to it."

"No you aren't, or you wouldn't try so hard to please everyone. You'll never be able to do that. Your approval needs to come from God, not the people around you. Only then will you be content."

Lilly hadn't looked at it that way before. She always tried so hard to be perfect, hoping to make up for her family's imperfections.

"Lilly, you need to accept the faults of the people around you. That's what true freedom is all about. I've talked to people in town. They all love you for who you are. Any time your name comes up, it's in a positive light. You're the one who puts the judgment in their eyes. Nonexistent judgment. Everyone I talked with had only good things to say about you."

Could it be true? Lilly contemplated his words. All this time she'd been so ready to expect the worst from the townspeople, but they'd really liked her all along. He had a point. Lilly was the one who didn't accept the way Nana and Annabelle acted. She was the one with the problem. She needed to let go and love them for who they were right at this moment.

"Oh, Caden, I've been so wrong!" she moaned, burying her face in her hands. "I've been the judgmental one, putting my thoughts and feelings on everyone else! How do I undo it all?"

Caden pulled her hands away so she had to look at him. The breeze played with his dark hair, tossing it about. "There's nothing to do, Lilly. Let it go. Love Annabelle and your grandmother for who they are. Then let God do the rest. I keep telling you it's easy."

Lilly felt a huge burden being lifted from her shoulders. She could see herself dumping the burden at Christ's feet, this time walking away without picking it back up. Why had she felt responsible for her family's conduct? Why did she think she'd be held accountable for their actions and behavior?

"Caden, thank you so much for showing me this!" She threw her arms around him and gave him a hug.

When she released him, Caden pulled her close, holding her a few moments longer. Embarrassed, Lilly tried to draw away.

"For a thank-you like that, I'll help you anytime," Caden teased, still not letting her go. "Now on to helping Annabelle. Will that earn me a kiss?"

"Caden!" Lilly blushed, but the fact that she still clung to his hand betrayed her true feelings. "You help Annabelle, then we'll talk about it."

"Ah, a woman of mystery," Caden stated. "But talking isn't what I had referred to. A kiss is the payment this pirate demands."

"I'm not going to live that down, am I?" Lilly asked ruefully.

Caden's blue eyes softened. "Lilly, I'd enjoy being your pirate for the rest of my days. As a matter of fact, in order to show you how I feel, I think I'm going to demand that kiss right now."

"You are not!" Lilly broke loose and moved away, laughing while playing along with his joke.

"But I am," Caden growled, looking the part of the feisty pirate. "Come here, fair maiden."

Lilly tried to stand, but nerves made her trip on her skirt. "No."

She laughed and Caden grasped her wrist, pulling her up against his chest. She struggled to breathe normally and failed miserably.

"Give me the kiss, or you walk the plank." He looked pointedly at the water lapping up on the beach. "And I do believe you already had that experience the day we met. So, what will it be? A kiss or a dunk in the water?"

Lilly froze, speechless. Surely he wouldn't dare. She didn't need a repeat performance.

She closed her eyes and tilted her face up toward Caden. His lips had barely brushed hers when they were interrupted.

"So, what do we have here?"

Caden released Lilly, stood, and pulled her protectively behind him in one fluid motion.

Three of the roughest-looking men Lilly had ever seen stood before them. They made Ned and Stan from the saloon look like innocents.

"We wanted to know what you really did in town these days," the largest man said. "We thought maybe you were having second thoughts about your involvement."

"Looks like he's pretty involved, all right," another man sneered.

"Watch what you say," Caden warned. "Go back to the ship. I'll be there shortly."

Surprisingly, after a short hesitation, the men obeyed. Lilly sank to the ground. Caden knelt down in front of her, pulling her into his arms.

"Thank God," he whispered, burying his face in Lilly's hair. "Lilly, if you only knew how important it was that those men saw us embrace instead of catching me in town, you'd never doubt God's hand in your life again."

Caden's comment confused Lilly. Was he saying he knew they were coming and this had all been an act? Or did he refer to Edith when he mentioned town? What had they meant about his involvement? Surely he didn't work with those men.

She searched his eyes for answers. He put a finger over her lips. "Don't ask. Please. You have to trust me. For now that's all I can say. I have to go."

Lilly stayed on her knees, watching Caden run after the awful men. It seemed Caden always left her behind, and she wondered if soon it would be forever.

Chapter 6

The Appleby carriage bounced down the rugged road. Deep sand made the buggy hard to control. Lilly used every bit of concentration to keep it out of the ditch. The rain had burrowed small canals alongside the road, and if she lost control, she wouldn't be able to get back on track without help.

With July only days away, the temperature was steadily climbing. Lilly had no problem remembering to wear her hat in the heat. The shade it provided was a welcome respite.

Tall oaks draped with Spanish moss formed a canopy overhead, cooling the air immensely. Though pleasant in the shade, Lilly knew the unprotected beach would be unbearably hot. Still, she had to make this trip. If Caden truly planned to leave, she wanted his opinion of Annabelle while she had a chance.

Annabelle sat perched beside Lilly, apparently enjoying the view. She pointed to a small path leading into the brush. "Remember when we used to sneak through there and pick the wild berries off Old Lady Winston's bushes?" she asked.

Lilly was shocked, not used to Annabelle making small talk.

"And she'd chase us into the swamp, if she caught us, holding that broom but carrying it like a shotgun?" Lilly found herself laughing at the memory, still surprised that Annabelle had brought it up.

"Until the day we came face to face with that huge alligator and decided Miss Winston was the lesser of evils."

Lilly shuddered at Annabelle's words. They had been terrified. Miss Winston, a lonely old woman, had ended up loving the girls' company until she'd passed away a few years back.

"Lilly, why did you stop bringing me along when you went out?" Annabelle asked with a directness that caught Lilly off guard.

She knew the reason, but how to tell her twin? *I love you, but you were an embarrassment to me?* Lilly was ashamed of her actions. Annabelle's behavior only drew unwanted attention when the tonic ran low. With the tonic, she seemed more normal, and most people didn't even notice her mechanical behavior. Those outside the immediate family didn't understand how focused Annabelle could get when taking the tonic. She'd go for days without sleep, furiously obsessed with whatever project interested her at the time.

The sleep deprivation affected Lilly the most because she shared a bedroom with Annabelle. Her twin would stay busy into the early morning hours, keeping Lilly awake long past a reasonable hour. Eventually an exhausted Annabelle would begin to act strangely due to tiredness she couldn't seem to understand.

Lilly shrugged off her thoughts and returned her attention to Annabelle's uncomfortable questions. "I've missed you, Annabelle, that's why I brought you today. We'll go down to the beach like old times."

Whether Annabelle accepted her answer that avoided the actual question, Lilly didn't know, but at least she let the subject drop. It wouldn't be like old times because Annabelle would be distant as usual. She could carry on a conversation, yet she did so without emotion. The loss of her sister's warm, friendly personality from their childhood bothered Lilly deeply, but she determined to follow Caden's advice, loving and enjoying her sister as she was.

Lilly parked the carriage near the place where wild growth overtook the road. She grabbed a bundle that contained their lunch and drinks, then led the way through the trees. Small roots that zigzagged across the ground made the walk treacherous until they reached the sandy part of the trail. Here, though walking became easier, they still had to fight the overgrowth that constantly threatened to reclaim the path.

Annabelle dragged behind, so busy touching and observing everything on the way that she couldn't keep up. The palmettos fascinated her, regardless of the fact that there were plenty near their home. Lilly felt another pang of guilt. She'd left Annabelle behind much too often.

Lilly waited for Annabelle even though she was anxious to see Caden. Hopefully he'd be there. She hadn't seen him since the day the three rough men had showed up. It unnerved her. What was going on? Though she'd made the trek to the beach several times, Caden was never there. She hadn't seen him in town either and couldn't get up the nerve to ask about him at McCarthy's General Store.

If truth be told, she didn't want to learn that Caden had left the area. She would rather hope he was just offshore on his schooner until so much time had passed that she couldn't deny his departure any longer.

Lilly reached the clearing slightly ahead of Annabelle and walked out from the protection of the trees. The water—placid in the unusually still air—ranged in hues of green from mint to emerald, fanning out to reach the dark blue of the deep water where the sandbar dropped off.

Lilly knew from experience that she'd be able to see the bottom for quite a distance, would be able to watch the fish swim and the crabs hunt for food. But other than the beautiful view, the beach was deserted, and Lilly's heart fell.

She placed the bundle in the shade, and she and Annabelle waded out into the water. Annabelle actually laughed when her feet sank down into the wet sand. Lilly decided the day would be a success even if Caden didn't appear.

As she scanned the horizon, a cool splash of water hit her neck. Startled, she looked back at Annabelle, seeing the old gleam in her eyes.

"You aren't going to stand there and let me get away with it, are you?" Annabelle asked, splashing Lilly again.

"Absolutely not!" Lilly retorted, bending over and scooping water to fling at her sister. The war was on, and the sisters played with abandon. The experience reminded Lilly of old times when it was the two of them against the world, when they were content to speak only to each other in the language they'd invented as tots.

Suddenly they heard the sound of clapping coming from shore. The two sisters froze. Whipping her head around, Lilly was surprised to see Caden standing with another man, amusement written on both of their faces.

The two men were complete opposites: Caden in his pirate black and the other man, fair hair pulled back from his face, wearing a white shirt tucked into tan trousers. Caden's ruggedness, dangerously handsome, contrasted with his friend's classic good looks that bordered on beautiful.

Lilly sloshed to the water's edge. "Caden! I didn't see your boat. How did you get here?"

Caden tugged her out of the water, not seeming to mind her drenched condition. Her hair, though wet, still felt presentable. Her dress was another story. Annabelle looked the same.

"It's great to see the two of you having a good time," Caden said softly, watching Annabelle as she trudged toward them. He turned to his friend. "Lilly, I want you to meet Brody. Brody, Lilly."

Lilly flushed, mortified that Caden had to introduce her in this condition. And after catching them in such an undignified water fight!

"You look radiant," he whispered while Brody reached a steadying hand out to Annabelle. She allowed him to help her to shore, but Lilly noticed that her sister had slipped back into a distant, serious demeanor.

Brody and Caden exchanged a glance, then Brody said something quietly to Annabelle. When she nodded, he walked with her up the beach.

Caden turned back to Lilly, his smile devious. He nodded at the twosome walking away from them. "I'm ready now."

"Ready for what?" Lilly asked in confusion. She glanced back at her sister.

"My kiss," he prodded, the silly grin still in place. "You promised."

"I did no such thing!" Lilly laughed, hardly expecting that her first words with Caden would have to do with kissing.

"Yes, you did. I told you that if I helped Annabelle, you'd have to give me a kiss. And you agreed."

"I agreed to talk about it," Lilly argued, torn between throwing herself into his arms and running the other way. "Besides, I don't see you doing anything for Annabelle. Brody's the one taking her for a walk. Very subtle."

"Excuse me," Caden interrupted, "but Brody is the expert on opium addictions. His mother had one. So I am helping Annabelle by putting Brody in her life."

"I see, but if Brody is the one helping my sister, then he's the one who has earned my kiss." Lilly started to go after them, but before she could complete her first step, Caden swung her around and pulled her into his embrace.

All signs of teasing gone, fierce possessiveness filled Caden's eyes. "Listen here, my lady. If any kissing is to go on with those lips, it will be with mine, not Brody's."

"Ah, the pirate has a jealous side. I believe the Bible has something to say about that in Romans 12:9. 'Let love be without dissimulation.' And yes, I've looked dissimulation up, Caden. It means 'to hide under a false appearance,' which is like hiding love behind jealousy."

"Love?" Caden raised his eyebrows, and Lilly wanted to crawl into a hole, dig like a clam, and disappear into the shore with a poof of sand.

"Are you trying to tell me something?" he pursued.

"I-I didn't mean that how it sounded," Lilly stuttered.

"Okay, how did you mean it?" Caden obviously enjoyed this. Lilly did not.

"We'd better go find Annabelle." She looked down the path for a glimpse of her sister.

"Annabelle is in good hands. Brody will watch out for her. He's a good man." Caden stepped into Lilly's line of vision, effectively blocking her twin from sight. "So back to what you were saying."

"It wasn't important," Lilly hedged.

"I know one way to distract me. Might take care of the

jealousy problem too." His eyes darkened, and he gently cupped Lilly's face with work-roughened hands. "Kiss me."

Lilly licked her lips, which were suddenly dry. "Um, that's the only way?"

"Yes. Otherwise I want to know what you had to say about love," Caden prompted, his thumbs caressing her skin, muddling her thoughts. "I think you were saying. . ."

Lilly leaned forward, pressing her lips against his, not wanting him to say it again. The moment their lips met—before they could even call it a decent kiss—Edith's voice called out from behind Caden.

"Yoo-hoo! Caden! There you are! I've chased you all over town." Her voice wavered to a stop as she took in the sight of Caden with Lilly.

Caden muttered something unintelligible under his breath.

Lilly huffed in frustration.

Caden chuckled softly. "You know that jealousy comment you made a few moments ago? I think you'd better check your emotions about now and see what *you* come up with."

He stared at her, his mouth quirking in a half smile. "If looks could kill, Edith wouldn't make it off this beach alive."

"Not funny," Lilly grated. "You better go see what she chased you all over town for."

With that, Lilly turned and stomped down to the water. *Jealous, my foot. How presumptuous of him!* She could hear Edith chirping away behind her.

"I didn't interrupt anything, did I, Cade?"

Caden, Lilly silently corrected. *Caden with an N. Cade? What was that? A little pet name, huh? Well, it sounded pitiful coming from Edith's mouth.* How Caden could think Lilly would be jealous of someone like that was beyond her. *Hrmph. Shows what he knows. Oh, great. Now I sound like Nana.*

Edith's syrupy voice was enough to give a person a stomachache. Not syrupy in a sweet, maple-sugar type of way, but syrupy in more of a castor-oil way. The kind of syrup that choked you as it went down.

Lilly glanced over her shoulder and saw Edith with her hand proprietorially on Caden's arm. Her blood boiled. Stalking up the beach, Lilly grasped Caden by his other arm. He flinched at her tight grip, but Lilly didn't care. If he wanted to keep that arm intact, he'd better release the other from Edith's clench.

Lilly was momentarily distracted by the huge muscles under his sleeve, but the sight of Edith clinging to his other arm quickly reminded her why she was there.

"Hello, Edith, and what can we do for you today?" she asked sweetly.

Caden coughed, and it sounded suspiciously like the word "jealous" was hidden in the noise. Lilly elbowed him in the ribs.

Edith looked confused, then wary. "I need to talk to Cade in private."

Caden grew serious. "Anything you have to say can be said in front of Lilly."

Lilly wanted to kiss him.

He draped an arm around her shoulder, making his feelings known. Lilly blushed.

Edith glared, not bothering to hide her anger. "Never mind. It wasn't important."

She turned her glare onto Lilly. Anger laced her words. "You'll be sorry. He's leaving soon, and you'll be left behind."

Turning on her heel, she stalked off up the path.

Stopping at the edge of the trees, Edith spun around for her final cutting words. "I'd watch him if I were you, Lilly. You might want to check a bit further into who's setting the fires at your mill." She paused. "And I don't think the mill is all we need to worry about."

With that she disappeared into the trees.

After she'd left, Caden turned to Lilly, rubbing the sore part of his arm. Lilly could see the hurt inflicted by Edith's words reflected in Caden's eyes. "I don't know why she said that. I think we might have trouble."

"I don't care. I resent her insinuation. She isn't usually like this. I don't know what has gotten into her lately. She seems to have changed since you came to town." Lilly glanced toward the trees where Edith had last stood. "I don't like the way she was acting."

Caden cleared his throat. "You mean hanging on my arm and talking to me? You did the same thing if I remember correctly. I'm not sure I see a difference."

"The *difference* is that you were about to kiss me, *not* her. That gave me a right to hold your arm, *not* her."

"I believe I did kiss you, though it was much too short of a kiss because we were interrupted. Maybe we should try again." Caden moved toward Lilly.

Lilly sighed dramatically, feigning disinterest. "No. I'm finished kissing now. Maybe when I get that horrible mental picture of Edith clinging to your arm out of my head, we can reconsider. But for now? Not interested." She fluttered her hand at him with the last statement.

"I love your spunk." Caden studied her, then laughed out loud, a disarming smile on his face. "You're good for me, Lilly. I like who I am with you."

Lilly ignored him, not knowing what to say.

"Hmm, well, if you aren't interested, maybe I should go after

Edith and see what she says," Caden teased.

Lilly had to give him credit. He certainly knew how to get a rise out of her. She spun around and pushed. Suddenly Caden lay sprawled flat on his back on the ground. She laughed at his scowl.

"How can a tiny thing like you take down a grown man? I don't even know how you just did that."

Lilly dusted her hands, moving a few feet away from him. "I have brothers."

She stated the fact as if it explained everything.

Brody's laughter made them aware they were no longer alone. Caden mumbled something about no privacy and aimed his scowl at Brody.

Lilly offered Caden her hand, and he tugged her down beside him. Her skirt made an embarrassing sloshing sound when she plopped onto the sand.

Lilly reached into the pocket of her dress and pulled out a bottle. "We brought the tonic."

Handing it to Brody, Lilly anxiously watched his expression as he read the label.

Annabelle sank down next to her twin, anxiety written on her face.

Lilly took her hand. She knew it scared Annabelle to think that her tonic might be causing her problems.

Brody's face darkened. "Laudanum. Just as I thought. It's a form of opium," he said in answer to Lilly's questioning look.

Lilly didn't know whether to laugh or cry. She was thrilled to know what had caused Annabelle's personality change but devastated to think of all the wasted years during which the medication had robbed her of her sister.

Caden pulled her against him. "We can help," he whispered.

"It won't be easy, but we'll get her back to normal. I promise."

Lilly leaned her head against his shoulder. They sat staring out at the water. A secret smile crossed her lips. No matter what Edith had said, Caden's words didn't sound like the comment of a pirate about to set sail.

Chapter 7

Caden seemed nervous when, a short while later, he walked Lilly to the tree line along the back of the beach. He cleared his throat, then stared out over the water before speaking.

"Lilly, I'm going to have to ask you to stay away from here for the next few days. At least until after the Fourth of July."

His eyes searched hers, apparently to see how she took the comment.

Lilly laughed, sure he was joking. Why would he ask such a thing of her? When she saw that he didn't share her smile, she felt confused.

"Why?" Her mind raced with possible reasons, none of which made sense. Lilly had expected to spend the Fourth with Caden, celebrating the holiday and introducing him to her family and friends. "What will it matter if I come to the beach?"

Caden's jaw clenched, and his words were terse. "I can't tell you. I need you to trust me."

"I do trust you, but trust works both ways. You're asking something of me you aren't willing to give."

Lilly turned her back to him, arms crossed defensively. "Why can't you confide in me?"

"Lilly." Caden touched her shoulder, but she pulled away. "I'd tell you if I could. It has to do with my work."

"Oh, yes. Your shipping business is secret, so you need me off the beach. It all makes perfect sense now."

"Sarcasm does not become you, Lilly. I'll tell you exactly what it is all about as soon as I can. But it will be sometime after the Fourth." He stuck his hands into his pockets and backed away, putting an invisible barrier between them.

Lilly thought he looked more handsome than ever, the wind ruffling his black shirt and blowing his dark hair across his face, while his blue eyes begged her to understand. She wanted to corral the silky hair with her hands, pull it back from his face, peer into his eyes and, well, yank his hair backward until he told her what was going on.

Men were *so* exasperating!

Not wanting Caden to see the hurt in her eyes, Lilly called to Annabelle and stalked off up the path. Brody had already waved his farewell, so she didn't have to look back, but she did anyway in time to see a very desolate Caden watching her walk out of his life.

Lilly's father waited on the front porch, much like on that first day when she'd met Caden. *How perfect,* Lilly fumed, *full circle from beginning to end.*

"Lillian, I want to speak with you," her father stated in his no-nonsense voice. He motioned her into the parlor. Annabelle continued toward the back of the house.

"Edith came by this afternoon, concerned about your well-being." Mr. Appleby paced while he talked.

Lilly had to bite her tongue not to snort. With the way

Edith had been behaving for the past couple months, the only reason she'd come by the house was to get even.

Her father stopped his pacing and took the chair opposite Lilly. "She said you were alone on the beach with a disreputable man. She also said she'd overheard him talking to another man outside their store earlier in the day. They spoke of plans to conduct a raid, possibly of our town on the Fourth when we're all at the festivities."

"Father, if she overheard, she can't possibly know all that they were speaking of. You're assuming! I can assure you. . ."

"Don't interrupt me!" He stood, towering over her. "I'm putting word out for everyone to watch their homes, and I'm also adding security to the mill because she said he mentioned something about the fires. She's afraid he might be behind them."

"But Father, if you'd just listen. . ."

Her father went on as if she'd never spoken. "You're not to see him again until I clear this up."

Lilly stood to her feet. "I won't see him until after the Fourth. He told me he would be busy."

"You won't see him, period. We know what he'll be busy doing. My statement is final."

Lilly tried once more to defend Caden, but her father would hear nothing of it. She stalked up to her room and threw herself on her bed. She knew everyone was nervous because of the fires at the mill, but this response was too extreme.

Caden hadn't lied, had he? He'd said he worked in shipping yet now was all mysterious. Surely this had nothing to do with the work he'd mentioned before. But if he wasn't doing something illegal, why wouldn't he tell her what was going on? Lilly felt so confused.

She thought back to Edith's words. Could the younger girl

possibly be right? If competitors had hired Caden to ruin the mill, what better way for him to find out information than to get close to Lilly? Her heart felt as though it were falling, but she struggled to fight off the doubts.

She thought back to some of their many conversations over the past couple months. They'd been talking about freedom, and Caden had asked why Lilly thought life would be better if she could start over somewhere else where nobody knew her or her family.

"Moving away won't solve the problem. You can't let others control your life, Lilly, but it's lonely trying to do it on your own. Let God in. Whether this town or another, the only freedom you'll ever find is in Him."

Then she remembered another conversation: "It's one thing to believe, but a lot of people stop there. You have to live your walk."

"Live my walk? What do you mean? I've been a believer since I was a small girl. I've grown up in the church."

Caden went on to explain that it wasn't enough to go to church on Sunday and to pray now and then. "To really grow close to God, a person has to give their whole life up to Him. Constantly interact, pray, and wait to see what God says."

"But that won't be freedom at all!" Lilly had said in dismay. "Then I'm giving up everything to be under God's control."

"And only then will you have real freedom," Caden had replied with a smile. "Try it and see."

Lilly had tried it and could see what he meant from the peace she'd received. It was liberating. But it wasn't easy, and she knew she'd have to take life one day at a time, study her Bible, and learn more.

Surely the man who'd taught her all that couldn't be a fake.

He'd seemed so sincere. Lilly decided to put into practice what she'd learned from Caden: give God control of the situation and her life. She walked down to dinner with a slightly lighter heart.

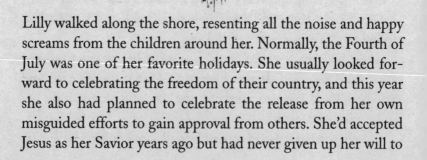

Two afternoons later, Caden sat in the bushes in the dim light, praying he wouldn't get caught. Tonight, if all went according to plan, they would raid the schooner, and Caden wanted to make it back safely to Lilly.

He didn't like the hurt and distrust that had shone from her eyes the last time they'd talked. But he knew he couldn't risk her getting hurt.

If all went well with the raid, he'd be free to seek her out and explain everything—and to help find out who was responsible for the attacks on the mill. It certainly wasn't him, no matter what Edith had hinted. Once everything was explained, he and Lilly would be able to plan a future together. He wanted her in his life, but for the present he needed to put such dreams aside and concentrate on his job.

Brody whistled, the sound much like the calls of the birds that circled through the trees behind him, and Caden signaled in return, disclosing his location. It was beginning.

Lilly walked along the shore, resenting all the noise and happy screams from the children around her. Normally, the Fourth of July was one of her favorite holidays. She usually looked forward to celebrating the freedom of their country, and this year she also had planned to celebrate the release from her own misguided efforts to gain approval from others. She'd accepted Jesus as her Savior years ago but had never given up her will to

Him, letting Him guide her daily walk.

Caden had once asked her, "How did you change when you asked Jesus into your life?"

The sad fact was that her life hadn't changed one bit. She had refused to relinquish the small hold she'd had on what she did instead of trusting Him to lead her through life's decisions.

Settling into the sand, Lilly closed her eyes. From now on, she'd pray and consult God before she did anything. Her first prayer was for Caden's safety in whatever he was doing; the second request was that he'd be a part of her future. She might not know what Caden was up to, but his actions didn't point to his being a disreputable character. She trusted him, no matter what, especially since he had helped bring her closer to the Lord.

Lilly felt freer than she'd ever been before. She watched her brothers and sisters splash with abandon and even caught herself smiling at their antics until she saw Edith sitting with her family on the sidelines.

Edith didn't wear a swimming costume like most everyone else. Instead, she sat primly with her parents, wistfully watching the others. Lilly glanced back at her own parents and saw the way they smiled and had fun, playing and relaxing with their neighbors and children.

Glancing around, Lilly noticed a few others from town seemed sullen. Suddenly, Lilly realized that all the people she'd sought to impress were the unhappiest people there. She wasn't about to let their unpleasantness rub off on her.

Glancing at Edith once again, Lilly knew what she had to do. Grabbing her satchel, she ran over to Edith and took her by the arm.

Edith looked frightened, then defensive. "Let me go."

"Come with me," Lilly pleaded. "I want to talk with you."

"I don't trust you," Edith said warily. "You're trying to get even with me because of what I said about Cade."

Caden. Caden. Caden, Lilly singsonged in her head with irritation before remembering her quest. Pasting a determined smile on her face, she turned to her nemesis. "I'm not happy about what you did to Caden and me, but I forgive you. Life's too short to go around holding grudges. Caden has helped me see that Jesus wouldn't want us to be that way."

Edith's expression showed utter disbelief at Lilly's words. Mouth gaping, she allowed Lilly to lead her to the makeshift cabana and pull her inside.

"Why aren't you swimming with everyone else?" Lilly asked, when they were out of earshot of the other beachgoers.

Edith turned up her nose. "It's completely improper."

Lilly didn't believe her. She'd seen the look in Edith's eyes while she'd longingly watched the others frolic in the water.

"Here, take this." She dug her new swim costume from her bag. "I don't need it right now. I'm going for a walk."

Edith's eyes lit up at the beautiful blue-and-white-striped swim dress. Lilly dropped matching white swim stockings into Edith's arms. White shoes completed the ensemble.

"I don't understand. You want me to wear this?" Edith's confused eyes met Lilly's. "Why?"

Lilly smiled. "Because I care about you and want you to have fun."

Tears glimmered in Edith's eyes. "But I've been so mean. I've caused trouble with Cade and with you. I've been so jealous."

Lilly felt sorry for her but did want to know the truth. "Why did you make all that up about Caden? Why did you want to hurt us?"

"You'll never know how guilty I've felt. So many times I

wanted to make things right, but I liked Cade so much. I was jealous that you seem to have all the good things: a big family, a twin sister, good grades, and now Cade. I wanted to—I don't know—I guess I just wanted what you had for once. I really did overhear him talking outside the store about a raid, but I told your father in a way that I knew he'd forbid you from seeing Cade. I'm so sorry, and I promise I'll tell your father the truth."

Lilly pulled the other girl into the circle of her arms, hugging Edith and knowing she'd done the right thing. "It's all forgiven, Edith. I'm sorry if we hurt you too."

Edith wiped at her tears and looked longingly at the swim dress once more. "Do you really mean for me to wear this? I've never seen anything so beautiful. I begged my parents to order me one when your parents ordered all of yours, but they said swimming costumes are frivolous and wasteful."

Lilly laughed. Her heart felt so light. "I really mean it. Enjoy yourself."

She thought about what Edith had said. Caden was right. All this time Edith had actually been jealous of her! Lilly was the one who had assumed Edith was one more person standing in judgment of her.

Edith scrambled to put on the costume, then self-consciously walked outside. Lilly tugged her down to the water's edge.

Leaning over, she whispered conspiratorially. "I have one request. Don't get out until Will is drenched."

Edith blushed. She looked over at Lilly's younger brother and nodded her agreement.

Darkness fell, and everyone lounged around in small groups, stomachs full after a successful clambake. Lilly wondered where

Caden was, sad that she wouldn't be able to snuggle up with him to admire the fireworks like the other courting couples.

Earlier in the afternoon Edith had spoken with Lilly's father, admitting she'd only heard bits and pieces of what the two men had said. She'd insisted that they'd mentioned a raid, so the town was still on alert.

Lilly didn't feel Caden had the potential to do anything so sinister. She knew in her heart he was innocent. He'd said they'd be apart until after the Fourth. Now that his mission was drawing to an end, maybe she could hunt him down. She had stayed away from their beach as promised; but though she'd watched for his ship from other locations, it never sailed her way. She resisted the niggling thought that he might have already left the area.

Deciding her father's demand that she stay far from Caden was no longer in effect since Edith had told the truth, Lilly slipped quietly up the dark path that led to the private beach. She'd waited long enough. Surely Caden's business was finished by now.

Upon reaching the small strip of sand, she was thrilled to see the outline of two men in the shadows. Caden and Brody. She grinned.

"Caden!" she shouted, jumping out to greet them. "I've missed you!"

"And I've missed you too, Darlin'." The gritty voice did not belong to Caden.

A chill raced down Lilly's spine. She knew that voice. It belonged to one of the awful men from Caden's ship. She turned, knowing if she reached the path, she could run away from them. She knew every step, even in the dark.

Strong hands grabbed her. Lilly tried to scream, but a

filthy, fleshy hand covered her mouth.

"Shut up, and you might not get hurt," the man hissed.

Lilly ducked her head, trying to avoid his atrocious breath. He held her tighter. The man smelled of sweat and liquor, nothing like Caden. She longed for Caden's fresh, salty scent.

What had she done? No one knew where she was, and hours might pass before anyone missed her at the town's festivities. Terrified, Lilly fought back the tears that filled her eyes.

The large man jerked her roughly around and dragged her down the beach.

Lilly used Molly's tantrum trick and went limp, making it difficult for the man to hold her. Grasping her arm with one hand, he slapped her face with the other. He pulled her to the small wooden boat, even without her cooperation.

The second man began to push the boat off the sand toward the water and headed toward the schooner.

Lilly didn't want to be taken to that horrible boat, only to end up a captive like the heroine in her story. She didn't want to walk any planks. And she certainly didn't want to be a captive of these awful pirates.

She tried to yell, but the man's massive hand stretched across her face, muffling the sound. Anger clouded his face, and as he clenched his fist to hit her, Lilly began to pray.

Chapter 8

J ust as the despicable man reared back to hit her again, fireworks from the schooner lit up the sky. Caught off guard, he turned to look, and Lilly saw a figure shoot out of the bushes, down the beach, and straight into her kidnapper's ribs, the force carrying him up and over the side of the small boat. Another figure hit the second man, knocking him into the water.

The squawk of a bird that could only be Peter joined the ruckus. Lilly whispered a prayer of thanks that Peter had obviously escaped the schooner again. Her captor howled in pain as the bird grabbed an ear with his beak.

Free to run, Lilly climbed out into ankle-deep water and scuttled on her hands and knees for the nearest bush. Yet her escape up the path was blocked by the fighting men. Crying, she watched the battle rage, listening to flesh hitting flesh.

Intermittent groans and oaths filled the air as the strange fireworks display continued from the ship offshore. Lilly could not imagine why the people on the ship were doing such an odd thing. No one had included offshore fireworks in the plans for the town's celebration, and if they had, they certainly wouldn't have asked someone to shoot them off in this remote location.

Unless her attackers broke away and started searching the bushes, no one would find her; but although she was safe, Lilly's tears continued to fall.

Moonlight reflected from the water as the clouds moved away, and Lilly could see another smaller vessel joining the first. She watched the smaller ship pull alongside the larger one. More boats came into sight seemingly from out of nowhere, surrounding the first two. Men poured out of the bushes, scattering along the shore, while several small rowboats lowered from the two ships and headed toward the beach.

Lilly's heart pounded in fear. What had she stumbled upon? Caden had tried to warn her, but in her usual impetuous way, she hadn't heeded his words. With so many men on the beach, she had no way to sneak back to the safety of her townsfolk. Suddenly, she wanted nothing more than to be in the center of the group of people who loved her.

Four men walked over to the two who'd grabbed her, took them by the wrists, and dragged them down toward the water. The two men who had pounced out of the bushes surveyed the area, speaking quietly to one another. One moved toward the water while the other headed Lilly's way.

Lilly held her breath in fear, willing her tears to abate. The man came closer, and Lilly couldn't move. If she did, he'd find her before she made it through the thick underbrush. She was trapped.

"Lilly."

The one word instantly soothed her troubled heart.

"Oh, Caden," she sobbed, crawling out and throwing herself into his embrace. "Caden."

She grabbed his shirt, burying her face against his chest, wanting to get as close as she possibly could. He smelled of freshness and salt air. Her pirate was back. He'd saved her from the villains, just like the heroes who saved the heroines in her novels.

Caden held her close, caressing her hair and back while whispering soothing words. She could hear his heart beating through his shirt, the tempo keeping pace with her own. He'd been scared too. Minutes passed while they held each other, each needing to know the other was safe.

Shifting, Lilly finally cupped his face, wanting to see him. The roguish smile was gone, replaced by anger and something else. . .fear?

Caden leaned down, pulling Lilly to him, and pressed his lips against hers. The fireworks from the kiss rivaled any of the ones she'd seen shot off from the ship. Time stood still. She was safely held in Caden's embrace. She grew lightheaded.

Caden's soft chuckle brought her back.

"Breathe," he whispered. "This isn't the time to swoon."

"Swoon and miss a moment with my pirate? I don't think that's possible."

He held her close, and Lilly was content to snuggle in his arms, her face against his strong chest. She wanted to relish every moment but was having trouble keeping her eyes open.

Brody approached with a cool wet cloth. "How's her head?"

Lilly could hear him but couldn't seem to move. She felt Caden pick her up and lower her to his lap, then felt his soothing hands explore her head.

Lilly cried out when his fingers brushed against her face. She could tell from the pain that the area would soon have a bruise to show where the awful man had slapped her. As Brody applied the soothing cloth to the tender area, Caden snarled about the two men who had hurt Lilly.

Lilly heard voices from far away. Caden tried to shift her so he could stand, but Lilly refused to let go, wrapping her arms around his neck and clinging for dear life. Soon more people were swarming over the area, bringing lanterns that lit the area brightly.

"It's okay," Caden soothed, his smile tender. "We have all the smugglers gathered, and you're safe."

"Smugglers?" Lilly tried to make sense of it all. "I don't understand."

Her family pushed through the crowd, drawn along with everyone else in town by the fireworks at sea. Lilly's father's face reddened when he saw her in Caden's arms.

"What is going on here?" he demanded, his voice harsh with anger.

Lilly tried to get up, but her woozy head and Caden's hold kept her in place.

Brody joined them, taking Mr. Appleby's hand and making introductions. "Brody Hopkins. Lilly is fine. She unknowingly walked into a raid, but she's come out of it with only a bruise on her cheek."

Her father paled, looking to Lilly for an explanation.

"I didn't know, Papa. I wanted to walk over here to find Caden. Since Edith told the truth, I thought it would be all right. Some men grabbed me, and Caden and Brody fought them off."

She'd never seen her father so distraught.

"Is this true?" he asked Caden.

"Indeed, Sir, it is. We've been working undercover with the navy and the Revenue Cutter Service to catch an illegal shipment of cargo when it came in. The fireworks from the ship were from the smugglers, to signal the runners where to land.

Your daughter walked into the middle of it."

Lilly's father sighed, giving her a "we will discuss this later" look. He offered his hand to Caden, who had helped a shaky Lilly to her feet. She leaned against him, her head now throbbing from all the excitement.

"I owe you an apology, Sir. I assume you must be Lilly's pirate, Caden."

Lilly was mortified when Brody chuckled, and Caden laughed out loud.

"Apology's not necessary, Sir, and yes, the name is Caden Shaw. I'm sorry we haven't met sooner and under better circumstances. I'd like another chance to do this properly."

Lilly glanced up at Caden. Did he mean it? After the mess she'd made of his raid and the embarrassment she must have caused him, he still wanted to be around her?

"You saved my daughter's life. I'd like you to join us Sunday for dinner. In the meantime, now that everyone's safe, let's get back to the celebration."

Her father was always abrupt when upset.

"Papa," Lilly whispered when he turned to lead the way up the path. "They are going to help Annabelle. Her tonic contains opium, and that's what has been making her act so strange. Brody and Caden said they can help."

Mr. Appleby's eyes misted over with appreciation. He turned once more to the two men.

"I had no idea," he admitted to Caden. "What can we do?"

"We'll talk at dinner. Our part here is finished. For now, let's enjoy the festivities." Caden motioned for Mr. Appleby to lead the way down the path.

The townspeople turned in small groups to follow him, seeing that the situation was under control. Lilly noticed Brody gently guiding Annabelle by the arm.

Caden pulled Lilly aside, waiting until they were alone before heading up the trail. He held her close against him as they walked. Upon reaching the clearing of the beach, he settled with her on a soft blanket set out by her parents near the tree line.

Peter flew up to take roost on Caden's shoulder. Lilly's heart leaped at the sight. Once again he was the mysterious pirate in black, his brooding blue eyes searching hers.

"You had me scared, Lillian Appleby." He rested his forehead against Lilly's, his breath warm against her face. "Promise me you'll never do anything like that again."

Lilly laughed, her heart beating a staccato rhythm against her chest. "I wish I could, but these things seem to happen to me."

Caden sighed. "Then I'll have to make sure I'm around to rescue you when you need me."

"I like the sound of that," Lilly admitted, snuggling against him. The fireworks began, this time compliments of the Pirate's Point Women's League Fourth of July Planning Committee. Everyone seemed to be enjoying themselves, even without the parade.

Lilly's heart rejoiced as she celebrated the nation's freedom, along with her own. She had never felt better than she did right now: nestled in her pirate's embrace, celebrating the holiday with the family and friends she loved.

PAIGE WINSHIP DOOLY

Paige enjoys living in the warm panhandle of Florida with her family, after having grown up in the sometimes extremely cold Midwest. She is happily married to her high school sweetheart, Troy, and they have five, home-schooled children. The whole family is active in helping with several new ministries around town. Troy loves to teach all ages, while Paige prefers to work with younger children; and both enjoy the challenge of teenagers!

Paige has always loved to write; first trying poetry in grade school—*not* for her, though she was published in the school paper!—and then writing short stories all through her youth. While early stories were really fictional—such as made up stories about being adopted, with Sonny and Cher being her real parents (hey, it was the era, and it would have been so cool to sit on that piano and sing!)—she now writes more—hopefully—believable romance novels. Paige feels her love of writing is a blessing from God, and she hopes that readers will walk away with a spiritual impact on their life and a smile on their face.

A Letter to Our Readers

Dear Readers:

In order that we might better contribute to your reading enjoyment, we would appreciate you taking a few minutes to respond to the following questions. When completed, please return to the following: Fiction Editor, Barbour Publishing, Inc., P.O. Box 719, Uhrichsville, OH 44683.

1. Did you enjoy reading *Sweet Liberty?*
    ❑ Very much. I would like to see more books like this.
    ❑ Moderately—I would have enjoyed it more if _____
    _____
    _____

2. What influenced your decision to purchase this book?
    (Check those that apply.)
    ❑ Cover   ❑ Back cover copy   ❑ Title   ❑ Price
    ❑ Friends   ❑ Publicity   ❑ Other

3. Which story was your favorite?
    ❑ *Freedom's Cry*   ❑ *American Pie*
    ❑ *Free Indeed*   ❑ *Lilly's Pirate*

4. Please check your age range:
    ❑ Under 18   ❑ 18–24   ❑ 25–34
    ❑ 35–45   ❑ 46–55   ❑ Over 55

5. How many hours per week do you read? _____

Name _____

Occupation _____

Address _____

City _____ State _____ Zip _____

If you enjoyed

SWEET LIBERTY

then read:

German Enchantment

*A Legacy of Customs and Devotion
in Four Romantic Novellas*

Where Angels Camp by Irene B. Brand
The Nuremberg Angel by Dianne Christner
Dearest Enemy by Pamela Griffin
Once a Stranger by Gail Gaymer Martin

If you enjoyed

SWEET LIBERTY

then read:

The ENGLISH GARDEN

Centuries of Botanical Delight Brought to Life in Four Romantic Novellas

Apple of His Eye by Gail Gaymer Martin
A Flower Amidst the Ashes by DiAnn Mills
Woman of Valor by Jill Stengl
Robyn's Garden by Kathleen Y'Barbo

If you enjoyed

SWEET LIBERTY

then read:

★ ★ ★

United We Stand

Four Complete Novels Demonstrate the Power of Love During WWII

C for Victory by Joan Croston
Escape on the Wind by Jane LaMunyon
The Rising Son by Darlene Mindrup
Candleshine by Colleen L. Reece

If you enjoyed

SWEET LIBERTY

then read:

AS AMERICAN AS APPLE PIE

Four Contemporary Romance Novellas
Served with a Slice of America

An Apple a Day by Andrea Boeshaar
Sweet as Apple Pie by Kristin Billerbeck
Apple Annie by Joyce Livingston
Apple Pie in Your Eye by Gail Sattler

Available wherever books are sold.
Or order from:
Barbour Publishing, Inc.
P.O. Box 719
Uhrichsville, Ohio 44683
www.barbourbooks.com

You may order by mail for $5.97, and add $2.00 to your order for shipping.
Prices subject to change without notice.

If you enjoyed

SWEET LIBERTY

then read:

Magnolias

*Romantic History from the Deep South
in Four Complete Novels by Jacquelyn Cook*

The River Between
The Wind Along the River
River of Fire
Beyond the Searching River

If you enjoyed

SWEET LIBERTY

then read:

✳

Lamps

OF COURAGE

*Four Novellas Honoring the Valor of Nurses
Who Served Both God and Country*

By Dim and Flaring Lamps by Colleen L. Reece
Home Fires Burning by JoAnn A. Grote
A Light in the Night by Janelle Burnham Schneider
Beside the Golden Door by Renee DeMarco